'Jack Perkowski's story [is] a rare treat . . . His wise and ultimately optimistic account should be required reading for anyone starting a business in China' *Economist*

'If you want to do business in China, Jack Perkowski is your man. In *Managing the Dragon* he takes you into the heart of the Middle Kingdom and shows you the way with insight, humour and the kind of practical advice an entrepreneur or a down-home tourist needs to navigate this fascinating and often bewildering colossus of a country' Tom Brokaw, author and NBC news presenter

'Fantastic. I was riveted by it. I cannot believe what Jack Perkowski has accomplished and what an adventure he's had, how he lived through it, how he's succeeded, and how well written his book is. It reads somewhere between a novel, a how-to book, and a primer on a second business life in a developing country' Michael Eisner, former CEO Disney Corporation

'I love Jack Perkowski's book. It tells, with some bravado and lots of humility, the firsthand story of a man who dared himself to move to China to seize upon the greatest economic boom of our age. Perkowski invites us into his world [and] reveals what it took to build a world-class manufacturing company in a country where you need to set firm goals but reach them in an environment where the rules and circles of influence shift daily' Ted C. Fishman, author of *China, Inc.: How the Rise of the Next Superpower Challenges America and the World*

'*Managing the Dragon* is more than a great story about Jack Perkowski and his courage to move to the new frontier; it is a graduate degree in the trials, tribulations, and successes of starting from scratch in China. Jack captures the essence of doing business in China and turns it into a very compelling "how-to" guide' Timothy Manganello, CEO of BorgWarner, Inc.

'You have to hand it to Jack Perkowski. The working-class Pittsburgh kid [who] spent 20 years on Wall Street and became head of investment banking at PaineWebber could have rested on his laurels and enjoyed his personal wealth. Instead he chose in the 1990s to set up a new business in a difficult country and in a difficult industry he knew nothing about. . . . [His] book is worth reading, both for its insights into business in China and for its self-portrait of a relentlessly optimistic American entrepreneur who has persevered in spite of disasters and disappointments' *Financial Times*

Managing
the
Dragon

Building a Billion-Dollar
Business in China

Jack Perkowski

BANTAM BOOKS

LONDON • TORONTO • SYDNEY • AUCKLAND • JOHANNESBURG

TRANSWORLD PUBLISHERS
61–63 Uxbridge Road, London W5 5SA
A Random House Group Company
www.randomhouse.co.uk

**MANAGING THE DRAGON
A BANTAM BOOK: 9780553819984**

First published in Great Britain
in 2008 by Bantam Press
a division of Transworld Publishers
Bantam edition published 2009

Grateful acknowledgement is made to Hal Leonard for permission to reprint an
excerpt from 'She Thinks My Tractor's Sexy' by Jim Collins and Paul
Overstreet, copyright © 1998, 1999 by EMI Blackwood Music Inc., Jelinda
Music and Scarlet Moon Music Inc. All rights for Jelinda Music controlled and
administered by EMI Blackwood Music Inc. All rights reserved. International
copyright secured. Used by permission.

A CIP catalogue record for this book
is available from the British Library.

Addresses for Random House Group Ltd companies outside the UK
can be found at: www.randomhouse.co.uk
The Random House Group Ltd Reg. No. 954009

Typeset in 11.25/15.5pt Janson by
Falcon Oast Graphic Art Ltd.

2 4 6 8 10 9 7 5 3

Penguin Random House is committed to a sustainable future for
our business, our readers and our planet. This book is made from
Forest Stewardship Council® certified paper.

Printed and bound in Great Britain by Clays Ltd, Elcograf S.p.A.

To my mother, Adele,
and in memory of my father, John.

*They instilled in me the values of hard work
and determination, and their emphasis on the
importance of education was a strong and
constant influence.*
*Whether I was in Pittsburgh, New Haven,
Boston, New York, or Beijing, they provided
unspoken support and a strong anchor to
windward.*

Contents

Managing

the

Dragon

Introduction

She thinks my tractor's sexy
It really turns her on
She's always starin' at me
While I'm chuggin' along

—"She Thinks My Tractor's Sexy," KENNY CHESNEY

It was a warm, clear, starlit night in Tucson in April of 2006. I was sitting in the bleachers at Caterpillar's Arizona proving grounds, along with five hundred executives from the company and its key suppliers, listening to Kenny Chesney tout the merits of his tractor as an aphrodisiac and watching expert operators put a dozen CAT machines through their paces.

As the music blared and synchronized multicolored spotlights flashed, a pair of massive dump trucks—the kind used to haul coal from large mines in Australia—rumbled down the hill in the far background, disappeared into the valley below, and then suddenly reappeared to our right and sped past the stands, throwing up clouds of dust in their wake. The music was so loud that it drowned out the roar of their engines. Meanwhile, giant earthmovers pushed tons of dirt into the waiting buckets of enormous CAT loaders, the kind with rubber tires more than twice a man's height. And then, suddenly, the hillside in front of us erupted with lights and movement, as three smaller earthmovers popped out of hidden tunnels that had been burrowed into the bank.

It was about as impressive an equipment show as I have ever seen, or could ever hope to see, and I doubt I'll ever see anything like it again. I could've sat there watching and listening all night.

On that evening in Tucson, we were a long way from China—but China was on everybody's mind. Caterpillar had gathered us there, in the first-ever meeting of its 150 or so strategic suppliers, to roll out its Vision 2020, a strategy to become a $100 billion company by the year 2020. At the meetings during the day, CAT executives described the company's seven key success factors. Three could be found at most companies: people, products, and quality. Three were unique to Caterpillar: distribution, ability to be profitable through a trough, and velocity, or speed to market. The most interesting factor, though, was the seventh: China. Over the course of three days in Tucson, every senior CAT executive, from CEO Jim Owens on down, stood in front of the company's key suppliers and said that CAT had to be number one in China by 2020. If it wasn't, the company's position as the global leader in its industry would be in question.

It was a stunning announcement. Caterpillar, one of the most successful industrial companies in the world, was saying that its future viability as a global leader depended on how it did in China. CAT is a proud company, almost one hundred years old, and it has survived severe threats to its position before. In the late 1980s and early 1990s, CAT successfully withstood strong competition from Komatsu, its formidable Japanese competitor, while also finding a way to come to terms with its unions—thereby avoiding the legacy issues that now threaten the U.S. automakers. Renewed spending for natural resources exploration and mining, in the wake of sharp increases in the prices of raw materials that began shortly after the turn of the century, had pushed the company even further into the black, and the company was having its best years ever.

But here CAT was, at the top of its game in the spring of 2006, saying that the future was in China. A lot of companies have set their sights on China. But, to my knowledge, CAT was the first major company to draw such a clear line in the sand regarding China's importance to its future success.

The fact that the largest, most successful companies in the world are coming to the same conclusion as Caterpillar is testimony to how far China has come in the last ten years. There will be bumps in the road, and China's growth as an economy won't flow smoothly from the bottom-left to the upper-right side of the chart. But the fact remains that China will be the biggest, fastest-growing economy in the world in the twenty-first century. Any company that doesn't do what CAT has done, to make becoming a leader in China an irrevocable priority, may be relegating itself to a future as a second-rate player.

What makes China's continued development so scary, to companies and individuals alike, is that it's happening so fast. Like a large rock rolling down the side of a mountain, China's economy is gathering momentum and gaining speed. After a period of double-digit growth in the post-Tiananmen period of the early 1990s, the law of large numbers would have predicted that that kind of growth couldn't happen again. But China has defied conventional wisdom. Already one of the world's largest economies, China grew by at least 10 percent in 2003, 2004, 2005, 2006, and 2007. The country had $21 billion in foreign reserves in 1993; ten years later, in 2003, China was adding $200 billion or more of reserves into its coffers *each year*. By the end of 2006, China had more than $1 trillion in foreign currency reserves, an unprecedented amount that was growing by $50 billion each month. The entire world is watching to see what the country does with its cash hoard.

The accelerated pace of China's economic development has us all "riding on the back of a tiger," as the Chinese would say. It's dangerous, perhaps fatal, to try to jump off, but it's also exceedingly difficult to stay on unless you know what you are doing.

What do individuals and companies of all sizes need to know to be successful in China? Everybody has their own opinion, but if I had to boil down everything I'm going to tell you in this book into one important idea, it's this: you have to develop a strong local management team for your company here. There's no way around it. After operating in China for fifteen years, I've seen companies come and go, but those that develop good local Chinese management teams that understand the company's goals and can respond to the unique elements of the Chinese environment are those that stand the best chance of success. We tried several different ways to close China's management gap—and I'll walk you through all of them—before we finally arrived at the approach that ultimately saved our company. That story lies at the heart of this book.

On a broader level, I also hope to tell you a bit more about where China is today, from the perspective of practical experience, not theory or hypothesis. Most people assume that China is a bureaucratic monolith, ruled from on high in Beijing. Right off the bat, it's important to understand that this couldn't be further from the truth. China has historically been, and still is, highly decentralized. Edicts from Beijing don't necessarily carry the same weight that one might think. China's decentralization, as I'll discuss later, is part of the dynamic that causes the country to create overcapacity for every product. It also leads to extremely fragmented industries, which are only becoming more so—and not consolidating, as conventional wisdom would have it.

Despite its shiny facade, China is in a different place economically than the rest of the developed world. From the outside, the country appears to be modern, rich, and prosperous, the epitome of the rich new kid on the block with all of the trappings and swagger that go with that status. Underneath that image, though, lies a soft under-belly of incredible poverty for the vast majority of the country's population. Isolated from the rest of the world from 1949 to 1978, China underwent a thirty-year time warp that continues to affect the country in all kinds of ways. As a result, the cost perspective here is more similar to the United States of the 1950s than it is to the United States of today, a fact that permeates all aspects of the Chinese economy.

With a vast disparity of income levels across the country, and a fundamentally different—and lower—cost perspective throughout, the China market wants and demands the most sophisticated products in the world. At the same time, China's purely local market accepts products with the most rudimentary technologies that have the advantage of being cheap. Unlike developed markets, where companies with even slightly lower levels of quality and technology quickly fall by the wayside, the China market tolerates all levels of quality and technology.

Since China's opening in 1978 the greater availability of higher-quality, technologically superior foreign-made goods has not crowded out local companies, as many predicted. Instead, a "foreign/local" market, where foreign-invested companies compete toe-to-toe with the best of the local players, has been layered on top of a purely "local" market, where only local Chinese companies play. Prices, quality, and technology levels are high in the foreign/local market; in the local market, all three are low. The continued growth of a large local market for all products has created a vast breeding ground for new competitors, where purely local companies have the chance to gain production scale competing in familiar waters, immune from foreign competition. A pattern is now emerging where successful Chinese companies in the local market move up to hone their skills by competing with the best of the global competition in China's foreign/local market, and then make the leap outside of China to the international markets. The continuation of this trend could bring onto the world stage a whole new set of players and reshape nearly every global industry.

Even in technological innovation, where its record hasn't been strong, China is starting to move up the ladder. The continued growth of the Chinese economy, combined with the lower cost perspective here, has created a set of forces that is driving the need to develop more affordable solutions to the problems unique to China's large and growing market. You cannot assume that products designed for another consumer in a more highly developed and wealthier economy will continue to meet these needs. In more and more cases, these solutions will be developed in China.

I cover all of the themes just outlined, in addition to the story of how I got here, in the pages that follow. I do so fully recognizing that, largely because of what's happening in China today, the world order is changing so quickly that no one can honestly say that they've got it all figured out. When it comes to China, we're all in the same boat. Individuals, both Chinese and non-Chinese, and companies—large, small, Western, Asian, and Chinese alike—have to come to grips with what's going on here, *right now*. Western individuals and companies have to learn how to deal with a completely different culture, and Chinese individuals and companies have to learn how to integrate into an open, transparent, and global economy. Neither task is easy.

My own journey to China started in August of 1990, when I was sitting on my bulldozer on my farm in Lambertville, New Jersey, deciding how to spend the rest of my working career. (When I tell my CAT friends this story, they always ask me which CAT model I own. I'm forced to admit, somewhat sheepishly, that my bulldozer was an opportunistic secondhand purchase. When I made this momentous decision, I was actually sitting on a John Deere!) Was I going to continue in the investment banking field in the United States, or was I going to do something that I really wanted to do, which was to establish a franchise by identifying a long-term trend and putting together an organization to get ahead of that trend? It was simple, really. Was I going to keep doing what I was most familiar with? Or did I have the guts to do something completely different?

My experience, straight from Wall Street to the Great

Wall, is quite rare. Any number of companies have invested in China, and major financial institutions are now taking big stakes in China's leading companies. And interesting Chinese companies, from both the private and the state-owned sectors, continue to emerge all the time and are raising serious capital in the global markets. But in all my years in China, I've never heard of another Westerner who has come to China, equipped only with a concept and twenty years' experience, and built a company that has become a major player in one of China's largest industries. You've heard the warnings from circus performers before a particularly perilous stunt: "Kids, please don't try this at home." In some sense, this book should probably sound the same warning.

Some will say, with some justification, that it was foolish on my part even to have attempted any of this. China's tough. My decision in August 1990 came at tremendous personal sacrifice, and there isn't a day that goes by where I don't at least question whether I did the right thing. Will ASIMCO, the automotive components company that I founded in 1994, go on to become the truly great company that I believe it can be? Will history view my decision in 1990 to have been the "right" one? Nobody knows the answers to these questions. And, frankly, that's not what people are interested in. What they want to know is more basic.

"Is there anything in your experience, Jack," they ask me, "that can help us understand and make some sense of China?"

Every year, I make dozens of speeches and present-ations to audiences around the world. I view this as part of my job building my company's franchise, creating new opportunities, and sharing my experiences with others who are interested in coming here. Why is this last objective important? Quite simply, the more good people and good companies that come to China, the better it is for all of us. China is both developing and trying to integrate into a global economy at the same time. If this were a gymnastics meet, the difficulty rating would be a 10.0. The more talent, experience, knowledge, and tech-nology that come here, the easier the development and integration processes become.

Whenever I speak, the questions I get afterward always fall into three predictable categories. First, every-body is curious about how I ended up here. I was born in working-class Pittsburgh, educated at Yale and Harvard, and then worked for twenty years on Wall Street before moving to Asia and China. The line of my life follows fairly logical patterns until my decision to move to Hong Kong in December of 1991, when I abruptly abandoned my lifestyle in New York—and, most agonizing of all, began to spend long periods away from my three children.

Second, audiences want me to distill more than a dozen years of experience in China into a couple of sentences of wisdom. They want me to tell them the single most important thing I've learned. There's only one answer to this question, and my answer is the same in each case: it's absolutely imperative to build a strong local management team in China if you want to have any hope of long-term success.

And third, once the basics are covered, I often get a litany of questions dealing with how China works on a daily basis. How can the Chinese make things so cheaply? Is China's growth sustainable? How do you deal with the legal system and protecting your intellectual property? What's it like dealing with the government? What do the Chinese think of Westerners? How has the country changed since you've been there? What's it like to live there?

To address each of these major areas, the book is organized into three parts. Chapters 1 through 5 trace my progression from Pittsburgh to Yale, Harvard, Wall Street, and then the big leap east to Hong Kong and China. In these chapters I'll describe what I did, but also what I was thinking about at each stage. I'll touch on how I developed our strategy in Asia, and also on the things I learned that had the biggest impact on my thinking. Those early days in China were filled with any number of singular experiences, from my first taste of Chinese hospitality and *baijiu* to the novelty of eating "every part of every animal" and the many trips I made through the mountains to visit Mao's Third Front factories. Even I wouldn't believe some of it if I hadn't gone through it myself, and I'll share it all with you.

The second part of the book, Chapters 6 through 11, will touch on the management issue, the most important of all. I'll explain how we hit the wall running our business in China in 1997, and how we had to come up with our own way to close China's management gap. I'll tell you why our Plan A and then our Plan B both failed, and how—out of pure desperation—we lit upon Plan C, our "New China" management approach. I'll also discuss my views on why management is such an issue in China, and why it won't become any less of one over the next ten years. This section will close with three examples of how we implemented our new management strategy, culminating in the democratic election—unthinkable, until you've seen it—of a factory general manager in Hunan Province, Mao's backyard.

The third part of the book, Chapters 12 through 18, will address the key themes that I see in China—which, taken together, can provide answers to many of the questions about how the country works. Though the chapters will each cover different themes, they're all connected. I'll talk in greater depth about China's two markets, the different cost perspective in China, the way in which decentralization actually affects business practices, how intellectual property rights can be protected, how to deal with local governments, and a host of other topics that people consistently ask me to talk about. In this section I'll also give my best advice to those who are looking to start a business in China, what I think works and doesn't work. And last, I'll review the major challenges of running a business in China today, as well as the challenges the country will face in the coming decades.

Though other books have been written about China, this is the first attempt that I'm aware of to put in one place all of the lessons learned by somebody who has experienced the country firsthand, running a business through the ups and downs of fifteen memorable years. If what I've been through can help the reader in some small way to develop his or her own strategy, then I'll consider it to have been a great success.

Because I've gone through this as an individual—there was nothing more than me and a friend and an idea at the start—every mistake and every success has had a major impact on me personally, from both a financial and an emotional point of view. China has truly been a financial and emotional roller coaster for me. Maybe that's why I think a great deal about how all of these things fit together, and about where the country is headed.

The best thing I can do is to share with you what I thought, what I did, and how I felt at each step of my journey. In the interest of complete candor, I'll tell you that it will be easy for me to tell you what I did and what I thought. What gets harder for me is to tell you what I felt. As Carleen, my wife, and Sara, Douglas, and Libby, my three children, will tell you, I'm my father's son. I'm a very private person, and I tend to keep emotions and feelings bottled up. Much to the disappointment and frustration of the people around me, it's hard for me to tell them what I'm feeling sometimes, even though I know they have only the best of intentions in wanting to know. All four of them, plus Wayne Kabak, my agent at William

Morris; Jeff Himmelman, who has helped me to write this book; and John Mahaney, my editor at Crown, have pushed me to open up.

Western managers will often commit to a course of action or a target because they know it's required, but the Chinese never want to openly commit and risk disappointment and a loss of face. Instead of saying, "I will do it," more often they'll say, "I will try my best." I think here is a good place to take a page out of their playbook. On the matter of conveying to you, the reader, what I've felt at each step along the way, I can say only, "I will try my best."

Chapter 1

"Who Is Jack Perkowski?"

As Alan Oakley, editor of the *Sydney Morning Herald*, began to introduce me at the Global Business Forum in Sydney, Australia, in February of 2006, I stood nervously at the edge of the stage. In a moment I'd be addressing the assembled crowd of seven hundred business leaders and international media, and I needed to quietly collect my thoughts for the speech I was about to give on doing business in China.

I've spoken to any number of different audiences over the years, so that wasn't why I was nervous. Not many people with substantial careers in developed countries made the decision to come to China when I did, alone, and long before China was the rage. This aspect of my background, coupled with the growing presence of ASIMCO in China, has created a lot of opportunities for me to speak around the world. Though I still get the inevitable butterflies before stepping up to the microphone, I've done it so many times by now that I don't really think twice anymore, regardless of the size or makeup of the audience.

But Sydney, the first in a three-city tour that included

Melbourne and Auckland, New Zealand, was different. Former president Bill Clinton was on after me, slated to speak on a wide range of global issues. Next up would be Carly Fiorina, the former CEO of Hewlett-Packard who had put together the largest technology merger in history. After Carly's remarks on leadership, Michael Eisner would take the stage to talk about the many firsts he'd orchestrated as CEO of Disney. To say the least, this was an all-star lineup—and I was the leadoff hitter.

Carleen Giacalone, my wife, partner in China, and ASIMCO's director of corporate communications, tried to encourage me by saying that I was in the best spot. Leading off for President Clinton would ensure that all of the press would be there, she said, and that turned out to be true. But all I could think about beforehand was that one of the greatest communicators of all time would be coming to the stage right after me. How could I possibly get everyone's attention and have them remember me?

I'd been nervously anticipating this event for months, and I was determined to find some way to relieve the tension, both for me and the audience. I approached the microphone to a nice round of applause, though I could tell that people weren't sure what to expect.

"Before I was born," I began, "my parents thought long and hard about what to call me, and they gave me the name 'Jack.' When I went to China, the first thing the Chinese did was to give me a Chinese name.

"And now, after only three days in Australia," I said, scanning the great hall and beginning to crack a smile, "I find that I have a new first name: 'Who is? . . . '"

Knowing just what I meant, the audience broke into loud but sympathetic laughter, and the ice was broken. I had made light of the question that was clearly on the mind of just about everybody I'd been introduced to in Sydney since I'd gotten there: "I know who President Clinton is. I know who Carly Fiorina is, and Michael Eisner, too. But who is Jack Perkowski?"

ALTHOUGH THIS IS a book about China—about entrepreneurship, about doing something different from what's expected of you—I thought that the first thing I should do is tell you who I am, just like I did in Sydney.

Since 1994 I have been the chairman and CEO of ASIMCO Technologies, a China-based automotive components company that I founded in that year. With sales approaching $500 million, ASIMCO isn't a large company by U.S. standards. In China, though, we are one of the largest companies in our field. We are not yet a household name internationally, but our seventeen manufacturing facilities in eight different provinces and our fifty-two sales offices throughout the country give us a physical presence in nearly every corner of China. With over twelve thousand employees and a product line that includes diesel fuel injection systems, piston rings, starters, alternators, air compressors, brake products, and a wide range of castings, we are a significant factor in the Chinese automotive industry.

Apart from the numbers, there are a couple of things about us that most people find interesting. Because we were only an idea as recently as 1993, and we began focusing on the automotive industry (and specifically components) well before the rest of the world came to understand just how big China's appetite for cars, trucks, and buses would become, we are regarded as a visionary company. We were one of the first to understand that China's sheer size would require an extensive highway system and all types of vehicles to move people and goods around the country, just like the development of the U.S. economy had required some fifty years before.

Because I'm an American and our capital has come primarily from the United States, many people assume we're a U.S. company—but we're not. We're a Chinese company in every sense of the word. Our headquarters is in Beijing, where I've lived since 1993. Nearly all of our employees are Chinese, 85 percent of what we make is sold in the China market, and more than one-half of our sales are to purely Chinese companies. As one company after another now wants to leverage its non-China infrastructure to get a piece of the China market, ASIMCO is already well established here, and we're actually doing the reverse: we're seeking to leverage our China base to create a global company. We have had an office in the United States since 1997, and we opened offices in the United Kingdom in 2005 and Japan in 2006.

Perhaps more than anything, ASIMCO is known for the approach it has taken to developing local management in China. All of our factories in China are run by Mainland Chinese, and there is no position, including mine, that is not available to our Chinese managers. Case studies have been written about us, and our management approach is one of the reasons I am frequently asked to speak to audiences like the one in Sydney. In both 2001 and 2005, the only two years in which we participated, ASIMCO was named one of the ten best employers in China, ranking third in the most recent survey.

I often tell people that I won't be satisfied until I've built a $1 billion business in China, and we're halfway there. China being what it is, my guess is that the next half will be every bit as exciting as the first.

While we have succeeded in creating the franchise that first motivated my move to Asia, we still have a lot of work to do. In the chapters ahead, I'll tell you about some of our successes. I'll also describe some of the difficulties we've faced and how we overcame them to build our business in China.

But first, to the question in Sydney: "Who is Jack Perkowski?"

Growing Up in Pittsburgh

I come from a working-class background. My mother and father were born in the United States to parents who'd emigrated from Poland in the early 1900s. None of my grandparents spoke English, so I never had any direct communication with them, but I heard their stories from my parents. Like so many immigrants, they left Poland to escape something—poverty generally, or military service under the Russians in the case of my maternal grand-father. They came to America alone, in their mid to late teens, with no knowledge of the language, pennies in their pockets, and only the name of a distant relative to contact in a city they'd never heard of.

By heading to a foreign country with a different language in search of opportunity, my grandparents did the same thing in 1900 that I did almost one hundred years later. While it did take a certain courage to move to Asia and China in the early 1990s, in my mind it pales in comparison to the move my grandparents made. At least I could return to the States on a thirteen-hour flight, and my education, work experience, and financial security gave me a fallback position. They had none. Twenty-five years younger than I was when I left, they had no education and owned little more than the one-way ticket that brought them over.

Pittsburgh and western Pennsylvania were popular destinations because of employment prospects in the coal mines and steel mills, and the region attracted Poles, Germans, Italians, Czechs, Irish, and refugees from almost every eastern European country. (Despite changes in the steel industry and the city's fortunes since then, Pittsburgh retains a broad ethnic diversity that gives the city much of its spirit.)

My parents were typical of Tom Brokaw's "Greatest Generation." My mother, one of six siblings, finished high school and then worked as an AT&T long-distance telephone operator. My father was one of ten, and the Great Depression forced him out of school after the ninth grade and into work in one of the many steel machining shops in the Pittsburgh area. When the United States entered World War II, he joined the army as an infantryman, serving in the Pacific theater. He spoke fondly of the natural beauty and friendly natives in Australia, Fiji, and the Solomon Islands, but the jungle fighting and hand-to-hand combat must have been horrific. He could never bring himself to talk about it.

My parents' families knew each other, and my mother and father met briefly before he went off to war. Probably because my mother represented the new life he might begin if he could just manage to survive, my father wrote dozens and dozens of letters to her while he was overseas. (My oldest daughter, Sara, one of the most precocious children ever, once spent a week with my parents when my father was still alive, and her most vivid memory was cajoling my parents to pull out those letters. I can still hear her describing the three of them sitting around the kitchen table, reading every sentence, tears streaming down their faces.)

My father returned to the United States in May of 1945. My parents got married soon after, in January of 1946, despite the fact that they'd spent little time together and my dad was still recovering from malaria. Like everyone else, they had lost four precious years of their lives and were in a hurry to make up for lost time.

My sister Maryann was born a year later, and I came along nineteen months after that, on August 6, 1948. My brothers Dave and Frank followed closely, and then Evelyn, my youngest sister, came five years later.

My mother still lives in the house on Dorseyville Road that we all grew up in, on a hill surrounding the small town of Sharpsburg, which is part of the larger city of Pittsburgh. My parents bought the house in 1950 for $7,500, $7,000 in cash that my father had saved from his army paychecks and wedding gifts and $500 borrowed from an uncle. Growing up in the Depression had made my parents exceptionally cautious and conservative financially. They never borrowed, never had a checking account, and always paid with cash. As a result, they had no credit history and no credit rating, either.

I was particularly amused one day recently when my eighty-eight-year-old mother told me how a well-meaning cashier had pointed out to her that she could receive a 20 percent discount on her purchases if she signed up for the store's credit card. Always interested in a discount, my mother gladly filled out the forms—only to find that her application was rejected because she had no credit history. She had cash but had never borrowed, making her ineligible for a card that she would probably never use anyway.

My parents' attitude toward personal finances might seem strange to people now, but in fact it's not dissimilar from prevailing attitudes in China today. Credit cards are only a recent phenomenon, and usage is nowhere near what it is in the States. Carleen, who tends to the daily purchases in China, always has a wad of RMB in her purse, and she seldom pays with a credit card. (RMB is short for *renminbi*, the name of China's currency, which literally means "The People's Currency." One unit of RMB is a yuan, and for most of my time in China, one U.S. dollar has been roughly equal to eight yuan. Since China began allowing its currency to appreciate in July 2005, though, the number of yuan that one dollar can buy is getting closer to seven. Visitors to China are often confused when they hear residents also referring to *kuai*, but it's the same as referring to a dollar as a buck. One RMB yuan is equal to one kuai.)

Likewise, when my Chinese managers travel, in China or abroad, they always have cash. As recently as 2001, if you wanted to buy a car here, you needed to take a sack full of money to the dealer. The banks couldn't even transfer your funds, let alone make you a loan. As Americans continue to use credit cards to finance their daily needs and desires, the Chinese are still largely content to stick with cash.

The house on Dorseyville Road sits on three-quarters of an acre, and it was always planted intensively with every type of vegetable you could imagine. My parents would can the produce from the garden, so winter or summer we were virtually self-sufficient in terms of vegetables and fruit. For many years we also had about thirty chickens or so, which provided both eggs and meat. Growing up, our jobs as kids were to weed and maintain the garden and to gather eggs and feed the chickens.

We all went to the same grade school in Sharpsburg that my father had gone to, run by St. John Cantius, the Polish Catholic church. The kids there were either from the town of Sharpsburg, or from "up the hill," like we were. Sharpsburg, itself a miniature melting pot, had four schools and churches: Polish, Irish, German, and Italian. Kids from the different schools didn't mix very well. According to my parents and my uncles and aunts, a "mixed marriage" was when a Pole married an Italian. When I want to tease my mom, I remind her—always in Carleen's presence—how she advised me never to marry an Italian girl, because they're too demanding. My mother vehemently denies ever saying this.

My father worked for A. B. Chance, a metalworking company that machined various types of steel and iron products, but he lost his job when I was twelve and the company decided to move the operation to Missouri to take advantage of cheaper labor. (This experience, painful at the time, would later help me better understand the present-day trend toward the migration of certain jobs to low-cost countries like China.)

With Pittsburgh in recession, a tight job market, and five young kids who needed to eat, this was a tough time for us. We all did what we could to pitch in. My father took whatever jobs he could, my mother cleaned houses, my brothers and I had paper routes and mowed lawns, and my sisters babysat. Like all kids, we had our moments and occasional quarrels, but we were close as a family and we looked out for one another.

My mother's two sisters are both Catholic nuns, and my mother can best be described as "saintly." She was the understanding one, and she left it to my father to keep order. Though he wasn't particularly tall, my father was strong and physically imposing, with a big chest and big arms. When you combine that with his combat experience, he wasn't somebody whom anyone would particularly want to mess with. "Wait until your father gets home" was not a phrase we ever wanted to hear, and when we did, it pretty much ruined the rest of the day.

I remember a particularly poor lapse in judgment during high school. Coming home late one night, I found all the doors locked and decided to crawl through my parents' bedroom window. As I straddled the sill, with my right foot already through the window, it dawned on me how incredibly stupid this was. If my dad had awakened and seen somebody climbing into his bedroom window at night, I would have been knocked back over the porch roof in no time. Thank God he was sleeping soundly.

No matter how difficult things got economically, my parents always stressed the importance of education. Though they had no idea how we'd ever pay for it, they always encouraged our ambitions to go to college. We all went and managed, one way or another, to pay our own way, but my parents deserve all of the credit because of the steady drumbeat of encouragement that they provided. They didn't have a higher education, but instinctively they understood its importance.

Having grown up with these values—emphasis on education, strong work ethic, financial conservatism, self-reliance, and a strong family support structure—it's no wonder that I feel so much at home in China today. All of these traits are cornerstones of Chinese family life, and have been for centuries. Ask any Chinese parent and they'll tell you that the education of their child is the most important thing in the world to them. (That's part of the reason why Chinese kids do so well when given the chance.)

And you don't need to spend much time here to see that the Chinese are incredibly hardworking. When I made my initial trips through China, I couldn't help but be impressed by how hard the Chinese work, despite poverty that would drive most people to despair. Instead of sitting around, they were working hard to get ahead. As I rode through small villages in very remote parts of the country in those early days, I could feel the energy and see the activity: workers, backs hunched over, carrying loads of bricks up planks; farmers riding to market on bicycles loaded with fruit, vegetables, chickens, or whatever else was on hand; and street merchants with slabs of meat hanging in the front of their stalls. Everybody was working. Though the differences between the United States of the 1950s and the China of the last decade are pretty obvious, there was much about China that felt familiar to me.

"I Think I Want to Go to Yale"

For somebody from my background, having the opportunity to go to Yale was the turning point in my life, and I owe a great deal to several people who helped me through the process.

The first is Joe Wirth, my football coach in my senior year at North Catholic, which was something of a football powerhouse in those days. My senior year was my breakout season. Though I was only 175 pounds, which was light even then, I started at offensive tackle and defensive end, and our team won the Pittsburgh Catholic League Championship. I wasn't a great athlete, but I was a good one, and I found that if I worked especially hard at it, my quickness and mastery of the technical aspects of the game could compensate for my lack of size. My best game came against Aliquippa High, in the town where Mike Ditka, the All-Pro tight end and head coach of the Chicago Bears, grew up, when I blocked two punts and caught a tackle-eligible pass for a forty-yard touchdown.

As the season went on, the college coaches started coming around to prospect, and Coach Wirth pushed me and a few others with the grades to shoot for the Ivy League. Bob Egan, a Yale alumnus who was responsible for covering North Catholic for the Pittsburgh branch of the Yale Alumni Schools Committee, contacted me and paid a visit to my family at our home. I agreed to apply to Yale, and a month or so later I was on my way up the Pennsylvania Turnpike to see an Ivy League school for the first time.

The entire weekend was almost too good to be true. I walked around the Yale campus and the city of New Haven in a daze. For starters, I had the honor of staying with Brian Dowling, the star quarterback of Yale's freshman team, and his roommate, another freshman football player who happened to be from Pittsburgh. On Saturday, I watched Brian and Calvin Hill, who would go on to be drafted in the first round by the Dallas Cowboys, steamroll Harvard to complete the freshman team's first undefeated season in years. The Yale-Harvard game is the biggest social event of the year, and the Yale campus was awash with "Old Blues," prosperous-looking alumni in Yale hats, sweaters, and blue blazers, and with beautiful women decked out in long fur coats and carrying Yale banners. I'd never seen anything like this in Pittsburgh. I still remember standing in the middle of the Old Campus late on Saturday night, surrounded by the original buildings at Yale and statues of famous graduates like Nathan Hale, and thinking to myself, "This is where I want to go."

When April of 1966 rolled around, I checked the mailbox nervously each day, hoping for a fat acceptance letter from Yale. I got into Columbia but was wait-listed at Yale, which led to a bit of a confrontation in my living room with Buff Donelli, the legendary head coach at Columbia. Coach Donelli wanted me to forget about Yale and confirm my acceptance to Columbia, and he proceeded to give me the hard sell, telling me that if Yale really cared about me I'd have gotten in on the first try.

Finally, after several minutes of this, he looked at me directly and said, "Well, Jack, what do you want to do?"

Not happy about the negative sell, I looked him right in the eye and said, "I think I want to go to Yale." (My stubborn streak started early.) To my great delight, I received a telegram from Yale informing me of my acceptance the next day.

Coming from a working-class background in a city like Pittsburgh, education beyond high school (let alone at a place like Yale) wasn't assured—and, truth be told, not always aspired to, either. Until the recent "flattening of the world" that Tom Friedman describes in *The World Is Flat*, which has enabled workers in China, India, and other developing countries to compete with workers in developed countries, you could make more money working in a steel mill or an auto plant in the United States than you could as a teacher, or as many other types of knowledge workers. If you can make more money and retire after twenty years with a nice pension and a good health-care package, why go to college?

During my senior year, I worked at Kroger's supermarket part-time after school to make some money. One day, one of my coworkers there, a middle-aged guy who worked full-time for the U.S. Post Office during the day, asked me what I was going to do after high school.

"I'm going to Yale," I said.

Looking a bit puzzled, he asked, "Yale Lock?"

That was the world I left behind.

Yale, Football, and the World Beyond Pittsburgh

The world I became exposed to at Yale was quite a bit different. It really didn't matter where you were from, or what your father did. What mattered was what *you* did, inside and outside of the classroom. I had left a world with limited opportunities and crossed into a world where they were limitless.

I still remember one of my first days as a freshman, unlocking the door to my first-floor room in Durfee Hall on the Old Campus and striking up a conversation with a guy coming down the stairs. We'd never met before, but we started talking about what we wanted to do after Yale. He told me, quite matter-of-factly, that he wanted to be president of the United States. I knew then that I was a long, long way from Pittsburgh. My classmate didn't achieve his ambition, but the point is that he didn't think it at all unusual to set a goal that high. (Admittedly, the story would be better if it had been George W. Bush whom I met in the stairwell, but President Bush was two years ahead of me in New Haven.)

I realized pretty quickly that I wasn't as prepared for the rigors of Yale as were my classmates who'd been to the Andovers of the world. I had written only one paper in all of my years at North Catholic, so catching up in that area was a real challenge. In History 10 my freshman year, I finally managed to get a top mark on my final term paper after a year of hard work. The teaching assistant, who worked with me all year to improve my writing style, wrote the following just below my grade: "Jack: Although your writing is still semi-barbaric, it has improved tremendously since the beginning of the year. Keep up the good work."

I had to work especially hard, both in the classroom and on the football field, to keep up in that first year at Yale. I was still only 175 pounds when I arrived for the first day of practice, and I didn't play much on a freshman team that was full of kids who'd been "All-Something" in high school. I soon realized that my only chance at ever making the varsity was to dedicate myself to getting bigger, stronger, and faster. I threw myself into an off-season program, lifting weights to improve my strength and playing handball to improve my agility. (Today weight training is commonplace throughout all of football, but in 1966 it wasn't nearly as common.) I gained more than thirty-five pounds in three months and became one of the strongest players on the team. I continued my training over the summer, so that when I arrived back in New Haven for my sophomore year, I was a different person. Though I didn't play much, I suited up for the varsity games and got my playing time on the junior varsity squad, where I was voted MVP and received the Norman S. Hall Memorial Trophy for outstanding service to Yale football. I finally earned a starting job my junior year, where I had the particular good fortune to play alongside Brian Dowling and Calvin Hill in their last season at Yale.

My football career at Yale was a real high point in my

life. The Yale teams of 1967, 1968, and 1969 were some of the best in Yale football history. Carm Cozza, whom I had the privilege of playing under, is widely regarded as one of the greatest college coaches of all time. We were undefeated my junior year, but the 29–29 tie with Harvard, easily the most famous game in Yale football history and generally considered one of the most famous games in college football history, meant that we had to share the Ivy League title with our friends from Cambridge. We blew a 29–13 lead late in the fourth quarter and awoke to a headline in the *Harvard Crimson* that blared, "Harvard Beats Yale 29–29." (The most famous person on the field that day, it turned out, was Tommy Lee Jones, the Academy Award-winning actor who was a senior offensive guard for the Harvard side.) I was named Honorable Mention All-Ivy that year, and I was also privileged to receive the Gordon Brown Memorial Prize, given each year to an outstanding member of the junior class. This meant a lot to me, because it showed that everything had come together in the classroom as well. By my junior year, I was an "A" student and ultimately graduated cum laude.

Yale reinforced forever my view that hard work and perseverance can help you overcome any obstacle. It also gave me a great deal of confidence in what I could ultimately achieve if I set my mind to it. If you want something badly enough and are willing to work for it, chances are you'll get it.

Shaking Off the Coal Dust

From the very first time I went to China, everybody I met emphasized the importance of relationships to doing business in the country. People always refer to *guanxi*, which essentially means "connections" or "relationships," knowing the proverbial brother-in-law of somebody in power. I didn't have any reason to disagree with this view as to how to operate in China, but it always seemed strange to me because it implied somehow that relationships weren't as important in other countries like the States. That didn't make sense to me. After all, the importance of relationships was why Coach Wirth had recommended the Ivy League to me in the first place, and the Yale network I became a part of would rival any, including that of Tsinghua University in Beijing, which the Chinese will tell you is Yale, Harvard, Princeton, and MIT all rolled into one. Like Yale, Tsinghua turns out a new batch of government and business leaders every year.

Coach Wirth had been right about Yale. Jim Mourkas, who'd brought me up from Pittsburgh for my Yale visit, was a senior sales executive at Jones & Laughlin Steel Company (J&L) and had helped me a great deal in finding good summer jobs. The summer between my sophomore and junior years I worked in the accounting department of the J&L rolling mills, located on Pittsburgh's Southside, right along the Monongahela River. The next summer, I was a member of the company's audit group, which gave me a chance to see J&L facilities in Pittsburgh, Cleveland, and Oil City, Pennsylvania.

Though these might not sound like glamorous jobs, I was in management. I got to see operations and finance firsthand in a factory environment. On one of my first days at the rolling mill, the assistant plant manager, a Princeton grad, took great pains to point out to me that management had white helmets and hourly workers had brown helmets. When I ran into one of my former North Catholic classmates who was working in the mill, he couldn't resist ribbing me about my white helmet.

In the fall of my senior year, I applied to Harvard Business School and was accepted straight off—no waiting list this time. I deferred for a year to serve on active duty with the National Guard unit I had joined, and I began looking for a job in finance. (By my senior year, the Vietnam War was raging and we all had to figure out what to do about the draft. I viewed service in the National Guard as a good way to meet my military obligation without delaying the start of my career.)

One afternoon after the football season was over, I was in the Yale Co-op, shopping for my upcoming interviews with several of the New York banks. Carm Cozza happened to walk into the other end of the store and noticed me sorting through the silk ties.

"Perkowski!" he shouted from across the floor. "What are you doing with those ties? You're still shaking off the coal dust from Pittsburgh!"

Carm was from Ohio, and much of his staff was from the Midwest, too, so they always liked to tease me about my western Pennsylvania background. Teasing aside,

Carm was a class act. He was always there for his players, and he took a personal interest in each of us. I don't know how he did it, but no matter how many years had passed since I played, he would immediately say, "Hi, Jack," or "Hi, Perko," whenever he saw me at the games. During the school year, he got copies of our grades (just like our parents) and was especially proud of the fact that the football team had a higher GPA than the student body as a whole. He always liked to remind us that our grades were higher during the season, when demands were highest, than they were in the off-season when we had more time to pursue "other interests."

As Carm approached, I sheepishly put the tie I was holding back on the counter.

"What's the tie for?" he asked.

"I have interviews with some of the New York banks," I said.

"You should go to see Charlie O'Hearn," he suggested immediately. Charlie was the assistant to the president of Yale in charge of fund-raising. Carm's advice was always good, and I had now been trained for four years to do exactly what he said, so I called Charlie's office as soon as I got back to my room.

As I walked into Charlie's office a few days later, I was immediately impressed with the man I encountered: a stately, well-dressed elderly gentleman sitting serenely behind his desk, smoking a pipe. A partner at Scudder, Stevens & Clark, Charlie had taken the position at Yale in 1951 and had extensive contacts on Wall Street. He was also a legend at Yale, where he had lettered in football, hockey, and baseball; he was probably best known for having kicked a fifty-two-yard dropkick field goal, the longest in Yale's history, against Carnegie Tech (now Carnegie Mellon) in 1922. As a former Yale football player, Charlie was only too happy to help a young player along in his career.

"Which banks are you interested in?" he asked after I'd taken a seat and explained why I was there to see him.

"Bankers Trust, Irving Trust, Morgan Guaranty, and Chemical Bank," I rattled off. (Due to the consolidation that has taken place in the banking industry since then, Morgan Guaranty and Chemical are part of JP Morgan, Irving is part of Bank of New York, and Bankers Trust is part of Deutsche Bank.) I'd already had on-campus interviews with all four and had been invited for second-round interviews at each.

"I'll see what I can do," he said.

In the days that followed, I received carbon copies of letters that Charlie had written on my behalf to his contacts at each institution. As I made the interview rounds in New York City, at some point during each full-day interview I was pulled away and escorted to an office the size of a football field at the top of the building. There I'd be introduced to Charlie's friend, who more often than not just happened to be the chairman or vice chairman of the bank. Often the person was a Yale graduate, and we would spend time talking first about the bank, and then about Yale and the upcoming football season. I didn't know what *guanxi* was at the time, but even now I'd be hard-pressed to tell you how this was any different.

Wall Street

With Charlie's help, I landed a job at Morgan Guaranty, where I worked for a year before spending two years at Harvard Business School. I emerged from Harvard as both a married man and as a Baker Scholar, meaning I'd placed in the top 5 percent of my class. (I married Mary Brophy, a girl I'd met in my junior year at Yale, in June of 1971, just before entering Harvard.) In the summer of 1973, I went to work for PaineWebber (now part of UBS) as one of only two MBA graduates hired into the investment banking department, because I thought the firm would offer me bigger and more diverse opportunities than the traditional investment banking firms. For the most part, that turned out to be true.

The Wall Street that I joined in 1973 was completely different from the Wall Street of today. Giant financial firms dominate the business now, but back then Wall Street was a cottage industry. A handful of firms advised companies on how to raise debt or equity financing and then formed syndicates to underwrite and sell the underlying securities. The industry had a clubby atmosphere, and the relationship between an investment banking firm and a company was like that between a doctor and a patient. Little did I know, when I first got there, that the "Street" would change more in the next twenty years than at any time since the Great Depression.

I also couldn't possibly have known that the experience that I would gain on Wall Street would be the best possible preparation for what I would later do in China. I learned some skills, to be sure, but, more important, I saw first-hand how the development of the capital markets in the 1980s contributed to the growth of the U.S. economy. Seeing that gave me some perspective on what might be in store for China, as its capital markets broaden and deepen. I can only imagine the growth that will occur when similar changes take hold here.

The biggest differences between Wall Street then and the Wall Street of today are scale and complexity. When I joined PaineWebber in June of 1973, the Dow Jones Industrial Average (DJIA) was hovering around 900. After plunging to a low of 577 in the bear market of 1973–74, it would barely recover to 900 by the end of the decade. The Vietnam War, stagflation, the Iran hostage crisis, the oil crisis, and the death of Elvis Presley—these were the stories that dominated the headlines and depressed the equity markets.

During those years, initial public offerings (IPOs) and equity financings were few and far between due to a lackluster stock market. Junk bonds, or high-yield securities, as they are called today, had not yet been invented; leveraged buyouts, called bootstrap financings then, were much smaller (anything larger than $10 million was simply unheard of); and there were no private equity or hedge funds as we know them today. The biggest question on the minds of venture capitalists was how to exit their investments, because companies couldn't count on an IPO. While there had been a wave of mergers and acquisitions in the 1960s, so-called M&A activity was relatively sparse in the 1970s. Making a "hostile" (unsolicited) bid for a company's common stock was a no-no.

With the DJIA now trading well over 12,000, everything today is at least twelve times bigger and more complex. Companies, deals, fees, and the organizations that handle financial transactions have all grown exponentially over the last thirty years or so. Advances in computer technology, globalization, and the tremendous wealth creation of the past fifteen years have made capital markets deeper, more complicated, and more international. In 1973, Wall Street was the street in New York City where it all happened. With the advent of the computer and the free flow of information, Wall Street is now literally all around us.

WHAT PEOPLE DON'T realize, when they think about China, is that the Chinese capital markets are a lot more like the U.S. markets of the 1970s than they are like the global markets that we've become accustomed to today. A company can't just take its business model and superimpose it on China, unless perhaps that plan is thirty years old.

First, China's economy has been less than one-eighth

the size of the American economy for most of my time in China, so everything has to be scaled down accordingly. Apart from the large state-owned companies, a $50 million acquisition or financing is quite sizable in China, but in the United States it would hardly register in the deal sheets. (My general rule of thumb is to multiply by eight to get a rough equivalent between the two markets.)

Second, China's institutional infrastructure, from the legal system and the capital markets on down, is still at an early stage of development, at least in Western terms. Between 1949 and 1978, Chairman Mao's isolationist policies put China into a thirty-year time warp where most development came to a screeching halt. As much as China might like to, and as much as bankers, venture capitalists, and private equity professionals might like it to, the country can't simply hit fast-forward and arrive fully equipped in the present. It's going to take a while for the time lost during those thirty years to be made up, and for China to grow into itself.

The markets reflect this lag. At almost 50 percent, China has one of the highest savings rates in the world. But, as I write this, there's simply no efficient way to distribute the tremendous amount of capital generated each year by these savings to the companies or individuals who can use it best. The central government has recently opened up the banking system to competition, but for too long the bulk of the deposits have been tied up in four state-owned banks. The loan officers at these banks have never been trained in fundamental credit analysis. All they've ever really had to do is hand out "policy loans," which go only to state-sanctioned companies and are essentially governmental funding under a different name.

The Chinese stock markets are also undergoing reform, but they have to come much further still. They should be a vibrant source of equity financing for companies with a good story or a visionary plan, but thus far they haven't even come close. Deals can't be financed with leverage like they can in the States. Mezzanine financings don't exist, and mergers and acquisitions—which can normally be relied upon to force much-needed consolidation in industry after industry—simply haven't taken place at the rate or in the numbers necessary.

The most important and first step is for China to reform its banking system. In other countries, a healthy banking industry has formed a strong foundation for the development of capital markets generally, and there is no reason to expect that it will be any different in China. Slowly—thankfully—this is starting to happen. Goldman Sachs and a few other firms have bought significant minority interests in the large state-owned banks, and Morgan Stanley has been one of the groups that have obtained banking licenses and acquired majority owner-ship interests in smaller or start-up banks. (For reasons I'll explain more fully in Chapter 12, the latter approach, where foreign institutions can more completely control bank lending policies immune from government influence, is likely to be more effective over the longer term. But foreign investment of any kind will inevitably speed up the reform process.)

The upside of all of this is the potential for growth. The state of the U.S. capital markets when I entered Wall Street in the 1970s approximates where China is today, but as we know now, everything in the United States was about to change dramatically. These changes—increasing sophistication, diversity, and market depth, to name a few—helped propel the U.S. economy to new levels in the 1980s. The same thing needs to happen in China, and as that process of change gains momentum, the impact on China's economy will be similarly profound. Right now, China's lack of an effective capital market is its biggest problem. The flip side is that, over time, the development of an effective capital distribution mechanism will be its single biggest opportunity.

Investment Banking

When I eventually made the move to Asia, it immediately became clear to me that my biggest selling point, by far, was my twenty-year career in investment banking. Chinese officials, our Chinese and foreign partners, existing and potential employees, and our customers were all fascinated by Wall Street and the fact that I had a long, successful career in a world beyond their imagination. Investment bankers are everywhere in New York, but I represented something new and different in China in the early 1990s, and I used it to my advantage as best I could.

At PaineWebber, I started off in private placements, and then became an account officer; in both roles, I learned how to raise money and worked on all kinds of different deals, from the financing for Sea World to other, more nuts-and-bolts kinds of businesses. I got my first big break in 1982, when the real estate division was gutted by a rival firm and I was asked to run it—despite the fact that I had very little experience doing those kinds of deals. Starting with a staff of one, I hired the smartest people I could and rebuilt the department to the point where, after two years, we represented 40 percent of PaineWebber's investment banking revenues.

In September of 1984, Mike Johnston, the head of Capital Markets, asked me to be "cohead" of PaineWebber's investment banking division. When I asked what that meant, he said, "I want you to run it." I was thirty-six years old, younger than virtually all of the senior bankers. Despite the successes of the real estate group, the investment banking department was in a death spiral. Revenue had been flat for years, and hiring of new associates had been minimal, barely enough to replace those who'd left. Within two years, we increased the number of associates we hired each year from four to twenty and doubled our revenues, which would grow by another 50 percent the next year and an additional third the year after that.

In 1987, Don Marron, the chairman of the firm, asked me to lead negotiations with Yasuda Life, a Japanese insurance company interested in investing $300 million in

PaineWebber. We arrived at the key elements of a deal over that summer, and all was well and good—until the Yasuda Life negotiating team decided to fly to New York City to seal the deal on October 19, 1987.

That morning, I was actually feeling pretty good: a reporter from the *New York Times* had called me over the weekend to ask what I thought about the 100-point drop in the market the previous Friday. I'd almost forgotten about it, but when I got to work that morning I discovered that my picture was on the front page of the *Times*, next to David Rockefeller and Ross Perot, along with a quotation that turned out to be somewhat prescient: "This market has come very far very fast."

Whatever exhilaration I felt about being on the front page of the *New York Times* went out the window shortly after the opening bell. By the time the Yasuda Life team got off the plane, the stock market had plummeted more than 500 points—a stunning 23 percent—and our stock price had been cut in half. Over the course of the week, we renegotiated the terms of the deal and, all things considered, PaineWebber came out quite well. In the wake of Black Monday, that we could even close a deal of that size meant a lot about PaineWebber's staying power. (At the Christmas party that year, Don Marron cited me for having made the most important contribution to the firm that year.)

The Yasuda Life deal was the capstone to my investment banking career. I had started to grow restless, and I sensed that there wasn't much more room to grow where

I was. I had learned a lot on Wall Street. I'd raised all types of capital for all sizes of companies in varying market conditions; I'd helped rebuild an entire real estate group that had been decimated by high-level defections to a rival firm; I'd been handed a mediocre investment banking division and asked to grow it; and I'd managed to complete a deal the week of Black Monday in 1987 that helped keep my firm afloat. Through all of this, I gained confidence that I could raise capital for any venture that I really believed in.

I started by raising $250 million, with John Kluge of Metromedia (part of which is now the Fox Network). Our idea was to create a $1 billion leveraged buyout firm of our own, capitalizing on John's reputation as a savvy investor and my investment banking experience. What we didn't realize is that timing is everything, and unfortunately our timing wasn't very good. Everybody and their uncle wanted to start an LBO fund. At a fathers' meeting I attended at Buckley, my son Douglas's school, the headmaster opened by saying, "Okay, which of you fathers didn't start an LBO fund this year?" Needless to say, we weren't exactly ahead of the trend.

Which, I began to realize more and more, was what I was looking for. During my years on Wall Street, I had seen that individuals who are first to recognize and capitalize on important trends could build firms with unique franchises. If I was going to leave PaineWebber and truly strike out on my own, I didn't want to simply follow others, or chase after the same deals that everybody else was competing for. I wanted to be the first to discover something, and to capitalize on my discovery. This became a burning desire for me, and ultimately it was this restlessness, and the desire to do something truly new, that brought me to Asia, and then to China.

To this day, the framed galley of that front page from October 19, 1987, which the *Times* was kind enough to send me, sits near my desk in my Beijing office—a constant reminder of a world I loved, but left because it was somehow not enough for me.

Chapter 2

Stay in New York or Move to Hong Kong?

I n the spring of 1990, Bill Kaye, who ran PaineWebber's arbitrage activity, confided in me that he was also thinking of leaving PaineWebber. We'd become friends serving on various management committees together, and we'd stayed in touch when I went to work with John Kluge.

Bill told me he was interested in what was happening in Asia, and he showed me a *BusinessWeek* article that had caught his attention. The piece quoted Bill Simon, a former secretary of the Treasury who'd gone on to become a principal in a very successful LBO firm, as saying, "If I were forty, I would move to Hong Kong."

Bill and I scratched our heads.

"Why did he say that?" we asked each other. I was just forty-one at the time, looking for the right new direction in my career, and we both had a feeling that the former Treasury secretary was on to something. We decided then and there to figure out what it was.

Made in Hong Kong

Hong Kong Island, off the southern coast of China, has had a long and varied history. It's said that humans have lived along its coast for more than six thousand years, and the Chinese first settled there during the Qin Dynasty (220 to 206 B.C.). As European contact with China grew due to the trade in silk, tea, and other Chinese products along the Silk Road, Europeans began to arrive at the beginning of the fifteenth century, attracted by the deep-water harbor and the connection to Mainland China.

British trade with the Chinese grew particularly briskly, and in an effort to balance their purchases from the Middle Kingdom, the British increased their sales of opium to the Chinese. China's emperor, alarmed at the outflow of silver that this was causing, tried unsuccessfully to ban the sale of opium in 1799. Eventually, the Chinese felt compelled to take more aggressive measures, resulting in the First Opium War and the concession of Hong Kong Island to the British in 1842. In 1860, after further hostilities, the Chinese would also cede Kowloon, across the harbor, and Stonecutter's Island to the British. In 1898, Britain acquired the New Territories, an additional part of Mainland China, through a ninety-nine-year contract, and what is now known as the Hong Kong Special Administrative Region was formed.

As China's political landscape changed, first with the end of the imperial period in 1913 and then with the establishment of the People's Republic of China in 1949,

Hong Kong became a popular destination for refugees and exiles from the Mainland. British rule of law and Chinese entrepreneurship proved to be an explosive combination, and Hong Kong prospered. With its central location in Asia and extensive harbor facilities, the region became a low-cost manufacturing center for apparel and lower-technology goods like toys. (When I was growing up in Pittsburgh, labels saying "Made in Hong Kong" seemed to be on just about everything. Gradually, those labels were replaced with ones reading "Made in Taiwan" or "Made in South Korea." Today, of course, nearly all say "Made in China.")

By the summer of 1990, when I was first starting to look seriously at Asia, there was a great deal of talk about the 1997 handover from the British to the Chinese. Everybody thought that there'd be good trading opportunities in the Hong Kong stock market in the run-up to 1997, but nobody knew what to expect afterward. Some predicted disaster when Hong Kong returned to China, and others thought Hong Kong would only be the better for it, given how linked it already was to the Mainland. Whatever side you came down on, the biggest question for the region was what was going to happen to Hong Kong after July 1, 1997. The idea of China was out there, looming on the horizon, but nobody really knew what to make of it yet.

Since 1978, when Deng Xiaoping had opened China up to foreign direct investment, capital had begun to flow steadily into the country, beginning with the overseas

Chinese businessmen who invested in the special economic zones (SEZs) just inside China's borders. Joint ventures deeper inland followed, but then the Tiananmen Square incident on June 4, 1989, brought things to a halt. One U.S. firm after another pulled out of China, as did companies from other countries, and the sluggish Chinese economy stayed mired in a recession. Among other issues, the foreign companies who stayed had a hard time finding foreign exchange, and this lack of hard currency was a central theme in Jim Mann's book *Beijing Jeep*, the first about doing business in China from a Western perspective.

As the Westerners got out in the late 1980s and early 1990s, businessmen in Hong Kong and Taiwan continued to invest in the four SEZs that the Chinese had set up in the south—Shenzhen, Zhuhai, and Shantou in Guangdong Province, and Xiamen in Fujian Province. The central government had cleverly located these first SEZs in convenient areas: Shenzhen is just across the border from the New Territories; Zhuhai is a ferry ride from Macau, which was then under Portuguese rule but was scheduled to revert to China in 1999; and Xiamen and Shantou sit just opposite Taiwan across the Taiwan Straits.

It didn't take long for the SEZs to become veritable boomtowns, as overseas Chinese entrepreneurs moved their manufacturing operations from high-cost factories in Hong Kong and Taiwan to lower-cost factories in China. The population of Shenzhen was approximately three hundred thousand in 1979; by 1991, it had climbed to almost 2 million, and it's higher than 10 million today.

By 1990, the Hong Kong and Asian stock markets had started to tick upward. Hong Kong companies were becoming increasingly connected to China, and the Chinese economy was starting to show signs of recovery from its doldrums in the late 1980s. From a low point of 3.8 percent GDP growth in 1990, China's economy advanced by 9.2 percent in 1991 and 14.2 percent in 1992. After touching bottom at 2,000 on June 4, 1989, the Hang Seng Index, Hong Kong's version of the DJIA, had nearly doubled to 4,000 by the end of 1991. These upward trends, particularly in the Hong Kong stock market, created a drumbeat for investment in Asia's emerging markets. This is what Bill Simon had been talking about in *BusinessWeek*.

ALL OF THIS is clear to me now, but in August of 1990 I had only snippets of information to go on and saw only a small piece of the total picture. In general, this was a particularly tough and uncertain time for me. Professionally, the deal with Kluge hadn't panned out the way I'd hoped; on the home front, I had separated from my first wife, Mary, several years before. In our seventeen years together, we had three wonderful kids, but we had grown further and further apart as husband and wife. Finally, we decided that it was best if we went our separate ways and focused on being the best parents that we could be to our three children.

During the years when I'd lived in a separate apartment in New York, I'd used the time as well as I could. The apartment was about ten blocks from Buckley, where Douglas went to school, and about thirty blocks from Brearley, where the girls went, so I was lucky enough to be able to go to Douglas's wrestling matches and football games, to Sara's and Libby's gymnastics meets, and to the myriad school events that kids want their dads to attend. (I have particularly fond memories of walking Sara to school in the mornings.) I didn't know it at the time, but those years spent with the kids formed a strong enough foundation that when I decided to move to Hong Kong, they viewed it as a new adventure, not as the loss of a parent. I had their blessing and support from the start, which meant a great deal to me.

After finishing extensive renovations to my farm in New Jersey in the spring of 1990, I gave up my apartment in New York, moved there full-time, and began figuring out what I was going to do in my second career. Fortunately, I didn't have to think through this alone. By this time, Carleen Giacalone was an important part of my life. Carleen had worked in the corporate secretary's office at PaineWebber, where she dealt with various legal and board-related matters. Her experience would serve us well later, as she took responsibility for overseeing certain legal aspects of ASIMCO's subsidiaries as corporate secretary and training the Chinese staff to deal with foreign investors, directors, and corporate executives. As we started the company, we began to host numerous visits, meetings, and plant tours with investors and senior corporate executives from all over the world.

Carleen had to convince our Chinese staff that the high standards for professionalism and attention to detail taken for granted in the West were not unrealistic for companies located in China—and, in fact, were an important part of becoming a truly global company.

A New Yorker who grew up in Greenwich Village, Carleen also has a great sense of style. As ASIMCO's head of corporate communications, she has been instrumental in defining and projecting ASIMCO's brand image as a modern, professional China-based company. After a week of traveling through China visiting a series of typical Chinese companies, with ASIMCO the last stop on his tour, one of our Western visitors once remarked to me that sitting in ASIMCO's conference room in Beijing made him feel very much at home. This was exactly the type of image that we have sought to project and that Carleen has made possible.

Those are some of the reasons why Carleen was the ideal partner for me as I began thinking about Asia. Apart from the many contributions she has made to the company, she has been a great wife and has developed strong and loving relationships with each of my three children. It's difficult for me to imagine how I could have gone through this experience without the unwavering support she has provided over the years.

Taking the First Step

After deciding to look at Asia, the obvious question was "Okay, where do we begin?"

Bill noticed that a "Pacific Rim Conference" was slated for early September at the Fairmont Hotel, in San Francisco. It seemed like a logical starting point. We wrote out checks for $1,500, booked our flights, and had name cards made up for "The Pacific Group." (We were pretty proud of the name, but it wasn't very original. Over the course of the three-day conference, I must have collected twenty business cards that had the word *Pacific* on them somewhere.)

The conference actually turned out to be fairly useful. We met a lot of people and heard from a number of CEOs of companies in Hong Kong, Taiwan, and other countries in Asia. The presentations generally reinforced the notion that Asia was a vibrant region, becoming more so each minute, and represented almost unlimited opportunity. The governor of California, George Deukmejian, gave the keynote address, and I was somewhat surprised to hear him cite statistic after statistic in support of his claim that California was one of the largest economies in the Pacific Rim. Somehow, in my years of investment banking, I'd missed the news that California had seceded from the Union. "You learn something new every day," I thought to myself.

When the conference was over, we'd accumulated a stack of business cards—primarily from attorneys, accountants, consultants, and a wide variety of advisers, all of whom gave the impression that they knew a great deal about Asia, or at least had partners who did. We were surprised at how willing everybody was to be helpful.

Looking back now, I can see that people knew Asia was going to be a big opportunity, but nobody really knew what to do about it. We were all searching for the right formula.

During September we had a number of follow-on meetings with individuals and firms we'd come into contact with, explaining each time that we were thinking of repotting ourselves in Asia. We must have seemed incredibly naïve, two American hotshots thinking they could take on Asia, and never more so than when the inevitable question would arise at some point in each meeting.

"So you've been to Asia many times, right?" somebody would ask, almost as a statement.

"No, we've never been there," I'd say. Whatever momentum might have been building in the meeting pretty much stopped right there.

"That's incredible," they'd say. "How in the world can you decide to move someplace you've never been?" We somehow didn't think the idea was all that incredible.

Nonetheless, after yet another frustrating end to a meeting, I turned to Bill as we walked out and said, "Bill, I don't care if we just take a plane to Hong Kong, touch down at Kai Tak and then come right back. We have to at least be able to say that we've been there." That day we began to plan a six-week trip to Asia, beginning in early October.

With that decision, our meetings took a new turn.

"We're planning a trip to Asia," we'd tell the people

we were meeting with. "Where should we go? Who should we see?"

If those meetings were being held today, the discussion would be all about China and which cities we planned to visit. But in those days, as hard as it is to believe now, China never even came up. Opinion was divided: some suggested that we look at Taiwan, some made the case for Singapore, and still others talked about Seoul. When all was said and done, Hong Kong, with its international capital markets, well-developed legal infrastructure, and its role as the "gateway" to China, seemed to be the best place for us to begin. We decided to spend most of our time there, but to visit Taiwan and South Korea as well. (I also planned to pay a visit to my old friends at Yasuda Life in Japan.)

Organizing the trip and arranging a schedule proved to be surprisingly easy. At PaineWebber I'd worked a bit with Coudert Brothers, a law firm with a strong reputation in international work. The partners in New York arranged a conference call for us one evening with Gage MacAfee, Coudert's partner in Hong Kong.

After we explained who we were, Gage said, "If you move to Hong Kong, you'll easily be the most experienced bankers here." He also said he'd be happy to arrange a schedule for us while we were in town. It was a promising start.

Another person who helped us a great deal in our planning was Richard V. Allen, a foreign policy expert who had served in various roles in the Nixon and Reagan administrations, most notably as Reagan's first national security adviser. (I was introduced to Dick by one of my colleagues at PaineWebber.) After leaving government service, Dick had set up a Washington-based international consulting company. We had a brief conversation over the phone and decided to meet in his D.C. offices.

I liked Dick immediately. He's a colorful guy, and conversations with him are a unique experience, punctuated as they are with frequent references to "foxholes" and "incoming shells." Dick liked the fact that my farm in New Jersey is in the 609 area code, which was where he was from, and "where the real men are," as he put it to me that day. Forever after, he would always refer to me as "609."

Dick's contacts in Taiwan and South Korea were particularly strong because of the work he'd done in the White House, and he offered to set up meetings for us in both countries. In the end he actually did us one better, arranging for his travels to Asia to coincide with ours so that he could take us around himself.

(A smile came across my face one morning in October of 2006, when I saw an e-mail from Dick titled "Incoming." We'd been out of touch for a long time, but he was in Hong Kong and planned to be in Beijing the next week. I explained that I would be flying back from Germany on that Saturday morning and suggested dinner that night with Carleen at one of our favorite restaurants. Evidently he appreciated the extra effort to have dinner with him on the night I flew in from out of town, because his response was classic Dick Allen: "Jack—glad to make contact. 609 people are all the same." We had a great time with him, reminiscing about the early days in Asia and listening to Dick's war stories.)

With Gage arranging meetings for us in Hong Kong and Dick doing the same in Taiwan and Korea, we were pretty well set. Now all we had to do was book our flights and figure out where to stay.

I wouldn't normally have thought too much about any of this. But as we made the rounds and told people we were going to Hong Kong, I was surprised at how many times the first question we heard was "Where are you staying?" Not "Why are you going," or "Who are you seeing?" It was always said in a way that suggested to me that our answer would have some bearing on how seriously we should be taken.

There were probably a number of right answers, but we quickly figured out that one right answer was the Mandarin Oriental. Opened in 1963, the Mandarin was the first truly upscale hotel built in Hong Kong. The nods of approval that we received after we booked our rooms bolstered our confidence. It was our first real indication that in Hong Kong, with its British heritage, form would be at least as important as substance. With that last element of the trip nailed down, we were off.

No More Ducks Over Hong Kong

In those days, flying into Hong Kong's Kai Tak Airport was a hair-raising experience. Among pilots, it was commonly referred to as the hardest place to land a plane in the world. The runway was an isolated spar jutting out from Kowloon into Victoria Bay; it was close to the city, which was great once you were on the ground—safely. The pilot had to navigate around the mountains that enfold Hong Kong, and, instead of making a straight approach, had to make a sharp turn and begin the descent immediately. The plane passed so close to the nearby apartment buildings that you could almost reach out and grab the socks and T-shirts off the clotheslines that hung from the windows. As if that weren't enough of a challenge, the runway was short. If the pilot didn't land perfectly and stop quickly enough, the plane could end up in the water. This wasn't mere paranoia, either. A plane actually did this once, and for years afterward it could still be seen, its tail sticking up out of the water right at the edge of the runway.

We didn't know it when we booked our flights, but October is the perfect time to visit Hong Kong. The summer heat has broken by then, the temperature is mild, the skies are clear and blue, and the danger of typhoons is at its lowest. We were pleasantly surprised to have accidentally picked the right season, and it seemed like yet another good omen for our trip.

True to his word, Gage had set up a great schedule. Our first meeting was with Gordon Wu, chairman of Hopewell Holdings, a Hong Kong listed company that was building toll roads in China and Bangkok. A Princeton grad, Gordon likened owning toll roads in

Guangdong Province to owning a piece of the New Jersey Turnpike. In many ways, he was right.

We met also with Peter Woo, chairman of Wharf Holdings, another large infrastructure company listed in Hong Kong. He told us in depth about all of the work Wharf was doing to upgrade the infrastructure in Wuhan. Situated at the crossroads of central China and the capital of Hubei Province, Wuhan was and is a transportation hub for air, rail, and river traffic. The city is basically equidistant from Guangzhou, Beijing, and Shanghai, and the Yangtze, Han, and Xunshi rivers all converge there, dividing Wuhan into three cities. Wharf was planning considerable investments in Wuhan, Peter said. Given its central location, he considered it to be the Chicago of China.

(Several years later, at a reception in Beijing given by James Sasser, the U.S. ambassador to China at the time, in honor of the mayor of Pittsburgh, I learned that Wuhan was Pittsburgh's "sister city," no doubt inspired by the fact that both cities are surrounded by three rivers. I didn't know this when I met with Peter Woo, but I still think the Chicago comparison is more apt given Wuhan's size.)

Next up was Simon Murray, a former member of the French Foreign Legion and now a prominent banker in Hong Kong. At that time, he was running Hutchison Whampoa for Li Ka-shing, reputedly Hong Kong's richest tycoon. We also met with Richard Li, Li Ka-shing's son, who had just returned from Stanford Business School and would go on to form PCCW, which later acquired Hong Kong Telecom, the principal telephone company in Hong Kong. We had a nice visit with Victor Fung, a Harvard Business School graduate and professor who was running an investment fund and whose family had founded Li & Fung, Hong Kong's most successful trading/sourcing organization. And, last but not least, I reacquainted myself with C. H. Tung, whose family owned a large shipping company and whom I had met when I was running investment banking at PaineWebber. C. H., or Tung Chee Hwa, as he is also called, went on to become Hong Kong's first chief administrator when the territory reverted to China in 1997.

The four weeks we spent in Hong Kong were packed with meetings like these, with many of the area's leading industrialists and financiers. Oddly enough, they all seemed truly interested in meeting with us and made special efforts to do so. When he later found out that I was seriously thinking of moving to Hong Kong, C. H. contacted me on one of his trips to New York City and invited me to dinner with him and his family.

The Mandarin Oriental definitely proved to be the right place to stay, for a number of reasons. First, it was located in the heart of Central, Hong Kong's business district, which extended then only as far as the Pacific Place complex. (It has continued to expand ever since.) All of our meetings were within walking distance of the hotel. Second, this was before the Internet age. We couldn't just peck out a follow-up e-mail and be done with it. We had to rely on the hotel business center to type thank-you letters, and we marveled at the efficiency, professionalism, and diligence of the hotel's Chinese staff.

This professionalism wasn't limited to the Mandarin. Equally impressive were the organizational skills of Kitty, Gage MacAfee's assistant. Every morning, Kitty would have a new meeting schedule delivered to our rooms before breakfast, complete with the latest changes and the names and titles of everybody we'd be meeting with that day. It might seem like a small thing, but all of this re-inforced our perception that the work ethic and attitude in Hong Kong at least equaled (and probably surpassed) what we'd been used to in New York. We could only imagine what the potential for the entire region might be if this diligence and work ethic could be accessed in the right way.

Not all of our discoveries were as beneficial. On one of our first days at the Mandarin, we decided to try the Chinese restaurant on the top floor, where Peking duck was the specialty of the house. I can't say for certain, but I'm pretty sure that this was my first taste of Chinese food. I wouldn't have been caught dead eating Chinese food in Pittsburgh, and I can't remember ever having it in New York. I'm more of a steak and potatoes man, and Chinese food always seemed a bit too exotic for me.

But in Hong Kong, I fell in love with Peking duck. The crispy skin, the sweet plum sauce, the cucumber and onion slices, all wrapped up in those wonderful pancakes. It was so good that we ate on the top floor every day for a week. We would joke with each other that there wouldn't be any more ducks flying over Hong Kong after we left.

It was good, but it was also healthy, right? In the pre-Atkins days, even I knew that red meat was bad for you and fish, fowl, and vegetables were good. Didn't stop me from eating steak, but I knew that I shouldn't eat too much of it. Here in Asia, I'd finally found a delicious duck dish, complete with greens, that could help me balance my diet. That's why Carleen's utter shock when she heard that I'd eaten Peking duck every day for a week took me completely by surprise.

"You did what?" she scolded me over the phone. "Do you realize how many calories and grams of fat are in every serving?"

I had no idea. I miss it, but I now reserve Peking duck (or Beijing duck, as it's known in China) for days when I deserve a special treat.

The Outline of a Plan: "Capital, Management, and Technology"

In preparation for our meetings in Hong Kong, we had to develop an explanation of what we planned to do in Asia. From a hundred-thousand-foot level, this seemed pretty straightforward. Asia held more than one-half of the world's population, and the potential for growth was huge. Compared with more developed parts of the world like the United States, Europe, and Japan, where the average age is in the high thirties, Asia's population was young, in the low twenties on average. "Older populations save, younger populations spend" was the commonly accepted wisdom, and with its large, young population, Asia's demographic profile promised to provide above-average growth prospects for the region well into the twenty-first century.

To take advantage of this opportunity for growth, Asian companies were going to need the critical ingredients of capital, management, and technology. Providing these resources to good companies in Asia emerged as a solid baseline concept for our company. My twenty years on Wall Street had given me a great deal of experience gathering these resources, and I was fully confident that I could do so in Asia . . . if I were willing to move there. It was immediately apparent to me that this couldn't be done from an office in New York, as much as I might have liked to. It was clear that I would have to relocate to the region in order to make it work.

What I saw in Hong Kong was encouraging, because it was apparent that everything I'd been reading about was actually happening. Also, it had been so easy to arrange meetings with the leading businessmen, who had been so genuinely interested in what we had to say. I remember thinking at the time that it would have been more difficult to obtain meetings with people of similar stature in the States. The sponsorship by Gage and Dick was exceedingly helpful, but I also concluded that the leading Asian businessmen sensed that the world was flattening and that

Asia was becoming increasingly integrated with the global economy. They considered establishing relationships with professionals from the other side of the world to be in their best interests.

I also saw that we needed to change our thinking a bit. First off, it was immediately apparent that there was a great deal of capital already in Asia. Looking at the fortunes that overseas Chinese had amassed in Hong Kong and throughout the region, I didn't think it would be credible for us to just show up without visible, significant backing. To be taken seriously, we were going to have to find an institution (or institutions) to sponsor what we were doing. I now had my work cut out for me in the States, raising capital or finding sponsorship that promised capital, before I could even begin to think about moving.

The second new piece of information was China. Few of the people whom we had met prior to our trip to Hong Kong had even mentioned China. I suppose that was because nobody outside the region really had a clue yet about how important China had already become, and how much it was making its presence felt in the Asian economy.

Those in the region, though—particularly the overseas Chinese—knew exactly what was happening. One of the important takeaways of our meetings in Hong Kong came from the overseas Chinese businessmen we spoke with. They would spend five minutes talking about their very substantial business in Hong Kong, and then spend twenty-five minutes describing what they were trying to do in China. We came away from these meetings determined to take a hard look at the Mainland.

What was strange, though, was that this belief in China's promise as an investment opportunity didn't square at all with what we were hearing from the Western bankers, lawyers, and finance professionals who were based in Hong Kong and had similar backgrounds to ours. These individuals had typically worked somewhere else (New York, or, more often, London) and had moved to Hong Kong to get a piece of the action in Asia. To a person, nobody in this group was even considering China.

Whenever I met with a Westerner managing an investment fund in Asia, I'd always ask, "What's your biggest problem?"

Incredibly, the answer almost always came back, "Deal flow!"

"Too much deal flow?" I would ask, half jokingly.

"No, not enough."

This left me scratching my head.

"Wait a minute," I said to myself. "Here I am, contemplating moving halfway around the world because my macroeconomic analysis tells me that Asia is going to be the ultimate in deal flow. But then all of these experts here seem to be telling me that exactly the opposite is true."

Something wasn't right.

When I looked at Asian investment fund portfolios, I saw a hodgepodge of investments: a $2 million investment in a chain of pizza restaurants in Thailand, a $3 million investment in a small manufacturing company in Hong Kong, a $5 million investment in a small property company. Pretty uninspiring stuff. I was fresh from my meetings with the overseas Chinese who were talking about big projects, and I noticed a void. There was no trace of China as an investment theme.

"How about China?" I'd ask.

"Too difficult, no infrastructure."

"What do you mean no infrastructure?"

"No phones, no real legal system, no law, accounting, or investment banking firms."

Because all of this "infrastructure" existed in Hong Kong and the more developed parts of Asia, that's where these funds focused, not on China.

And so, in the eyes of the Westerners in Hong Kong, Bill and I must have seemed like naïve American cowboys to even raise the subject of China. One meeting, with Asia Capital Partners, stands out. As we described our plan to look seriously at getting into China immediately, the group could hardly conceal their amusement. We began to sense that we were more a source of entertainment than a potential collaborator, so we ended the meeting abruptly and walked out. On our way out the door, Bill and I looked at each other and didn't have to say anything; we both knew they were all having a good laugh at our expense. (In 2005, more than ten years later, I confirmed this with Andrew Korner, who was present at the meeting and had come to see me in Beijing. "We all had a good laugh afterwards," Andrew said, "but you were right to come to China when you did.")

At another meeting, we passed out business cards that we'd had made up in Hong Kong, English on one side and Chinese on the other.

"It looks like you'll be doing business on the Mainland," said a Chinese man from Taiwan.

"Why do you say that?" I asked, with a blank look on my face, detecting a trace of skepticism.

"The Chinese characters are simplified, not complex," he said, clearly skeptical of our chances in China.

I had no idea what he was talking about, but I soon learned. In order to encourage literacy, China has undertaken over the past hundred years to simplify the complex, traditional characters used in the Chinese language and to reduce the strokes to form simplified characters. Simplified characters are now used on the Mainland and in Singapore, while traditional characters are used in Hong Kong, Taiwan, Macau, and other overseas Chinese communities.

And so we were hearing diametrically opposed perspectives. The overseas Chinese were saying that China was the future, but Westerners in the region didn't want to go near it. We might have been naïve, but we began to detect that these differences between how overseas Chinese and Westerners in Hong Kong were approaching China might actually represent an opportunity.

The China Card

As I thought about it and learned more about how every-thing worked, what was going on became clear. The Westerners liked the infrastructure in Hong Kong and other parts of Asia, but they didn't seem to realize that there was a much bigger barrier to entry to getting real deal flow in those countries—namely, the overseas Chinese families who controlled those economies.

Over the years, émigrés from China had done a masterful job building businesses in every Asian country they'd landed in. As these businesses grew, they became the dominant economic and political force in country after country. Given the importance of family in Asian culture, this control became, in effect, control by groups of families.

The head of Sun Hung Kai Securities, a Chinese brokerage firm, alluded to this phenomenon in a discussion I had with him on one of my later trips to Hong Kong.

At one point he looked at me sideways and said, in a soft voice, that he was playing his "China card."

"What does that mean?" I asked him.

"Every week for the past thirty years," he said slyly, "the overseas Chinese have had their weekly poker games. That's where all the good deals get divvied up. If you're an outsider, not a member of the family, you can't play. It's difficult to get a real seat at the table, even if you try and marry into it."

"That," he concluded, "is my China card. I have a seat at the table."

I was surprised, but now I understood. Overseas Chinese businessmen, who effectively controlled the various economies of Asia, took all the good deals off the table before they even got to market. That left only the table scraps for the outsiders.

And so I came to a completely different conclusion from most of the Westerners I'd met in Hong Kong. Despite the advantages of infrastructure in developed Asian economies, I didn't see how I (or anybody else like me, for that matter) could develop a competitive edge. We'd never be invited to that weekly poker game. And even today, with all of the foreign capital that has flowed into the region over the past ten years, the economies of Asia remain in the tight grip of a small group of very powerful families. China, despite its lack of infrastructure, seemed to me to be an easier market for a complete outsider to crack, because I saw a different set of dynamics at work.

The Mayor's Two Hats

Since Hong Kong was always advertised as the "gateway to China," I can't blame those in Hong Kong for trying to get a piece of the action by encouraging the notion that China could only be accessed through them. From the minute I stepped off the plane, I was told over and over again that to get something done in China you simply had to have *guanxi*. Nothing could be done without it. You had to know the right someone to get anywhere at all.

But even before I visited China, I knew instinctively that this didn't add up. While families called the shots in the rest of Asia, the government and the Communist Party called the shots in China. Mike Johnston, whom I worked for at PaineWebber, once told me that it's easier to predict the actions of an institution than an individual, and China was certainly an institution. Individuals can wake up one day and decide, for no apparent reason, to reverse a decision made the day before. Emotions, health, and personality quirks can all come into play. But all institutions, no matter how irrational they might seem from the outside, have a logic to them. Once you understand the logic, you can start to predict how an institution will act in the future. China is an institution, not a family, and it has a logic. If I could figure it out, I'd have a chance, I reasoned.

Although it would be quite some time before I'd actually meet with Chinese officials in the flesh, I knew from what I'd read and heard that they weren't like government officials in the United States. Unlike the mayor of Pittsburgh, for example, the mayor of a place like Wuhan wears two hats. The first is the government hat: the mayor has to keep the buses running, the schools open, and the streets clean, much like his counterparts in the United States. Wearing the other hat, the mayor is, in effect, the CEO of the hundreds of companies in the area that fall under his control.

Like any CEO, he needs capital to build his businesses, management to make them as productive as possible, and technology to make them globally competitive. If I could sit down with the mayor, I imagined, and tell him that I could provide those three resources if he would be willing to share ownership with me, I didn't think I'd need an introduction by anybody. The logic of this position, and of the way China appeared to work, made this seem like a compelling approach to me.

I had yet to set foot in China, so all of this analysis was done in a vacuum. And yet it's amazing how dead-on my initial reasoning turned out to be. As the next chapter will describe, finding deals proved to be the least of our problems. Within a very short period of time, we had the local governments and factory managers lining up to show us investment opportunities. We had figured out the logic and had learned how to work within it.

This analysis of the deal dynamic in China has stood the test of time and is still valid today, with two important qualifications. The first is that capital isn't quite as pressing an issue as it was in the early 1990s. China's been running a large trade surplus for a number of years, and foreign direct investment has continued to flow into the country. But capital still cannot be taken for granted, even though it is more readily available. As long as local government officials are evaluated based on how much capital they attract to their city, it will remain a strong motivating factor.

The second qualification is that the central government has recently been encouraging "self-development" and has taken a tougher stance with respect to foreign companies or investors taking majority ownership of certain key enterprises in China. Due to growing competition in China, access to management resources, tools, and concepts will continue to be an important driver, as will the opportunity to gain access to global technology. But the Chinese have begun to realize that they can do some of this themselves, and that has reduced opportunities for foreign investors. In regulations published in 2006, the State Council effectively reserved the right to disapprove of share transfers of companies in a surprisingly long list of equipment manufacturing industries. This emerging economic nationalism (you could call it protectionism) has affected several highly publicized share transfers to foreign firms.

In 2006, the central government refused to allow the Carlyle Group—a large, Washington-based, politically powerful U.S. private equity firm—to buy an 85 percent stake in Xugong Group Construction Machinery, one of China's largest construction equipment producers. Thyssen Krupp's proposed purchase of a majority interest in Tianrun Crankshaft Company, China's largest manufacturer of heavy-duty crankshafts (of all things!), was also rejected. A potential joint venture between Germany's ZF Group and Hangzhou Advanced Gearbox Group met a similar fate, halting negotiations that had been ongoing for nearly three years.

Even Hong Kong was affected. Beijing stepped in when Richard Li tried to sell his stake in PCCW, which owns and operates Hong Kong's telephone system, to Texas Pacific, a U.S. buyout firm, and Macquarie,

Australia's largest financial organization. Beijing disapproved of the sale to foreign interests and supported a bid by a local group, which was later rejected by PCCW's shareholders as inadequate.

The recent trend toward economic nationalism is important. The head of Asia for a major multinational, which plans to obtain a leadership position in China by acquiring several of its major players, told me that he was having difficulty getting deals approved.

"If we were doing this three years ago," he confided in me, "this would have been relatively easy. It's gotten a lot tougher."

All of this said, capital, management, and technology are still hot-button issues in China. Though things here change constantly, China's managers and government officials still operate from largely the same script. Personal relationships can help, but they're no substitute for being in harmony with the economic and political winds. We've had operations in some cities for more than ten years, and we've been good for those communities and have developed strong relationships. Even still, like General Motors at an earlier stage of American development, we find it useful to remind our friends in the local governments on a regular basis that what's good for ASIMCO is good for them, too.

My First Glimpse of China

After all that we'd heard about China in those four weeks in October of 1990, Bill and I decided that we needed to at least get a peek at the country before we left.

One afternoon, we took the train to the end of its line in the New Territories. From the station, we took a taxi to the border area where, standing on a small hill, we could see the border with China and the guards standing watch over it. Straining to see as much as I could, I remember being slightly mesmerized. I could feel the mystery that surrounded the place, the aura of a long history and immense size. I certainly had no idea that I was about to spend so much of my adult life there, trying to figure out how it worked.

From there, we went on to Taiwan, South Korea, and Japan, all of which rounded out our perspective on Asia in general. Dick Allen met us in Taiwan, where he'd arranged meetings with key businessmen and government officials. Our most notable meeting was with Douglas Hsu, an urbane graduate of the Columbia Business School, who ran Far Eastern Textile, one of Taiwan's largest companies. While Taiwan's businessmen spoke privately about their aggressive plans for China, the government clearly had an uneasy relationship with the Mainland, so the connection to China was clear but not as visible as in Hong Kong. I remember the traffic in Taipei, particularly the large number of motorcycles. I had no idea that this was a vision of what was to come in China, where motorcycle production would go from 2 million a year when I arrived to more than 21 million a year today.

Another memorable night in Taipei was a much-advertised excursion to Snake Alley, famous for its night market and the various rare snake products featured there. Our meetings in Hong Kong had been all business, and nobody had shown us the local color. (In truth, we never strayed too far from our hotel.) Dick made up for it, giving us a good taste of Chinese nightlife in Taipei. For several days, he told us to get ready for Snake Alley. I kept asking him what it was, and he kept saying, "You'll see." My imagination ran wild. Exotic sex? Exotic food? Exotic entertainment? (I would later learn, not all from personal experience, that all three were available.)

I know now that night markets are a big part of Chinese culture, but this was my first experience with them and I was transfixed. The sights, smells, and sounds were all new to me. Row upon row of vendors selling everything from fake watches to designer clothes; food stalls and restaurants; massage parlors; and, yes, snakes, turtles, and other animals hanging on hooks, about to become part of somebody's meal. After killing the snakes and hanging them, the vendors cut them open and removed the internal organs. Some men, believing that it enhances their virility, eat the gallbladder and mix the snake testes with their beer, or whatever else they're drinking. (I think this was the place, more than any, where I felt farthest from home.)

South Korea and Japan were quite different and felt disconnected from China and from the earlier portions of our trip. In South Korea, what we noticed most was the martial law and the armed guards that seemed to be every-where. We met with members of the banking and business communities, but the country seemed to be on a completely different and independent path from the rest of Asia.

The same was true for Japan. When I explained what we hoped to do in Southeast Asia and China (our strategy had evolved as we'd been there), my friends at Yasuda suggested that we might act as a "very good bridge" between Japan and China. I knew that Japan had occupied China, and that there were some hard feelings as a result, but this suggestion was the first indication I had that history might get in the way of business for the Japanese. Though many Japanese companies are now expanding aggressively into China, and Chinese consumers love Japanese technology and line up to buy their cars, even today the strain between the two countries lies very close to the surface.

BY THE TIME we arrived back in the States in mid-November of 1990, Bill and I had covered a great deal of ground. We were by no means experts, but we'd gotten a wide and deep exposure to Asia. We were starting to get a handle on what we might actually be able to accomplish in the region.

I would make several trips back to Hong Kong in 1991, but my principal focus during that year was to try to find an institutional sponsor, some financial or industrial organization that believed in the promise of Asia (and China in particular) and might support what we were trying to put together.

I went through my Rolodex and networked harder than I've ever networked in my life. I must have had more than one hundred meetings with various people in the States in 1991, between my travels abroad. Unfortunately, they all ended the same way.

After listening patiently to what I had to say, the person across the table from me would say, "Jack, I agree. There's tremendous opportunity in Asia. But there's just one problem. You're not Chinese, you don't speak the language, and you've never operated there. How in the world are you ever going to make it work?"

I knew I could make it work, but I didn't have a good answer to that question. I never would, until I'd actually done something in Asia.

The definition of insanity, I read once, is to do the same thing over and over again but to expect a different result. By that standard, I was approaching insanity, and the question before me was simple. Do I stay in the United States and have another one hundred meetings in 1992, knowing that they're likely all to end the same way? Or, do I just pick up and move to Hong Kong?

The answer was simple, too. I packed my bags and booked a ticket to Hong Kong.

Chapter 3

A Blank-Sheet Approach to China

After the move, I was sitting in my new Hong Kong office, looking at our large map of China and reading an article about investment opportunities in a long list of Chinese cities I'd never heard of, all with names I couldn't begin to pronounce. Every one of them, it seemed, had dozens of projects available for investment—but all those strange names and places. I remember thinking to myself, "How in the world am I ever going to figure this out?"

After fifteen years in China, I don't claim to have all the answers, but the answer to that particular question was obvious: I just had to throw myself into it. I didn't know the language and had never studied Chinese history, so I had no choice but to dive right in.

After making my initial trips into China in 1992, I discovered one fundamental reality about the place: China changes constantly, and quickly. This is the first thing I tell people when I discuss doing business here. While such fast-paced change can be a scary prospect, it's also a tremendous leveler. What happened in China a thousand, a hundred, or ten years ago is important, but what's more important is what's happening today, on the ground. I personally enjoy learning about Chinese history, and I learn something about Chinese culture every time I read a book on the subject. But the simple fact is that knowing the ins and outs of China's many dynasties is interesting if you've got the time, but not terribly helpful in terms of figuring out how to do business today.

I started with a blank sheet of paper, and in hindsight this was an advantage. I could take China for what it was, as I saw it, unencumbered by any prior knowledge or expectations about the country. Instead of worrying about whether I understood the "context" of Chinese culture or history, I simply put what I saw into the context of my own twenty years of work experience and developed my strategy accordingly. When people think about China, they often get tangled up in its complications. My advice is to start with the simple facts about the country, build on them using your own experience and judgment, and always stay conscious of the way in which China is changing.

When I set up shop in Hong Kong in early 1992, I had my work cut out for me.

I also had very little time for personal matters, which affected some other decisions. Having lived and worked all her life in New York City, Carleen was game for a change and ready to come to Hong Kong. (Well before I had even thought about Asia, we both went to a fortune-teller on the Lower East Side who uncannily predicted that there would be ships in Carleen's future. Although I don't believe in such things, I was impressed by how prescient that turned out to be every time I looked out at Hong Kong's busy harbor. I would have been even more impressed if she'd seen millions of cars and trucks.) After discussing it, though, we agreed that Carleen should stay in New York until I got a better sense as to whether this was going to work. Everything seemed so temporary and up in the air. I only brought a few suitcases with me from the States, and I got a monthly room rate at a Sheraton hotel in Kowloon.

My first job was to form an investment vehicle so that Bill Kaye and I could bring in outside investors and at least earn some management fees to cover expenses. I went to work putting a vehicle in place, and by the middle of 1992 we had formed a limited partnership and had taken in the first $35 million, which grew relatively quickly to $100 million. (This fund was purely an investment vehicle for investing in publicly traded equities in Asia; we'd have to raise a different fund for investments in China.) While this was going on, we found permanent office space, and with money under management, life in Hong Kong began to take shape. I took an apartment in the Atrium, a Marriott-run serviced apartment facility next door to the office, and had the shortest commute I've ever had in my life. Carleen left PaineWebber and moved over at the end of 1992.

In the summer of that year, the kids made their first trip to Asia and Hong Kong. Sara was fifteen, Doug, fourteen, and Libby, nine. Although they stayed in school in the States, they spent nearly every summer with me, either in Hong Kong or Beijing. They watched my concept grow from that first office in Hong Kong to an office in Beijing, our first factories in China, and, finally, to a company with a global footprint. As difficult as it was to live on the other side of the world from my three kids, I firmly believe they are the better for it. Sara attained a healthy perspective on how one-half of the world's population lives; Doug found fuel for his entrepreneurialism; and Libby developed her love for languages and everything international. All of them gained at least entry-level ability to speak Chinese.

Hong Kong and Beijing (as we'd find out later) are great places for kids to spend summers. Every year, thousands of students from all over the world descend on these cities to study the language and travel the country, providing an ideal opportunity to learn about Asia and also the rest of the world. Having factories all over the country gave the kids the chance to visit parts of China that few people see. Sara still talks about her fall semester in Harbin; Doug, his one-week trip across China by train and his summer at our factory in Shanxi Province; and Libby, her trip to Hengshan Mountain in Hunan Province.

One Sunday, the four of us made our first trip to China. We signed up for a hotel tour that took us from Hong Kong to Shenzhen, Guangzhou, and then back to Hong Kong, all in one day. One of the stops in Shenzhen was billed as a visit to the city's "museum"—which was really just a big room with a scale model of the city in the center. Pasted on the walls were dozens of charts showing the growth of the city in terms of population, gross domestic product, investment, exports, and a host of other measures.

Looking around the room and seeing the lines on every chart running from the bottom left to the top right, indicating exponential growth, Sara turned to me and said, "I can see why you moved here, Dad."

That made my day. Having her and her brother and sister understand why I had made this dramatic change in our lives was extremely important to having their support.

China's Hidden Buying Power: Free Drinks in Tianjin

Once we had a growing amount of money under management, the Hong Kong brokerage firms started to call, peddling their research and looking for a piece of our business. True to its chairman's words, Sun Hung Kai Securities played the "China card" by organizing trips to China for potential clients. One of the cities they liked was Tianjin, a major port city in the north not far from Beijing, and they had a trip planned for early September. I agreed to go along, with a group that consisted of about twenty-five Hong Kong Chinese investment professionals and me, the lone Caucasian.

I'd never heard of Tianjin before we made our plans to visit. Even though it's one of China's major cities, with a population of 8 million people, it's not well known outside the country. Sun Hung Kai was clearly promoting Tianjin because it had strong connections there, but it's also an important city, one of only four in China that enjoy provincial status. The others on that exclusive list are Beijing, Shanghai, and Chongqing.

Aside from that brief, one-day trip to China with my kids during the summer, this was my first real trip into China. In Shenzhen and Guangzhou, I had been a tourist. Now I was traveling as a potential participant in the economic development of the country, and I was excited.

We had a direct flight from Hong Kong to Tianjin, which surprised me. I couldn't imagine that a city I had never heard of might have international flights. What's more, we stayed at a very nice, modern Sheraton hotel—another surprise—in the center of the city. Sun Hung Kai liked Tianjin because of its infrastructure, and their assessment was right. I was impressed by the many modern expressways, complete with cloverleaf interchanges, which had already been built. There weren't very many cars on the roads yet, but the city was poised for growth.

We spent several days in Tianjin, visiting a number of factories that were looking for investment and joint venture partners.

At the first factory, the general manager introduced his business entirely in Mandarin. I sat patiently through the forty-five-minute presentation, figuring I'd be able to get a five-minute summary from one of the Hong Kong Chinese managers whom I'd befriended on the bus ride over.

As we left the meeting and were walking out, I pulled my friend aside and quietly asked, "Can you please give me the short version of what the general manager said?"

"I'd like to," he replied, "but I only speak Cantonese and don't understand a word of Mandarin. I don't know what he said, either."

That was my introduction to the language issue in China. Each region, each area, and sometimes even each city has its own dialect, and if you aren't familiar with it (even if you're Chinese), you have no idea what people are saying. This would make China unworkable if it weren't for the fact that Mandarin functions as the official language of the country and is, more or less, universally spoken throughout China. (Because Hong Kong had been separate from the Mainland for so many years, and Mandarin was not taught in the schools, many Hong Kong Chinese can only speak Cantonese, the dialect used in Guangdong Province in southern China.)

As an example, Wilson Ni, ASIMCO's head of global sales and marketing, is an extremely well-educated Beijinger, but he can't understand a bit of Shanghainese. He also has a great sense of humor, and whenever we're traveling I like to wind him up about the rivalry between Beijing and Shanghai. Without too much provocation, I can usually get Wilson to begin by recalling his first trips to Shanghai.

"I used to hate going there," he'll say, "because all the announcements in the department stores were in Shanghainese, which only people from Shanghai could understand. At least now they make them in Mandarin." Visibly worked up by then, Wilson will go on with more Shanghai stories for as long as I let him.

To be sure, there are strong regional differences and rivalries between the different parts of China. If you ask Beijingers about their cousins to the south, they'll tell you that all the Shanghainese are farmers. If you talk to the Shanghainese, they'll say the same thing about their fellow countrymen in Beijing. When I first arrived in Asia, there was considerable speculation that China might break apart someday because of this regionalism. I never bought that, and I always thought the argument that China was not one but many countries to be a bit over-done. (No one considers breakup a realistic possibility anymore.) In the end, despite the rivalries, differences, and varied dialects, China is one country.

Thankfully, there was some translation at our other meetings and plant visits in Tianjin, so I could get a flavor for what was being discussed. We visited a steel-processing factory that was actually quite presentable—in a new building, with all-new equipment—but it didn't have any business. It wasn't even clear that the operators knew how to run the equipment. In addition to capital, it was going to need some customers and a lot of know-how, I thought to myself. Getting a plant like that started would be a challenge.

I began to think about a business model where I might match opportunities like this steel plant with companies in the West that could provide capital and know-how. On subsequent visits to Tianjin I brought over representatives from M. A. Hanna, a company that I knew from my investment banking days, which was interested in linking up with a rubber-compounding facility in China.

There was, of course, a great deal of logic to this classic mergers and acquisitions approach. The reality, though, is that many Western companies have been very tentative toward China. The very largest global companies now have aggressive China plans, but you don't have to go too far down the list to find large companies that have little or no presence here. Trying to get companies seriously interested in China has proved to be a difficult sell. Everyone was interested in looking, but no one was buying. While this has changed somewhat recently, I'm still surprised by how many companies aren't here in any significant way.

Another surprise was the unexpected affluence of Tianjin. In 1992, China's GDP was approximately $480 billion. Based on a population of 1.17 billion people (though estimates vary, and many experts say it's actually closer to 1.5 billion), average per capita income then was $412. The assumption most Westerners like me made was that nobody had much money or spending power in China.

That assumption wasn't entirely true. On that first trip, I was sitting at the bar in the Sheraton after one of the dinners held in our honor when a young Mainland Chinese woman sat down next to me and struck up a conversation in English.

After some small talk, she asked me, "Have you heard of Anshan Steel?"

"No," I said. I didn't even know where Anshan was.

"My uncle's in the army and has some connections to the company," she said vaguely. "Perhaps you'd like to meet him?"

Not wanting to be impolite, I said, "Sure, I'd be happy to meet him."

Minutes later, her uncle showed up, dressed in his green army officer's uniform, covered with gold braid and stars. I began to wonder what I was getting myself into.

With my new friend translating, her uncle and I spent a couple of minutes discussing the steel industry in China, and he invited me to visit Anshan. (Although I later learned that Anshan is one of China's largest steel companies, I never did take him up on his offer.)

It turned out to be a very pleasant conversation, and when it was over I tried to pay the bill. He wasn't having it, which was my first shock. Despite the high Western prices for drinks, he insisted on picking up the tab. I was even more shocked when he whipped out the fattest wad of 100-yuan bills I had ever seen in my life. Whatever he did with Anshan Steel, it involved a great deal of cash.

However poor China might have seemed based on the aggregate numbers, individuals were definitely starting to get rich in 1992. The buying power was greater than a lot of people outside the country could have imagined. The same is still true today. The recent rapid growth of the Chinese automotive industry, fueled by consumers spending $15,000 to $30,000 on cars, took many industry watchers by surprise for all the same reasons.

"Per capita income in China is only $1,000," skeptics about China's potential to be a major auto market would say to me. "So how can the Chinese possibly afford to buy cars?"

It sounds logical, but time and again generalizations like this have proved to be wrong. A high savings rate, double-income families, the support of an extended family, and relatively low living costs result in a large pool of untapped purchasing power. Moreover, the numbers are skewed because 50 percent of China's employment is still in agriculture, where incomes are very low. In the larger cities, China has an emerging middle class that is already larger than the populations of most countries. It should come as no surprise that China is now one of the largest markets in the world for designer clothing, expensive cars, top-shelf liquor, and other luxury goods.

I went back to Hong Kong after that first trip to Tianjin encouraged. I had seen a couple of factories that, with some work, might turn out to be pretty good opportunities. And clearly, everyone, from the local government to the factory managers, wanted to do business. They seemed very open to foreign capital and made all the right noises about needing to improve their managements. I began to speak with people I knew in the steel industry to see if I might do something with the steel-processing center. This seemed to be a promising approach, and I was willing to see where it led, though I knew that it was still too early to draw any hard-and-fast conclusions.

Déjà Vu All Over Again

My next trip to China came several weeks later. Arthur Andersen, the firm handling our accounting, was cosponsoring a conference in Shanghai with *Euromoney* magazine, and I was invited to attend.

Established as a military airport in 1907 and opened up to civilian traffic in 1963, Shanghai's Hongqiao Airport is one of China's oldest. In 1992, it looked it. The terminal was dirty and dark without any features that were remotely modern.

The expressways and overpasses that move traffic around the city today were also not yet in place back then. Pudong, which now boasts a tremendous and famous skyline, had only been named a special economic zone the year before. Where Shenzhen had reminded me of Houston, Texas, in the 1970s—a young city with new and modern buildings—Shanghai wasn't there yet. It was clearly a more vibrant city than Tianjin, but it didn't have the same feeling of unbridled capitalism and unchecked growth as Shenzhen. It felt to me that the farther north one traveled in China, the farther behind was the time line for reform. (Now, of course, looking at Shanghai at night makes it seem like the city—and all of China, for that matter—is on steroids.)

By that time, just a few weeks after my first real visit to the country, I had been struck by another simple fact about China: its sheer size. I knew that China had a lot of people, but I didn't realize until I started traveling the country just how big it really is. Almost to the square kilometer, China is the same size as the United States.

China's physical size is the reason that every industry here was then, and still is, fragmented. Historically, business in China has been done regionally and locally, with every major industry replicated in each large city and province. An average province in China has approximately 50 million people, more than most countries, and I was told once that China has seventy cities with a population of 1 million or more. (Lately, the number being bandied about is one hundred cities.) Knowing the history of development in the United States, it seemed logical that, as China's telecommunications and transportation infra-structure improved, industries would begin to consolidate and operate nationally.

It began to make more sense to me to pick an industry, not a set of individual companies, and develop a strategy for creating the leading company in that industry in China. The company would then benefit from the inevitable consolidation instead of falling victim to it.

As I thought about the steel-processing company in Tianjin, another reality hit home. To make a sensible decision about that company, I would first have to know everything there is to know about its finances, operations, and potential market, but I would also need to have a view as to how it would fare in a consolidating industry in China. On top of that, I would have to understand how it fit into the global market, and how it might fare against global competition. It seemed like a lot of work for what might only be a $10 to $15 million investment. With an industry strategy, a great deal of learning could be spread over many investments, and we could realize economies of scale in the investment process. (Due to our focus on automotive, ASIMCO knows as much about China's automotive industry as any company in the world.)

An industry approach made sense intuitively, but it begged the question of which industry. When people would talk about direct investment in Hong Kong, nine times out of ten they would be referring to real estate and property investments. After all, that's where much of Hong Kong's wealth had been made. But that didn't make any sense for me, because at least 6 million people in Hong Kong knew more about property than I did, so I had no competitive edge. I was hoping that the speakers at the *Euromoney* conference might give me some other ideas.

One of the featured presenters at the conference was Dr. Stefan Messmann, a senior executive with Volkswagen. In his remarks, he explained to the roughly three hundred people in attendance that Volkswagen viewed China as one of its key growth markets. The company had already invested more than $350 million in two joint ventures, in Shanghai and Changchun, and had clearly taken an early lead in the race to develop China's automotive industry.

I was surprised. At that point, it wasn't clear that China even had an auto industry. The streets were filled with bicycles and a couple of trucks here and there, but passenger cars were few and far between. The ones you did see were typically imported Mercedes, which usually belonged to government officials. But here was a high-ranking Volkswagen official saying that China was going to develop a major automotive industry. More important, he was saying that Volkswagen, a major player in the global industry, was counting on China for a great deal of growth. I sat up in my seat and started to listen more closely.

When he finished his presentation, Dr. Messmann opened the floor for questions.

As he surveyed the room, a hand shot up. "What's your biggest problem?" somebody asked.

Without a moment's hesitation, Dr. Messmann replied, "Our biggest problem is getting an adequate supply of high-quality parts."

When I'd been in investment banking, I had called on a number of companies in the automotive components area. Though times were tough then, in the late 1970s, I looked back at financial statements from the 1950s and 1960s and saw that these companies had all been very profitable. This had been America's growth period in autos. GIs returning from World War II, people like my dad, wanted to get on with their lives and were buying houses, refrigerators, and cars in huge numbers. As General Motors, Ford, and Chrysler expanded production, components companies could literally fill up their plants for the year after three golf dates with buyers from the Big Three. If Messmann was right, the same thing was now about to happen in China forty years later.

"Wow!" I thought to myself. As Yogi Berra had said, "This is déjà vu all over again!"

I was so excited after Dr. Messmann's presentation that I raced to the lunchroom and jockeyed for the seat next to him. I slipped a card into his hand and asked if I could meet with him at a later date to learn more about the types of components that he actually needed. It was just the kind of jump start I had been looking for.

After the *Euromoney* conference I started to do more research on the automotive industry. The more I learned, the more attractive it seemed. Whenever I returned to China after that trip in September of 1992, I would always ask what the two or three best opportunities were in whatever city I happened to be visiting. Invariably, people would mention components companies.

What I learned about China on my subsequent trips gradually convinced me that the automotive industry might be a logical place to start. Naturally, there were other opinions.

"Of all the industries you could have picked," some prospective investors would say to me, "why automotive components? It's a mature industry." And that's true. In developed economies like the United States, automotive is a mature industry. But Dr. Messmann's words, along with what I'd seen with my own eyes, convinced me that it could be a growth industry here. Even as early as 1992, if you believed that China was going to continue to grow, it simply had to follow that China would develop a large, robust automotive industry. There's no other way to move people and goods around a country so large without a system of highways and plenty of trucks, buses, and passenger cars to go along with it.

When I tried to explain my strategy of building a national components company to the people who'd been around China a lot longer than I had, they would look at me like I didn't really understand the country.

"China's not one country," they'd tell me. "It's a series of local, protected markets."

I knew this, too. But as I began to talk with the global assemblers, they echoed what Dr. Messmann had said: they wanted better quality, service, and price than they were getting from their local suppliers in China. As the China market developed and became more sophisticated, I believed that the global automakers would favor companies that could provide the right balance of all three. Granted, it took China's entrance into the World Trade Organization (WTO) in late 2001—and the increased competition in the China market that resulted from it—to finally break down local protectionism, but the handwriting was already on the wall as early as 1992.

Importance of Majority Ownership

Another important conclusion that I came to after these first few trips to China was the importance of majority ownership and management control. In all of the meetings I had in 1992, I was pleasantly surprised that most of the managers spoke about profits, and the need to make them. With their socialist, centrally planned backgrounds, I had thought that *profit* wouldn't even be in their vocabularies. What I didn't know was whether these managers even understood what the word *profit* actually meant, and whether they meant what they said. After all, they had to know that emphasizing the importance of profits was important to attracting capital, and that's what Westerners wanted to hear.

I was encouraged by what I was hearing, but I concluded relatively quickly that we would never do anything in China without majority ownership and the ability to control management. Our goal couldn't be merely to create the best company in the industry in China. Our goal had to be to create a company that was globally competitive. However good the companies in China might be, they were going to have to change to keep pace with developments in the global economy. Change is always difficult, and I wanted the ability to control it as much as we could.

We were helped in our strategy by the fact that China was discussing a new automotive policy in 1993, which, when formally published on March 12, 1994, named the motor vehicle industry as one of its "pillar industries."

The government knew that China had to develop its transportation infrastructure, and it also knew that the automotive industry would provide employment and lead to technological development as it had in the United States and other countries. (Automotive and its ancillary enterprises account for approximately 10 percent of global GDP.)

The central government also knew that China needed a vibrant components industry if it was ever going to develop a globally competitive automotive industry. Bearing this in mind, China's planners included in the policy the ability for foreign companies or investors in the components industry to take majority ownership interests. Now there are a number of industries in which foreign investors can own a majority (or even 100 percent) of an operation in China, but this is the only instance I know of where China specifically encouraged it as part of an official policy. Like Dr. Messmann, the government was frustrated by how slow foreign components companies had been in following their global customers to China. This policy was meant to encourage them to do so, and it also presented an interesting opportunity for us.

While in Shanghai, I met a partner in Arthur Andersen's Shanghai office who wanted me to meet Tim Clissold, a British accountant and Mandarin speaker whom the firm had hired to help its clients find opportunities in China. Tim had worked as an accountant for the Lufthansa Center, a real estate joint venture in Beijing, before joining Arthur Andersen.

Tim and I met upon my return to Hong Kong, where he also lived, and he expressed interest in working with me to investigate the components idea and any others that we might develop. (Ultimately, we would look at other industries—everything from beer and plastics to cement and building materials.) Having the support of Arthur Andersen, which had negotiated many joint ventures in China on behalf of its clients, was a good first step. Adding Tim, with his language capability and seeming knowledge of China, was a logical choice to help me take the next steps. We agreed to work together and immediately made follow-up trips to Tianjin, Shanghai, and other cities in China.

On one such trip to Tianjin, Tim arranged for two university students he'd met while studying Mandarin at a Beijing university to sit in on our meetings and act as translators. Their names were Rock and Corner. (That's right. I couldn't believe it either, "Rock" and "Corner.")

Late in the first day, after we'd spent a bit of time together, I couldn't help but ask the obvious question: "So, how did you both get your names?"

"Our English teacher," they said in unison, not thinking their names at all unusual.

"I got my name because I like rock-and-roll music," Rock explained.

"And I got mine because I had a corner desk in the classroom," Corner added.

It may seem like a silly story, but there are several important points to be made. When you start doing business in China, you will need a Chinese name, and if you're not careful you'll end up with a name in Chinese that appears as silly as a name like Corner does in English.

I'm particularly sensitive to this because it happened to me. When I was getting cards made up for one of my trips to China, a Chinese analyst we'd hired in Hong Kong (not a Mainlander) thought it would be clever to play off the "P" in my last name and give me a Chinese name alluding to Puyi, the last emperor of China. I never questioned what he had done and didn't get a second opinion, but I could see from the puzzled looks I received when I handed out my card that something wasn't right. I soon figured out what was wrong, and changed it immediately. The one I use now plays off the characters "jie ke," which are based on the pronunciation of my name and are appropriately neutral in meaning.

More important, this experience taught me to be careful about whom I take advice from with regard to China. If somebody speaks Chinese or is of Chinese origin, the natural tendency is to take their word or advice at face value. As I learned, this can be dangerous. Even among my Mainland colleagues today, some of whom I've now known for many years, I still try to get several opinions on just about anything of importance. And no matter what, I never allow myself to forget to test that advice or opinion against my own common sense and experience. Where China is concerned, no one has all the answers.

Beginning the Marathon

By the end of 1992, I had come a long way in my thinking about China and what I might do. The idea to pick an industry, instead of specific companies, made sense based on what I'd seen, and majority ownership was clearly a prerequisite for creating a globally competitive company. The components sector of the automotive industry fit nicely with those core elements. The auto industry was going to benefit from China's development, though it wasn't yet obvious just how large China's appetite for all types of vehicles would become. The fact that the global components suppliers hadn't yet come to China indicated that many industry experts didn't buy in to the future of China's auto industry. That lack of presence created a vacuum in which we could operate; it also prompted the Chinese government to give additional benefits (allowing majority ownership for foreigners, for example) to those companies that stepped forward and invested.

It all seems pretty straightforward today. Nearly everyone now acknowledges that China is on track to become the largest automotive market in the world. But back then, the idea of creating a national components company in China was a novel one. With respect to ownership, companies today would prefer to own 100 percent, or at least a majority, of their operations in China, but that was not commonplace, either. In order to benefit from China's development, many investment funds were formed between 1992 and 1994. None of them adopted an industry strategy, and nearly all purposely only took minority positions (in most cases specified as no more than 30 percent ownership). Nobody said anything about taking an active role in management. Even the large multinationals were content to take minority interests in their Chinese joint ventures, in effect delegating the job of management to their Chinese partners.

To be fair, the approach I started to develop in 1992 appealed to many of our potential supporters, but not to all. Some were uncomfortable with an industry focus, regardless of the industry, because it offered no diversification. There was general skepticism about whether China would ever develop a viable automobile industry, and concerns about the ability to produce quality in China were universal. Looming in the background also was the question of what would happen when the big components companies got serious about China. Wouldn't we be swept aside when the established global players finally decided to get in? And on top of that, what did majority ownership really mean in China?

"Does it give you 'hire and fire' rights?" everybody asked me.

My standard answer was "I don't know. But I'd rather have it than not have it."

I NEVER SAW Dr. Messmann again after that presentation he made at the *Euromoney* conference, but that was the moment where everything changed for me in China,

where I started to see a path to doing something meaningful. That said, I'm sure he thought I was a real nut. I
didn't even represent a company yet (or at least not one he
recognized), and I'm sure he was constantly being bom-
barded by people with all of their various ideas about what
they were going to do in China. Most people never
actually saw them through.

That's really the ultimate difference. It's easy to have
big ideas about China. I've seen many companies become
infatuated with doing business here but then leave at the
first hurdle or sign of trouble. This has become so
commonplace that a "show me" attitude has developed.
Representatives of well-established companies are often
surprised when the head of China operations for their
best customer at home tells them that no firm commitments will be made until the supplier has manufacturing
capability in China. "When your plant in China is up and
running, come talk to me" is the standard reaction to
presentations about China plans. The purely Chinese
customers are even bigger skeptics.

When I started traveling through China, one piece of
advice that I frequently got was "Remember, Jack, China
is a marathon, not a sprint." I've found that to be true, but
it's interesting to see how many people—even some of
those who gave that advice in the first place—forget it
after the first mile. As 1992 turned into 1993, we would
begin that first mile ourselves.

Chapter 4

One Hundred Factories in Forty Cities

I began 1993 with one purpose in mind: to determine whether the automotive components strategy made any sense, and to prove that I could access deal flow on the Mainland.

Like most newcomers, I believed China was highly centralized. If you made a comprehensive deal with a powerful central government entity in Beijing, I figured, that would pave the way for cookie-cutter deals in the provinces. It didn't even occur to me that I might have to go to each city and province in China to find and negotiate individual opportunities. Accordingly, my initial efforts were focused on finding some organization in Beijing to bless and facilitate our plan to invest in the components industry. After all, wasn't that exactly what the central government was trying to encourage with its new automotive policy? In January of 1993, I made the first of what would be many, many trips to Beijing from my base in Hong Kong.

Beijing has changed enormously over the past ten

years. Today it's a modern city, with a constantly changing skyline, a new airport that has undergone two major expansions since 2000, and six ring roads encircling the city center used by 3 million passenger cars each day, more than in New York City.

Not so in 1993. Back then, the Beijing airport had a 1950s-style terminal building, which was always packed with travelers. Terminal 2, the first major expansion, was completed in 2000, and the original terminal, Terminal 1, has since been redone, replete with Starbucks and high-end retail shops. (My colleagues who are relatively new to China refer to Terminal 1 as the "new terminal," which I find amusing. It'll always be the "old terminal" to me, even though the makeover has been so complete that, with the exception of a few familiar features, it's hard to remember what it looked like before.)

The road into Beijing from the airport is a six-lane expressway today, with a new, overhead high-speed rail system running alongside it. In 1993, it was a two-lane, tree-lined road, the "Old Capitol Airport Road," where people walked and rode bicycles amid the beaten-up trucks and horse-drawn wagons. There was just about every form of transportation imaginable on that road, and passenger cars were few and far between.

Several different types of vehicles served as taxis, depending on how much the passenger was willing to pay. At the bottom end of the spectrum was a locally made minivan that the Chinese referred to as "small bread," because it looked like a loaf of bread on wheels, particularly with its yellow color. These taxis were cheap, at 1 yuan (about 12 cents) per kilometer—especially since six people could be stuffed into one of them—but they were also unsafe, and the passengers usually got a healthy dose of carbon monoxide before the ride was over. While still used in other cities in China, they have been taken off the streets of Beijing. For 1.2 yuan per kilometer, one could ride in a red Daihatsu Charade ("Xiali" in Chinese) made by Tianjin Auto Works; a red Citroen ("Fukang" in Chinese) made in Wuhan cost 1.6 yuan per kilometer; and, at the high end, a Volkswagen Santana was available for 2 yuan per kilometer. Today, virtually all of the city's taxis are Hyundai Elantras made in Beijing, and a ride costs 2 yuan per kilometer.

While much has changed since, Beijing had already begun to develop by the time I arrived. The Third Ring Road was completed in 1992, replacing another two-lane, tree-lined road; and the Lufthansa Center, featuring the Kempinski Hotel, had just been built. The Kempinski was the most recent high-end hotel to come onto the scene, but foreigners also frequented the Great Wall Sheraton, the Palace, and the Beijing Grand Hotel. The Holiday Inn Lido, which is right across the street from our office today, was about halfway into the city from the airport, but it was considered to be in the boondocks back then.

What I remember most about Beijing in those days was that if you arrived after eight o'clock at night, it was just about impossible to find anything to eat. There were no restaurants outside the hotel that stayed open that late, and even the three in the Kempinski—a coffee shop, an upscale Western restaurant, and the Sichuan Restaurant— were closed by then as well.

Except for a place called the Moon Bar across the street, there was nothing to do outside the hotel complex. One time when the kids were in Beijing, we ventured over to check it out. Dimly lit, musty-smelling, with very few customers, it was as unappealing inside as it had appeared from the outside. We sat in a booth, had some Cokes and beer, and, with nobody around to hear how badly we sang, took turns on the karaoke machine. Not exactly my idea of a night on the town.

Beijing is much different today. There are a great number and variety of restaurants, many of which are open well into the night. It's not quite New York, but there's more variety here in terms of types of food than you'll find in most of the major cities of the world. In 1993, the only Western restaurants in Beijing were the ones in the major Western hotels. Today, there are any number of stand-alone Western restaurants that are the equal of those anywhere.

Ai Jian (Mr. Ai)

Tim Clissold's key contact in Beijing was a man named Ai Jian, a former member of the Red Guard whose university education had been interrupted by the Cultural Revolution. Mr. Ai (I have always referred to and addressed him in this way) ended up being sent for "reeducation" to a farm in northeast China, but he eventually made his way back to Beijing. He never completed university, but, to his credit, he taught himself English and became a midlevel official in the Ministry of Foreign Trade and Economic Cooperation (MOFTEC); the ministry's job was to promote and oversee foreign investment and trade. Due to his language capabilities, Mr. Ai was often asked to accompany foreign delegations from companies interested in doing business in China, and he even traveled abroad on several occasions. This was highly unusual for Chinese at the time, and it gave him his first glimpse of the world outside China.

Mr. Ai is slender, with dark black wavy hair and gold-rimmed glasses. When we first met, he seemed pleasant enough, though a bit shy. By that time he had met many foreigners, but it was obvious to me that he was nervous. He had never met somebody from Wall Street.

We got over any uneasiness quickly, though, and got down to the task at hand. Tim had told Mr. Ai about my interest in automotive components, and Mr. Ai had set up a meeting for the next day with representatives from the China National Automotive Industry Corporation (CNAIC). To a newcomer like me, CNAIC seemed to be just the kind of central government organization I was searching for.

Everyone now agrees that China will be the largest automotive market in the world by 2020. A large land mass, at least 1.2 billion people, and an economy that has been in overdrive since 1978 spell massive needs for transportation. Despite its bright future, however, the country's auto industry had a rather inauspicious start in 1953, more than thirty years after autos had already become a rather big business in the United States and Europe, when China established First Auto Works (FAW) in the northern city of Changchun to make trucks. Since then Second Auto Works, or Dongfeng Motor Company, and China Heavy Duty Truck had been formed, and for all intents and purposes these three companies (or offshoots of them) form a substantial portion of China's truck industry today.

While truck making in China started in the 1950s, the passenger car industry is a creature of a later time. The first joint venture with a foreign company, Beijing Jeep, was completed in 1984 between Beijing Automobile Industry Corporation (BAIC) and American Motors (later acquired by Chrysler). The most successful of the early entrants, Shanghai Volkswagen, a joint venture between Shanghai Automotive Industry Corporation (SAIC) and Volkswagen, was formed one year later. But the explosive growth in China's passenger car industry would not occur until China entered the World Trade Organization in the early years of the twenty-first century.

By the time we arrived, a lot had changed. Government control over numerous industries had lessened over the years, and many supervisory authorities, like CNAIC, had lost a great deal of power. Once responsible for overseeing China's entire auto industry, CNAIC's authority had been steadily reduced to the point where it had become a shadow organization.

Naturally, we didn't know this at the time and only pieced it together much later. China then, like China now, isn't known for its transparency. Finding out who actually owns a particular factory or company, who has the power and the decision-making authority, is very difficult. Understanding the exact nature of CNAIC's relationship to the factories under its supervision was elusive. Things aren't always what they seem. That's why I caution newcomers to China not to get too hung up on setting senior-level meetings in Beijing. It's nice to meet high-ranking officials in impressive-sounding organizations, but whether these officials can actually help is a question mark. In most cases, the work gets done, and decisions get made, at much lower and more local levels.

Mr. Dong and Mr. Lin

After our initial meeting, which was with relatively low-level managers, we had follow-up meetings on subsequent visits to Beijing with progressively more senior members of CNAIC management. One of these was with Dong Jianping, an upper-middle member of management who was said to be responsible for components, whatever that meant.

CNAIC's offices were in an old, traditional, multistory building in the center of Beijing. We were met in the lobby entrance by an underling and led up several flights of stairs, down a long, dark hallway, to a reasonably appointed meeting room at one end of the building. Immediately upon taking our seats, the ever-present hot water lady appeared with her thermos, dutifully filling the teacups beside us. Soon thereafter, Dong appeared with several of his colleagues.

In virtually all of the meetings described in this and subsequent chapters, the Chinese officials whom we met with spoke little or no English, so the meetings were conducted entirely in Chinese. Mr. Ai always translated for me. In most cases, the interpreters from the other side were young, inexperienced, and difficult to understand. After a few halting attempts to translate what his or her boss had said into English, the other interpreter would yield and Mr. Ai would jump in and translate for the other side as well. Given the importance of "face" in Chinese culture, I always felt sorry for the interpreters when they stumbled like this. They just hadn't had enough chances to use English in a real-life setting.

After exchanging a few pleasantries, I launched into a description of our plan for creating a leading components company in China. From his body language, it was obvious from the start that Dong was skeptical, quite suspicious about how real we were.

"How much money do you have to invest?" was the first question he asked me.

"One hundred fifty million dollars," I said, after only a second's hesitation.

In that one second, I'd realized that if I told him we didn't have any capital now but would be raising it once we'd done our homework, we'd never get a follow-up meeting. I didn't like to misrepresent our situation, but I was confident that I could raise the capital if the opportunity was real. After all, we had quickly raised capital for the fund that was managed by Bill in Hong Kong. While that money was earmarked for investments in publicly traded securities throughout Asia—and could not be used for illiquid, private investments in China—it did indicate investors' appetite for investing in this part of the world.

If I'd had enough time in that meeting, and Dong had been more knowledgeable about the capital-raising process in the West, I'm sure I could have convinced him that it was worthwhile to spend time with me. As it was, it was much simpler and easier to just tell him we had the capital in hand. Even with that, he didn't offer up any joint venture candidates, or any specific assistance for that matter. He kept his cards close to his vest.

Nonetheless, Mr. Ai continued to work his contacts at CNAIC, and a dinner in our hotel with one of its top leaders was arranged for several weeks later. Once again, I raised the topic of CNAIC helping us to identify possible joint ventures, but I received only a vague and non-committal response. After several more meetings and dinners, the senior management of CNAIC suggested that we employ CNAIC as a "consultant." Without any evidence of what they were going to do for us, I wasn't about to pay them a consulting fee.

By now, six weeks had gone by since our first meeting, and I was scratching my head. Something was wrong. It was already March, and after countless meetings and dinners with the higher-ups, we were still no closer to any real deals than we had been in January. More meetings would have been a waste of time, and I certainly wasn't about to pay for any more dinners. In fact, Tim, Mr. Ai, and I joked that dealing with CNAIC was like practicing tai chi: a lot of circling, hand and arm movements, but never any real contact.

Sensing our frustration (and no doubt feeling it a bit himself), Ai Jian recalled a contact he had at a company called Norinco, which he believed had some automotive activities. Otherwise known as China North Industries, Norinco had originally been the Fifth Machine-Building Ministry, responsible for manufacturing and supplying weapons and munitions to the Chinese army. With a great number of factories across China and a growing opportunity in the motor vehicle industry, Norinco had already begun to dedicate a portion of its production to the manufacture of products for civilian use.

After reviewing a promotional brochure clearly showing that Norinco was in the automotive business, Mr. Ai set up a meeting for us with Mr. Lin, a Norinco bureau chief.

A kind, silver-haired man in his fifties, the type of person you would love to have as a grandfather, Mr. Lin immediately struck me as someone who was determined to help in any way that he could.

After my customary introduction, with Tim and Mr. Ai sitting on either side, Mr. Lin finally opened a door.

"We do indeed have components factories," he explained. "In fact, we have more than one hundred factories dedicated to the automotive industry." Approximately thirty were involved in the assembly of all types of vehicles, he told us, and about seventy were involved in the manufacture of components.

What he described was pretty interesting. Here was a large company that appeared, unlike CNAIC, actually to *own* some factories that made components. And because it also had assembly operations, Norinco would be a natural customer as well as a joint venture partner. I couldn't imagine a better scenario.

Expecting more tai chi, I asked the $64,000 question: "Can we have a list of all of Norinco's components factories?"

Without hesitation, Mr. Lin nodded "Yes."

After months of vague answers, I wasn't ready for his immediate and positive response. Recovering from my initial surprise, I explained that Tim and I would be leaving for Hong Kong that evening, and that we'd love to get our hands on the list before we left.

"Where are you staying?" Mr. Lin asked matter-of-factly.

"The Kempinski Hotel," I replied. "And our flight's at 6:00 P.M."

"I'll have the list delivered to your hotel this afternoon," he said. After shaking hands and saying our good-byes, we headed off to our next meeting, wondering whether Mr. Lin would really deliver the list as promised.

When we returned to the Kempinski later that day, I was pleasantly surprised to find an envelope waiting for me at the front desk. Tight on time, I grabbed it without even looking inside, and Tim and I hopped into a taxi for the airport. When I was finally seated on the plane, I opened the envelope and quickly scanned the sheets of paper inside.

True to his word, Mr. Lin had listed, in English, all seventy of Norinco's components companies, including their locations, products, and approximate output. When we landed in Hong Kong that evening, I told Tim that we should return to Beijing immediately, and we booked a return flight for that Sunday. Tim called Mr. Ai and asked him to schedule a follow-up meeting with Mr. Lin on Monday. At that meeting, Mr. Lin gladly offered to arrange factory visits, and we set a schedule for the following week. We were finally going to see what a components company in China looked like.

Mao's Third Front

In the 1970s, Mao Zedong became concerned about the vulnerability of China's military/industrial complex to bomber attacks from the Soviet Union, Japan, and the United States. In response, he undertook a major campaign to locate military factories in the mountains and other out-of-the-way locations in China's interior. So-called Third Front factories, they represented China's third front against a future enemy, with the coastal areas and China's major cities as its first and second fronts. Because it was a quasi-military organization, many of Norinco's factories were Third Front factories and were located in remote parts of the country, such as the mountains of Sichuan Province. Accompanied by Mr. Lin, we began our visits to these factories with a series of trips to Chongqing.

Chongqing is more than three thousand years old, and it's one of the largest cities in the world, with a population of over 30 million people. It served as the capital of the Nationalist government during World War II, and the city sits on the edge of a plateau in the upper reaches of the Yangtze River in the middle of China. It's known as a city of mountains, rivers, and fog, and my first reaction on seeing the city in the distance as we crossed the bridge on the way in from the airport was of the color gray. Chongqing has always been a heavily industrial city. By 1993, it had already developed as a major automotive and motorcycle production base, which was largely the result of Norinco's activities. Chemicals, steel, aluminum, and other industrial products were also made there.

With all of the industry and coal burning, Chongqing struck me as a very dirty and unpleasant city at the time. Having said that, Carleen, Douglas, and I took a trip down the Yangtze in the summer of 2003 that originated in Chongqing. I hadn't been in the city for at least seven or eight years and still carried with me my initial impressions. Compared with what I saw then, I was quite impressed with how much the city fathers had done to improve the city and its environment. We stayed at a very nice Hilton Hotel, and the city didn't seem nearly as gray as I remembered it.

Despite the dirty surroundings on that first trip, we managed to find a reasonably nice Holiday Inn, where we stayed that first night. The next morning, Mr. Lin and one of his colleagues met us downstairs at 7:00 A.M., and we began our "two-factories-a-day" schedule. They had arranged a van, and we all piled in. Over the next several months, this scene was to be repeated over and over again in Chongqing, Chengdu, Changchun, Harbin, and countless other cities where Norinco had components factories.

The Norinco factories were true to their billing, enormous facilities built into the mountains and cities unto themselves. It was nothing for a factory to house twenty thousand people, with the workers and their families all living within the factory gates. Each factory had a central area for recreation, and after dinner you'd see hundreds of people standing around, talking, and playing various games. Surrounded by mountains and with no local town or entertainment nearby, there really wasn't much else to do.

One factory we visited was five kilometers long and one kilometer wide, nestled in a narrow valley between two mountain ranges. The young man who was assigned to translate for us, a cheerful guy with a cherubic face, explained that the surrounding mountains hid the factory and made it less accessible to bombers. I couldn't help but agree with him.

As we were making small talk, waiting for our meeting to start, I asked, "What do you do here for fun?"

"I like to watch MTV," he said, a devilish smile crossing his face. Not what I expected. Slowly but surely, even remote places in rural China were starting to open up via modern technology.

The factories themselves were great complexes of ancient Soviet-style buildings, many of which were half-empty. A good number of the structures were off-limits to us, and though our hosts always denied it vehemently, we suspected that these buildings were devoted to the production of military weaponry. On one of our visits, we were accompanied by several representatives of JP Morgan, which was considering working with us on the components program. As we sat around the conference room, the factory manager assured us that the factory didn't make military goods of any kind. Seconds later, our discussion was suddenly interrupted by a loud explosion, followed by several moments of silence as we all turned and looked at one another, wondering what had just gone off.

Norinco is a well-funded organization with plenty of access to capital, and even in 1993 it was already doing a significant export business. As a military company it got more than its fair share of capital from the central government. This capitalization was obvious as we visited the factories under its umbrella. Invariably, the workshops where the production was actually done contained nothing but old and worn equipment. But, in separate buildings, we'd often find brand-new imported equipment still covered in plastic. The desire to close the thirty-year technology gap between China and the rest of the world was clearly there—they'd bought the most modern equipment they could get their hands on—but nobody knew how to use it.

Watering the Dark Earth of Heilongjiang

When we first set up our offices in Hong Kong, the design company gave us a framed map of China as a gift, and we regularly used it to identify the locations of possible factory joint ventures and other points of interest. When my daughter Sara was at Andover, she befriended an exchange student from Qiqihar, near the Russian border in the far north of China. One afternoon, Tim and I were looking at the China map on my wall, and I pointed out the city where her friend lived.

"We'll never have to go there," Tim immediately responded.

Three months later, we were planning additional visits to Norinco factories with Mr. Lin, and up popped Qiqihar as the location of one of the company's brake factories.

On these weeklong outings to scout possible joint ventures, Tim, Ai Jian, and I (and sometimes Carleen) frequently traveled to places that were two or three hours of hard driving from the nearest city, along roads that quickly deteriorated into dirt and mud passageways. In some cases, the roads didn't even make it all the way to the factory itself. In one spot, we had to take a ferry across a river because there was no bridge. How in the world raw materials got in, and finished goods got out, was a question to which I never got a satisfactory answer. In China, though, the seemingly impossible always somehow gets done.

On our way, we'd usually pass through several villages, on narrow roads made even more narrow by the stalls that farmers had set up to sell their meat and produce. We'd literally crawl through the villages, and if the car window was open you could reach out and grab whatever was being sold.

In many of these places, nobody had ever seen a foreigner. In one small village, we slowed to a stop and I decided to get out and stretch my legs. As the car door swung open and I stepped out, a poor elderly woman nearby shrieked. With my stocky frame, light hair, and big nose, I must have looked like the reincarnation of the devil himself.

A number of Norinco's factories were in the north, and many were situated near Changchun, the home of First Auto Works and FAW/Volkswagen. Changchun is a relatively young city in China, only two hundred years old, and it's located in Jilin Province, in what used to be known as Manchuria, in the middle of China's industrial heartland. Because many of the more modern buildings were built during the honeymoon period between Mao and Stalin, the Russian style is prevalent throughout the city, and many of Changchun's broad streets had Russian names. One of the city's main streets was named Stalin Street in 1948, and that's what it was still called when we first visited in 1993. (The honeymoon long since over, the street was renamed People's Street in 1996, caused no doubt by the demise of the Soviet Union and Russia's change of fortune in the aftermath.)

On our first visit to Changchun, Mr. Lin arranged for us to have dinner with Deputy Mayor Wang, who was in charge of industrial development for the city. While he was interested in the possibility of us doing joint ventures with the Norinco factories in Changchun—and thereby bringing much-needed capital to his city—Deputy Mayor Wang also had some components factories under his wing, and he offered to introduce us. From then on, we began to schedule separate trips to Changchun to visit factories controlled by our good friend Deputy Mayor Wang, and this opened up a second channel for joint venture opportunities.

One factory that we visited was a rubber factory with a production line from Italy. The factory manager was a bit eccentric and over the top, and we decided pretty quickly that this wasn't an opportunity we wanted to pursue. But, for whatever reason, the company wouldn't take no for an answer. Every time we traveled to Changchun, a representative of the company would be waiting for us when we arrived at the hotel. When we got back from dinner, yet another person would be waiting patiently in the lobby. When the factory's managers even followed us to Beijing, I started to feel like we were being stalked. You can imagine our shock when we returned to the Kun Lun Hotel in Beijing, where we had a one-room office, and found several people from the company waiting for us. I don't know how we shook them, but eventually they gave up.

We did eventually make that trip to Qiqihar. Mr. Lin had arranged for us to visit a factory in Harbin, a city even farther north than Changchun that's famous for its winter ice festival. After a quick dinner, we embarked on what turned out to be a seven-hour van ride through the night to Qiqihar, arriving in the factory well after midnight.

On the way, we stopped by the side of the road to "empty our water," as Ai Jian described it. Standing side by side and staring out at the pitch-black northern China sky, we watered the dark earth of Heilongjiang Province and compared notes about where we both were in 1973, in the midst of China's Cultural Revolution. Ai Jian reminisced about his work on the farm that year, when I'd been worlds away, at Harvard Business School and then at PaineWebber. Back then, I had no idea what more than 1 billion people in China were going through. I remember being struck by how two people of the same age could have had such totally different experiences in a modern, twentieth-century world. I was also struck by how the trauma of such a large part of the world's population could have been kept hidden from the rest of the world for so long. That simple moment is one I will always remember.

Breaking the Logjam

After we'd visited a number of Norinco's factories, Mr. Lin began to introduce us to the more senior members of Norinco's management. We eventually met with the general manager of the company and had a number of meetings with the two vice general managers, Mr. Wang and Mr. Tian. Norinco is a very large, serious, and powerful company, so when you get to those top levels you're reaching into the top leadership of China itself. I was particularly impressed with Mr. Wang. He was tall, had a great deal of bearing, and carried himself with confidence. I could easily imagine him running a Fortune 500 company.

I hoped we could cut a deal with Norinco in Beijing, which could then serve as a framework for the joint ventures with (what we thought were) its wholly owned subsidiaries. We were anxious to avoid the pain of negotiating joint ventures with multiple partners, but again this proved to be wishful thinking. When the time came to negotiate the individual joint ventures, the powers that be in those companies couldn't have cared less about what we'd discussed or agreed to with the higher-ups in Beijing.

But we'd only learn all of this later. In the meantime, Mr. Wang told us that several organizations—the civilian arm of the Aviation Ministry, Norinco, and others—were sponsoring a major exhibition in Hong Kong in July of 1993. They hoped to attract foreign investors and partners by displaying their various wares at the exhibition, a kind of "guns to butter" showcase that might be a way for defense-related organizations to accelerate the development of the civilian sides of their businesses. Mr. Wang suggested that it would be a good thing for us to sign letters of intent in Hong Kong with seven of the Norinco factories we had visited.

On Wall Street, signing a letter of intent (LOI) was a serious event. It usually followed fairly rigorous negotiations that had already hammered out the key terms of the agreement. Usually legal and accounting due diligence were all that remained undone, and everyone was pretty confident that the transaction would go ahead. When signed, an LOI in the States is typically made public and can potentially have a significant impact on the publicly traded securities of the parties to the agreement.

In China, an LOI has a somewhat different meaning. It's the first step in the joint venture process, and the Chinese company has to file it with its supervisory entity in order to get the process started. Once the supervisors have signed it, the LOI signifies that the Chinese company can now work with its potential partner to pre- pare a "project proposal" and then a "feasibility study," both of which have to be approved by the relevant authorities. Under this system, a Chinese company could conceivably have LOIs signed with several different potential foreign partners. There was nothing exclusive or final about the letter itself.

Mr. Wang wanted us to sign in Hong Kong because he thought it would encourage other potential investors to look at Norinco's factories. We ultimately did what he had suggested, and we signed seven LOIs at the exhibition, with great ceremony. There was a high level of interest in the event in China, and it was covered heavily by the Asian media. The business sections of several of the Hong Kong papers showed pictures of me signing.

Though we hadn't planned it this way, these public signings also broke the logjam with CNAIC. Dong Jianping saw the newspaper articles, concluded that we were serious, and sent a message through Ai Jian that he wanted to meet with me the next time I was in Beijing.

When we met, Dong immediately produced a spreadsheet listing twenty of what he considered to be the best components factories in China, along with their locations and products. While CNAIC did not have any formal connection to most companies on the list, Dong had gotten to know their general managers over the years, and he had tried to help each of them obtain government loans and find joint venture partners or sources of technology. It was his knowledge and personal relationships, not his position with CNAIC, that turned out to be most valuable. Now taking a personal interest in our mission, he said that he'd personally arrange and accompany us on our visits. The list that Dong produced that day turned out to be the best single list of potential joint venture partners that we ever received, and we eventually consummated joint ventures with several of the companies on it.

By July of 1993, only three months after we'd been at a stalemate with CNAIC, we were visiting factories that had been introduced by either Norinco, the City of Changchun, or CNAIC. Everywhere we went, we met with representatives of the local government, each of whom had components factories under his supervision. Our network broadened. We'd gone from not being able even to find factories to visit to essentially having the entire universe of Chinese components companies available to us. By the time we were finished, general managers of factories from all over China would come to Beijing, call us from the lobby of the Kun Lun, and tell us that they'd like to discuss the possibility of doing a joint venture with us. Little did they know that the only capital I had at that time was my American Express card. Fortunately, it was platinum!

By August, I was exhausted. We'd been visiting two factories a day since March, traveling under difficult conditions and staying in too many factory guesthouses and "one-star" hotels. We had eaten way more food than anybody should eat, and we certainly drank more *baijiu* (I'll explain in a minute) than any human should consume in a lifetime. One day I counted them all up, and I realized I'd visited more than a hundred factories in forty cities throughout China.

This was enough. The last factory we visited during this phase was a rubber factory in Wuxi. To say that I wasn't excited about having to make this visit is a severe, severe understatement. I was tired, irritable, and ready to get on with the next phase of the program—figuring out how to raise the capital.

To make matters worse, this particular factory made no sense. It made rubber parts for the automotive industry, but it also made floor tiles. It was hard for me to understand, through all of the translation, exactly which part of the business the management considered to be more important. I remember deciding then and there that the investigation phase was over for me. It was time to try to take the next step in my journey.

Chapter 5

Eating, Drinking, and Sleeping on the Long March

Whenever I describe our "Long March" through China during those first nine months in 1993, people always want to know what it was like to travel through China then. Beyond the deals we signed and the factories we visited, what was China like in those earlier days? Undoubtedly, it was the most interesting and fascinating nine months of my life. On those trips, I had an opportunity to visit places that few foreigners had ever seen, at a point in time that is now lost forever. While most cities in China haven't changed nearly as much as Beijing and Shanghai, the fast-food restaurants, super-markets, new buildings, and modern cars that are now seen in even seemingly remote parts of the country simply weren't there in 1993.

Unlike our modern world of credit cards, booking online, and e-tickets, traveling in China back then was done the old-fashioned way. You made your reservations and bought your airline tickets at an airline ticket office or travel agent. There was a six-month waiting list for a

landline in Beijing, so telephones were few and far
between, and there were certainly no cell phones. Credit
cards were a novelty, so hotels, meals, and even plane
tickets often had to be paid for in cash. Even getting
enough yuan for a weeklong trip was itself an adventure.

At the time, the exchange rate was set at 5.5 yuan to
one U.S. dollar. As foreigners, though, we weren't
officially allowed to use the local currency; instead, we
were supposed to exchange our dollars for foreign
exchange cerificates (FECs). This was okay, until high
inflation in the early 1990s caused the real value of the
RMB to decline substantially, and the local currency could
be purchased much more cheaply outside official
channels.

Being the entrepreneurs that they are, many Chinese
went into the currency trading business, and an active
black market developed. If you walk down many Beijing
streets today, vendors will whisper "DVD? DVD?" as you
pass by, in the hope of selling you a DVD of a just-
released Hollywood hit for 10 yuan (a little over one
dollar). Back then, you might just as easily hear "Change
money? Change money?" as you passed by a stall selling
sneakers. If you nodded yes, you would be quickly pulled
into the back, where the money changer would begin
haggling over the exact exchange rate to be paid. At the
RMB's low point, 12 yuan could be purchased for one
dollar, more than twice as many than at the official rate.

Needless to say, no one in their right mind used FEC
when you could pay less than one-half by purchasing and

using the local currency. For a while, taxi drivers and shopkeepers would refuse to take yuan, arguing that foreigners weren't allowed to use the local currency and had to pay in FEC. Instead of arguing, common practice was to calmly put the yuan on the counter or the front seat of the taxi and walk away. Eventually, they got the point.

Exchanging money at stalls was one way to get your hands on local currency, but before China had pizza home delivery, it also had "yuan home delivery." If you called a certain number, a bag-carrying foreign exchange specialist would arrive at a stairwell nearby, and the exchange would be made. With such a large gap between the official and the real exchange rate, China did the only sensible thing. At the beginning of 1994, it eliminated the FEC and revalued its currency by setting the exchange rate at RMB 8.3 to $1. There it stayed until July 2005.

Every Part of Every Animal

"You name the city or province, and I was there during the first nine months of 1993," I often say when people ask me about our investigation phase in China.

"Also," I always add, "during that period I ate every part of every animal, with the emphasis on *every*."

The follow-on comment always gets a laugh, but understanding China's food culture was a large part of my learning experience. Make no mistake about it, food is very important in Chinese culture. Meals are not just times to fill one's stomach. They're meant to be shared with family and friends and to build new relationships.

The Chinese have a saying about their brothers in Guangdong Province in the south of China, "If it has legs and isn't a table; if it has wings and isn't an airplane; if its back is to the sun, and it isn't a peasant hunched over working in the field, they will eat it."

To a certain degree, this applies all over China. Almost every imaginable type of animal, bird, or insect might end up on the table, and the Chinese make full use of every animal that they raise, catch, or kill. No doubt remembering tough times when having enough to eat could not be taken for granted, the Chinese don't let anything go to waste. Traveling through China, I've had it all. Cow's intestine, duck's tongue, chicken feet, dog, snake, scorpion, eel, turtle, and (the reason I can claim to have eaten every part) deer penis, which I had the pleasure of eating one memorable evening in Changchun.

Most foreigners make the mistake of asking what something is before sampling. My practice is to just go ahead and eat. If it tastes good, continue. If not, stop. If I'd been told ahead of time that I was going to be eating duck's tongue, for example, I might have been a bit turned off. But when they came out, little orange things mixed in a spicy sauce with green beans, they tasted quite good. The unusual consistency told me that they were something I hadn't had before, but I didn't need to know what they were. Similarly, I never would have thought that I could eat scorpion. But deep fried and spread over a bowl of chips, they tasted like any other crispy, salty snack I might have in the States.

The Chinese spend a great deal of time on present-ation and preparing dishes in an appetizing way. Of all the factories that we visited, the 228 Clutch Factory in Changchun took the prize in the presentation depart-ment. (Often, Chinese factories are named according to a numbering system. I am certain there was a reason for assigning "228" to this particular factory, but I never asked, and was never told, why.) Every time we went there, the kitchen staff went out of their way to arrange dishes of radishes, carrots, small tomatoes, and other vegetables into the shape of a dragon, a peacock, or some other colorful bird or animal. The dishes were so artful and so vibrant and colorful that the cameras came out of their bags almost instantaneously, nobody wanting to eat anything before it had been commemorated on film.

At most of the dinners we went to, the Chinese hosts would go to great lengths to describe the way in which each dish was particularly good at serving some particular function. The hot and spicy foods of Hunan and Sichuan, our hosts told us, are good for cleaning out the insides and releasing the heat in your body. Turtle and any male organs are good for a man, while other dishes are said to be good for a woman, or for your skin. I don't know if any of this is true or not, but I've gotten the same explanation for the same dishes no matter where I've gone in China.

Baijiu: China's White Lightning

Naturally, you don't get food without drink. The Chinese in the north have a saying, "If you have three dishes, you should drink. If you have four dishes, you should drink and talk." After formal factory visits and official meetings, the drinking portions of the meals were often a chance for personalities to come out, both mine and our host's. Though it doesn't happen nearly as much today, in those days most of the meals we had featured China's drink of choice, the infamous *baijiu.*

Baijiu, to put it mildly, is an acquired taste. It's a clear alcohol, made from rice or a variety of other grains, and it can have an alcoholic strength of up to 65 percent. Over the years, I've heard foreigners describe it as tasting like gasoline, lighter fluid, or kerosene. It's serious stuff. To make matters worse, it has a way of sticking with you. The next morning, nobody needs to tell you that you had a "*baijiu* night" the night before, because you can still taste it.

Most of the time, *baijiu* is served in mercifully small "cups," which contain less than the typical American shot glass. Generally, the routine is to down the contents of the cup in one gulp (usually following a toast) and then wait for the inevitable aftershock. The waitress is never far behind, hastening to fill your glass so you are always ready for the next toast. The small glasses make a *baijiu* night somewhat manageable, though there was one dinner in Anhui Province where they filled the *baijiu* almost to the top of regular-size water glasses. That was a rough night.

When we would travel to, say, Harbin in the north, invariably the dinner host would set the stage for the rest of the evening's events by explaining that the people there needed to drink a lot because of the extreme cold. Then, a week or two later, we'd find ourselves in a city like Nanjing, designated as one of China's "fiery furnaces," and our hosts there would explain that people in Nanjing liked to drink a lot because Nanjing is so hot. And, naturally, when we were in Sichuan, our host would explain that people there had to drink a lot because the food is so hot and spicy. The only rational conclusion I could draw in 1993 was that people all over China liked to drink.

And because I was a foreigner who might bring capital, our Chinese hosts would always roll out the red carpet when we came to town. When we were visiting two factories a day, it was like having two New Year's Eve celebrations a day, *every day*. We'd get up, drive two hours to a factory, get a factory introduction, a tour, and then an invitation to lunch, where I'd give my patented "capital, management, and technology" speech about the resources we'd bring. Food and *baijiu* would flow throughout. Then we'd get back in the car and drive two more hours to the next factory, where the process would repeat itself and end up with a dinner. More "capital, management, and technology," and more food and *baijiu*. Needless to say, it was considered impolite to refuse what you were offered. More important, though, drinking with the Chinese showed that you were a good sport, that you wanted to form a relationship, and that you were willing to accept China on its terms.

Even though the Chinese generally have a lower tolerance for liquor than Americans do, there's always one Chinese in the crowd with an iron stomach—the "designated drinker." The hosts use this individual, plus an assortment of tricks, to get the foreigners to drink much more than they should. This always seemed to be an objective for our hosts, as a way of making sure we had a good time and would remember their factory or city after we'd gone.

But, as you've probably already suspected, they'd play tricks to tilt the drinking advantage their way. One of the most common ploys was for our host to tell the waitresses to pour water into his glass but to keep refilling ours with *baijiu*. Most Americans pride themselves on being pretty strong drinkers, but if you're not aware that these instructions have been given, you can spend a whole evening downing *baijiu* while your host does the same without any noticeable effect. You have to be up close to smell the clear liquid itself in order to tell the difference.

Despite these deceptions, though, there is a strong sense of fairness in China. After gaining some drinking experience in the country, I learned that it's perfectly okay to challenge your Chinese counterpart if you suspect that this is going on. The way you do this is to offer to exchange cups, your *baijiu* for his water. Once you've made the offer, there's no way for your host to refuse. I did this in Beijing one evening years later when we were having dinner with a group of managers from BAIC, our Chinese partner in our fuel injection business. Mr. Zhang, who was on the joint venture board, made a great show of going to each table and toasting everybody. When he came to me, I offered to exchange cups, and I've never seen somebody's jaw drop so far. At that moment, he realized that I'd been learning my lessons in China.

There were other ways for the Chinese to get you to drink more than they did. When Douglas was sixteen, I took him on a trip with me to Sichuan Province. The designated drinker there took great delight in showing Doug how he could take a cup of *baijiu* and appear to throw it in his mouth—all the while tossing it over his shoulder instead. (Don't wear an expensive suit when you try this one.) There's also the straightforward approach, which is to invent reasons why the Western guests should drink more than their hosts. "I've brought three of my colleagues here to meet you, so for every cup I drink, you should drink three." Or, "This is your second trip to this city, so for every cup that I drink, you should drink two." You get the point.

One of our lunches in Sichuan Province still sticks in my mind today. I had fully launched into my capital, management, and technology speech when I felt a tap on my shoulder. I turned around to see one of the waitresses with a glass of *baijiu* in her hand, offering to *ganbei* (a bottoms-up toast) with me.

Ever the gentleman, I responded by saying, "I never refuse to drink with a beautiful woman," and we drank.

It was a fatal mistake. I sat down, resumed my speech, and about five minutes later, felt another tap on my shoulder. Another waitress, another glass of *baijiu*, and another offer of *ganbei*. How could I refuse after drinking with the first? If I did, wouldn't she think I was trying to tell her that she wasn't beautiful? Down it went.

I sat down and resumed my speech yet again, though this time admittedly a bit more slowly. When I received the next tap only minutes later, I knew that when I turned around I'd see yet another waitress with yet another glass of *baijiu* and another offer to *ganbei*. What I didn't expect to see, when I happened to glance toward the entrance to the kitchen, were seven more waitresses lined up, all patiently waiting their turn!

Every place we went, there was always a new experience like this. One of our favorite hosts was Mayor Wang, the deputy mayor for industry in Changchun, whom I mentioned in the last chapter.

Mayor Wang was a colorful character, and I always looked forward to seeing him. In his midforties with black hair, dark glasses, and a round face, Mayor Wang always looked a little bit heavier, and a little bit rounder, than he actually was. This was due to the several layers of woolen underwear that he typically wore underneath his suit pants. (Changchun is very cold, and the buildings were not evenly heated, so it was not uncommon for office workers to wear layers of clothing, even indoors.)

Among other things, Mayor Wang will always have a warm spot in my heart for having introduced me to the delicacy of deer penis. In the middle of one of our dinners, the waitress put a bowl of brownish-colored soup in front of me. It was a cold night in Manchuria made for hot soup, so I dug in. After a few spoonfuls, I noticed a flesh-colored object floating in the middle of the bowl. Thinking it was some type of root vegetable, I didn't bother to ask what it was and took a bite. Clearly, this was not a vegetable! I caught Mayor Wang looking over at me out of the corner of his eye, and I looked up at Tim who nodded knowingly. Afterward, he broke the news to me about what I had eaten.

In one of our lighter moments, when we were drinking and talking about all of the joint ventures we would do in Changchun, Mayor Wang promised to sponsor me for membership in the Communist Party. "Of course," he said with an impish smile on his face, "you'll have to pay your dues in FEC."

Dinner with Mayor Wang was usually followed by a trip to one of the "nightclubs" operated by the city of Changchun. Intentions were good, but these were always painful affairs for us, mainly because everybody in the clubs looked like they'd studied ballroom dancing in an Arthur Murray dance studio. We would have been happy to just sit, have a beer, watch the activity, and listen to music. Instead, each of us was approached at the beginning of each song by a young lady asking us to dance. On other occasions and under different circumstances this might not have been a bad thing, but the combination of our inability to communicate and our pitiful attempts to blend the ballroom dancing style of our partners with the "white man's overbite" style of dancing that we practiced in New York made these moments pretty uncomfortable. (On those occasions when Carleen, who is on the tall side, was with us, Mayor Wang's staff searched the city to find a particularly tall male to be her dance partner. Carleen was always delighted, of course, to be introduced to her date for the evening.)

Sleeping on the Road

The Kempinski Hotel in Beijing was the oasis we returned to at the end of each week. I can't tell you how nice it was to get back to the clean, soft sheets of the Kempinski after whatever we'd been through that week. In most cases, the factories we visited were located in very, very small towns, most barely villages, and in many cases there were no hotels. Each factory typically had a guesthouse, and that's where we would often stay. Some of them weren't too bad, but many of them were pretty awful. They all smelled like smoke, and the beds had sagging mattresses and blankets so dirty you wouldn't even dream of lying on them without a full set of clothing, including your over-coat. The water in the shower wasn't always hot, either—at one place, they told us that hot water would only be available between 6:00 and 7:00 A.M.—and most times barely a trickle came out of the showerhead.

The bathrooms were always an adventure. Carleen and I checked into one guesthouse and found that the bathroom floor was covered by a thick, wet, dirty film. We had no idea what it was, and we had a tough time deciding whether to take our shoes off and risk contracting some unknown disease or keep them on and risk ruining them forever.

The hotels we stayed in weren't much better. One of our potential investors came to breakfast one morning with numerous stories about the uninvited four-legged guest that had visited him the night before. Another rat sighting occurred at a meeting I had with a deputy mayor in the meeting room of the best hotel in that city. As the mayor and I sat side by side in front of the television cameras, I turned to listen to his pitch about the benefits of investing in his city, only to find my attention wandering as I watched a rat scurry all the way up the curtain hanging at the back of our chairs.

A Taste of Italy in Nanjing

One of the most memorable visits of my entire time in China occurred in late 1993, in Nanjing. With our relationship with CNAIC growing by the day, we were invited to spend three days visiting components factories that were part of Nanjing Auto Works (NAW), one of the companies under the supervision of CNAIC.

The visit was organized by Lu Zaihou, a wonderful man and the chief engineer of NAW at the time. Mr. Lu retired in early 1994 and later came to Beijing to personally deliver a handwritten note in English, telling me that he admired our strategy and wanted to work for ASIMCO. I hired him on the spot, and Mr. Lu worked for us until the end of March in 2000, when he retired a second time and gained the distinction of being the first person ever to officially retire from ASIMCO.

This visit to Nanjing was one of our higher-profile visits, and we were told that because of the importance of the occasion we'd be meeting with Mr. Gu, the general manager, and that he would personally host each of our three dinners. This was quite an honor. Typically, the general manager, particularly of such a large company, wouldn't be present during the first visit at all. Mr. Gu was quite a senior figure in the Chinese automobile industry, and he knew all of the vice premiers of China and the senior-most leadership of the country.

After our first day of meetings, we showed up for dinner at the appointed hour and met Mr. Gu. He was an important official, to be sure, but he was also quite an interesting personality. In his late fifties, Mr. Gu was of average height and stocky build, which gave him a certain presence when he walked through the door. At the same time, his salt-and-pepper hair, combed loosely to one side, lent him a boyish and slightly disheveled air. He had traveled extensively to Italy to meet with members of the Fiat Group, the most important company in Italy and NAW's global partner. He loved Italy and spoke often about it. Carleen, who was part of the ASIMCO delegation on this trip, swore that he spoke Chinese with an Italian accent.

After the small talk had ended, Mr. Gu announced at the first dinner that each of the three nights would have a different theme. The first night would be "beer night," and we would drink only beer. The second would be "*baijiu* night," and we would drink only *baijiu*. The third night was to be the most special of all, because Mr. Gu had been saving several bottles of cognac for, you guessed it, "cognac night" on the final night of our stay. No matter what their alcoholic content, all three liquors were to be drunk in the same manner: glasses full, bottoms up. Going into these dinners, I was pretty sure I could handle nights one and two, but I was worried about night three. The prospect of downing cognac in large quantities didn't sound terribly appealing.

We got some idea of what we were in for on the first night, when the waiter brought around a very popular pork dish in China called *kourou*. This dish is essentially a slab of pork, covered by a one- to two-inch-thick slab of fat. When the dish arrived, Mr. Gu immediately cut off a large piece of the fat and put it in his mouth.

"The fat's good for coating the stomach," he said, looking right at me. This was ominous. He meant that it would provide at least some protection against the onslaught of alcohol that was about to come.

"You should do the same," he encouraged me and the others.

On the second night, I made the mistake of wearing a new tie, one I'd paid a fair amount of money for in New York and especially liked. At one point during the dinner, when we were already well into our *baijiu*, Mr. Gu looked, noticed my tie, and suggested that we exchange. Mr. Gu's tie wasn't bad, yellow with some type of a black pattern, but I knew what I had paid for mine. I didn't honestly see how I could refuse, so I reluctantly undid my tie, being careful to leave the knot in place. If I minimized the handling, I figured, and nothing was spilled on it before the end of the meal, I would get it back in the same condition. I just assumed that each tie would be returned to its rightful owner at the end of the night, we'd have a few laughs, and that would be it. I never saw that tie again.

And then the much-dreaded "cognac night" arrived, the most raucous of them all. I still remember Mr. Gu, who lived near the restaurant where we were eating, pedaling by on his bicycle while clutching several bottles of cognac. (I have no idea how he got home.)

During dinner, desperate for a break, I got up and headed down a long, dark corridor to the men's room. On my way back to the table, I passed Mr. Gu headed the other way. When I returned, Carleen decided to go to the ladies' room, and apparently passed Mr. Gu on his way back to the table.

A native New Yorker who grew up in the West Village, Carleen doesn't rattle easily. When she got back to the table, she told me nonchalantly that, in true Italian fashion, Mr. Gu had pinched her bottom.

"Don't worry," I turned to her and said with a smile. "He pinched mine, too!"

* * *

IT GOES WITHOUT saying that things have changed a lot since those tours I took in 1993. For one thing, hotels are much improved throughout China, and even small cities have a decent place to stay now. With more airports, more flights, and better roads, the driving time to a larger city (and a good hotel) is a lot shorter than it used to be.

Food is still a focal point, but I find that the Chinese are a bit more relaxed about it these days. If we have a tight schedule, the person hosting our meeting might have food from Kentucky Fried Chicken or McDonald's brought in. This couldn't have happened in 1993. Those chains existed only in Beijing and Shanghai back then, but even if they'd been more widespread, nobody would have thought serving fast food to be an acceptable practice. At meetings just before lunch and dinner in 1993, attention would visibly begin to drift as we approached the meal hour. Today, we often meet well beyond what many might consider to be a reasonable lunch or dinner time, and nobody seems to mind.

The infamous *baijiu* is, of course, still present, but wine has made some big inroads. More often than not, and particularly at lunch, you'll see wine more frequently now. The host will still always ask me, as the guest, what I'd prefer, and in 1993 that choice was clear: *baijiu*. I was only being asked so I could confirm the selection that had already been made. Today, I have to look for some hint as to what the host really wants to serve.

Eating and drinking habits may have changed somewhat, but the spirit of the Chinese people I've met has not. The Chinese are gracious hosts who want to do business and like to have fun while doing it. Over those nine months, I went to many remote parts of China, places that not many foreigners—or even Chinese, for that matter—have ever seen. Throughout, I found myself consistently impressed by the attitude of the Chinese people. No matter how poor their condition seemed to be, I always found them to be positive, upbeat, and fun-loving, with a genuine sense of humor.

After all of the hospitality the Chinese showed me, and after seeing the strong work ethic of the Chinese people, I couldn't help but come away with a great deal of respect for them. Whatever the politics, and never mind the bad actors that we would ultimately come across, I have grown to admire the intelligence, attitude, and industry of the vast majority of China's population. I came away from all of those factory tours impressed by the wealth of opportunities that existed in the country. Even more, I found myself impressed with China's biggest asset of all—its people.

Chapter 6

Developing Our New China Management Strategy

Once the investigation phase was over, I moved very quickly into the implementation phase. Raising capital proved relatively easy. I had done the work, developed a good strategy, and managed to attract strong partners—and we all got lucky with the timing. While it took six months to complete our first joint venture, we then proceeded to put together the core of the company by completing a half dozen more in short order.

And that's when everything came to a screeching halt. As a result of a sluggish auto market (brought on by an economic austerity program) and our head-on collision with China's "management gap," we had to regroup and reevaluate how we were going to manage and grow our business in China. The years between 1996 and 1998 were some of the darkest for ASIMCO. We managed to work our way through them through sheer perseverance, and because our strategy was correct. Through this, I have learned that getting the strategy right is one of the most important things that a company can do.

WHILE I WAS traveling through China in 1993, I kept in touch with my contacts on Wall Street. In particular, the executives at Dean Witter, a large securities firm at the time, and Trust Company of the West (TCW), a money management firm, became interested in emerging markets such as China and in what I was doing. As my concept began to take shape, both sent their own experts to China to see firsthand what was going on in the country and its auto industry. I took them to some of the factories we had already seen, and we visited several of the leading car and truck assemblers together to get their take on the components strategy that I was developing. The result of these discussions was the formation of Asian Strategic Investments Corporation in September 1993. Dean Witter, TCW, and the company that Bill Kaye and I had formed were the shareholders, and the idea was that it would act as the general partner of a limited partnership that we planned to put together later in the year.

As we began to write the private placement offering memorandum, we found ourselves using the acronym ASIMCO throughout the document. The name stuck. The only change would come in 2004, after an ownership restructuring, when we added the word *Technologies*. (We did so to emphasize to our employees, customers, partners, and shareholders that being a technology leader would be the key to the company's future success.)

I didn't realize it at the time, but having a name that begins with "A" is one of the smartest things you can do when starting a new business. Sounds like a superficial point, but it isn't. Even though we were newcomers to the automotive industry, ASIMCO's name was always listed first at industry conferences and in industry publications—ahead of more established, world-famous players like Bosch, DaimlerChrysler, Delphi, Ford, and General Motors. Only half tongue in cheek, I routinely advise MBA students bent on entrepreneurial careers to give any company they establish a name that begins with the letter A.

After I returned to the United States from Hong Kong in December of 1993, TCW and Dean Witter set up meetings with potential investors and we set about raising the funds. In six weeks over the Christmas holidays, we reached our goal of $150 million. Before I even knew it, this phase in ASIMCO's development was finished.

The fund-raising went smoothly for a number of reasons. First, I'd already spent a considerable amount of time in Asia and China, had done a great deal of work on the ground, and was committed to living in China and seeing the program through. That level of personal commitment was important to potential investors. Second, our industry focus and insistence on majority ownership proved to be a unique and compelling strategy.

Third, we had strong institutional support from TCW and Dean Witter. Last, and most important, our timing was good. We caught the tail end of the initial rush to invest in China. If we'd started six months later, when Zhu Rongji's austerity program to combat inflation began to take hold and interest in China began to wane, we probably wouldn't have been successful. As I'd learned in twenty years on Wall Street, timing is everything in the capital markets.

From the beginning, we knew that there was a management gap in China, though we would not have articulated it in quite that way at the time. To address this issue, we told investors that we would recruit an expatriate team of Western managers from the automotive industry to augment the efforts of the Chinese managers. While I was raising capital, I began to look for a person to head up this effort. We hired Korn Ferry to conduct the search, and I began to interview candidates from Detroit between meetings with investors.

"What, No China?"

Despite the risks and the costs inherent in hiring expatriate managers, the need to do so seemed obvious at the time. I wasn't a manufacturing or operations expert, but I'd visited many factories in the States and knew what a well-run factory should look like. Most of the factories I'd visited in China didn't look anything like the ones I was used to seeing. Instead of the lean, focused factories

I'd seen elsewhere, the factories in China were sprawling, state-owned complexes that were generally dirty, not well lit, and loaded with too much work in process inventory. All were highly vertically integrated, meaning that they did everything, but nothing very well. Many had Dickensian-style foundries, dark, dirty workshops where a worker might pour molten metal by hand wearing nothing but sandals. There were no safety glasses, safety shoes, or earplugs, and the workers—of which there were clearly far too many—all looked dirty and poor. The only impression you could draw was that China was indeed a third world country, and that its manufacturing processes were rooted in the 1950s. You had to have some imagination, to put it mildly, to envision what these factories might become.

Given these surface impressions, it was easy to underestimate the management abilities of the Chinese and to overestimate what a foreigner could do. I was guilty of this myself. When I first saw these places, I thought, "My God, what we need here is some good old-fashioned U.S. management to get these places organized and cleaned up!"

The most important thing to me was our ability to create globally competitive operations, and I was pleased with the candidates I began to see. Korn Ferry had surfaced some very capable managers, people who were excited about the opportunity and who could help me upgrade the kinds of factories I'd seen in China. I was optimistic about bringing them onboard.

My backers, though, were upset that none of the candidates had China experience.

"What, no China?" they asked me.

I was trying to find the most capable managers in the automotive industry, but they thought we needed people who had worked in China. This was a battle that I chose not to fight, but should have. It was one of the biggest mistakes I made in putting the company together, and it cost us several years in our development and a lot of money. That's why I always advise companies, "If China is important, get your best people there. Whether they have China experience or speak the language is beside the point."

Requiring that our automotive operations expert have China experience might seem like a reasonable request, but in the context of China's automotive industry in 1994, it severely limited the universe of available managers to choose from. At the time, there were only three foreign-invested automotive joint ventures with any length of history in China: Beijing Jeep, Shanghai Volkswagen, and Guangzhou Peugeot. Foreign investment in the components sector was virtually nonexistent. Even today, with a greater universe of managers who have had experience in China, I believe that specific industry, product, or technical knowledge should be weighted more heavily than China experience. Often it isn't.

The management team that we ended up with was led by Don St. Pierre and included individuals who'd worked with him at Beijing Jeep. Don is a likable guy, and he clearly had experience in China. I had read the book *Beijing Jeep*, in which he came off as being resourceful and feisty—not a bad thing, I thought, for what I figured would be a pretty rough-and-tumble environment. But the team he put together was mediocre at best, and I soon found out that they were creating more problems than they were solving.

In addition to the operations team, we hired several young university graduates to act as translators and financial analysts. As the fund-raising became more certain, Tim Clissold brought on Michael Cronin, a fellow Brit whom he had met while working for Arthur Andersen in Australia. Michael's job was to conduct the due diligence on all of our investments and to oversee the documentation. He later would become ASIMCO's chief financial officer.

The Birth of ASIMCO

We closed on the fund on February 28, 1994, and what's now known as ASIMCO Technologies was officially born. Don St. Pierre had already joined the company, and we held a press conference at the newly opened Hilton Hotel in Beijing to announce the formation of the company and our plans for China. We rented five rooms in the Hilton (there was literally no office space in Beijing at the time) and began our search for joint venture candidates. After more than three years of hard work, we were finally in business.

After some initial false starts where our requirement for majority ownership proved to be a major stumbling block, we completed our first joint venture in August of that year. Once the Chinese managers heard that we had actually made our first investment, and obtained majority ownership at that, the drumbeat was sounded. Soon all of China knew. Before the Internet and the proliferation of cell phones and text messaging, it was amazing how quickly word got around the country. One by one, the people we'd been negotiating with came back to the table and agreed to our terms, including majority ownership.

As we got under way, important people began coming to the table. One was Wang Jianming, a legend in China's auto industry and the larger-than-life chairman of Yuchai. Of partial Korean descent, Chairman Wang, as everyone calls him, is a stocky guy with a round face, a thick neck, a deep voice, and a presence that is felt the minute he steps into a room. He never wears a tie, simply dress slacks and a dark sport shirt, usually a black collarless T-shirt with a pocket on the left. He carries it off, even though most would consider it inappropriate business dress. When sitting, he reminds me of the Giant Buddha statue in Leshan, Sichuan Province. Surprisingly, though, his five-foot, nine-inch height makes him appear considerably smaller when he stands up.

Chairman Wang is a deep thinker and true visionary, and a teacher at several universities. He often elaborates on grandiose business concepts in a high-level Mandarin that even my Chinese colleagues tell me is very unusual. I once asked him to speak to our general managers, which he graciously agreed to do since he's our largest customer. Like everyone else in the room, I was anxious to hear what he had to say. Henry Huang, who works with me on government affairs and relationships with our Chinese partners, usually translates for me. As Chairman Wang spoke, Henry did his best, but after a while he told me that the language Chairman Wang was using was so complicated that it made it nearly impossible for him to properly translate the meaning into English.

Chairman Wang is a legend because he personally built Yuchai from a small company located in the city of Yulin, in the remote Guanxi Autonomous Region in the southwest corner of China, into the country's largest diesel engine company. (In Chinese, *chai* refers to diesel, hence the name "Yuchai.") Unlike most diesel engine companies, Yuchai is not affiliated with a truck manufacturer, and it did not have a captive market with a parent company. Chairman Wang was somewhat of an outsider, without the strong central government support afforded the more traditional state-owned companies. He became the industry leader through the sheer force of his personality and will, and his story is nothing short of remarkable.

When they heard that Chairman Wang wanted to meet me, some of my more traditional Chinese managers told me that they doubted Yuchai would be successful. I suspect that, because Chairman Wang is outspoken and not afraid to speak his mind, many in China have secretly hoped that he would fail. He has proved them all wrong.

I described to Chairman Wang my investigation into China's auto industry, my vision for the future of the industry, and my plans to form a leading components company to take advantage of the void that existed in that sector.

Chairman Wang was visibly impressed. "You have a good understanding of China for a foreigner," he told me. He wasn't one to hand out praise lightly, so I took this as a great compliment.

My observation on the weakness of China's components sector resonated with Chairman Wang's own analysis. Recognizing that having a good supply base would be key to Yuchai's future success, Chairman Wang had initiated a program whereby Yuchai began taking equity positions in its important suppliers. With a common vision, we agreed to join forces and look at companies together.

One of the first investments Yuchai made was in a company that supplied it with diesel fuel injection systems. Chairman Wang offered us an opportunity to participate as the first part of our collaborative effort. (We would end up working together to identify a number of different components companies for ASIMCO to invest in.) In September of 1994, we purchased most of Yuchai's investment in a fuel pump manufacturer in the city of Hengyang, in Hunan Province, with Yuchai retaining a small ownership interest in the company. It was the second joint venture we completed in China, and this operation has since become the backbone of our current diesel fuel injection business and one of our most successful operations.

In addition to offering us an opportunity to become the majority shareholder in a well-positioned, successful company, the introduction by Yuchai was the start of a long-term strategic relationship between Yuchai and ASIMCO and solidified my personal relationship with Wang Jianming. Yuchai remains the largest diesel engine company in China and ASIMCO's largest customer. Because we supply a wide range of products, we are also Yuchai's single most important supplier.

Chairman Wang is a close business associate, but he's also become a good friend. We've faced many of the same issues. Early on, he had a vision of what he wanted to do, but he had to defy incredibly steep odds to convert Yuchai from a small maker of agricultural engines in the 1980s into China's largest diesel engine manufacturer. Along the way, he attracted foreign investment, took the company public on the New York Stock Exchange, and was put through the wringer by troubles with his foreign investors. His experiences are a mirror image of my own. Every time we meet, we attend to the business at hand and then spend some time just catching up, bringing each other up to date on other aspects of our business and personal lives. When we are having these discussions, he will invariably look at me at some point in the conversation and say (through the translator, of course), "Jack, it's a pity that we can't communicate directly." We have so much in common that I, too, would love to have a free-form discussion with him. Feeling as helpless as he does, I have no choice but to respond, "Chairman Wang, I agree. It's a real pity."

We completed seven joint ventures by the second quarter of 1996, and the guts of the company were formed. By the end of that year, we would go on to complete five more deals. With a fairly sizable operation now in place, our attention shifted from looking for new opportunities to managing what we had.

Confronting China's "Management Gap"

As each new operation came into the fold, it soon became apparent that managing companies in China was going to be an even more difficult challenge than we had imagined. The fast growth of China's automotive industry from 1992 to 1995 had masked some underlying problems in our businesses. As the market cooled in 1996 and 1997, they began to come out of the woodwork.

The problems weren't new; we just hadn't seen them. Terrible market conditions in 1997, the uncertainty caused by the Asian crisis, and other macroeconomic and industry factors brought them to the surface, like rocks in a river that only become visible when the water level drops. Some problems were specific to our particular operations, but most were symptoms of the fundamental problems of doing business in China. We had to learn to deal with them to become a viable company.

China in the early 1990s produced approximately six hundred thousand vehicles per year for its domestic market. Most were trucks. Between 1992 and 1995, the market almost tripled to 1.5 million vehicles, with an expansion in truck production and the introduction of new passenger car programs fueling industrywide growth. As the truck market grew, truck assemblers began switching from gasoline to diesel engines because of the performance characteristics of diesel engines. Between 1992 and 1995, automotive diesel engine production quadrupled to more than 460,000 units. This was very good for us, because most of the factories that were now a part of our company sold to the diesel engine and truck markets. (At that time, the number of passenger cars produced in China was less than the number of trucks. Those that were assembled in China used a high proportion of imported parts.)

We didn't know it at the time, but the slide in sales that we experienced in 1997 actually started in 1996. As 1996 began, sales were growing by about 20 percent—not bad, considering that China was still feeling the impact of the austerity program that Zhu Rongji had instituted in 1995. Responding to double-digit inflation, Mr. Zhu, then the premier and the economic czar of China, had instituted a tight credit policy designed to rein in inflation. This in turn triggered a period of deflation that continued through the rest of the 1990s, and even into the twenty-first century. Sales of new vehicles slowed dramatically, and the industry grew moderately from 1996 to 2001. China's accession to the World Trade Organiz-ation at the end of 2001 provided the spark that reignited the growth of China's automotive industry and created the conditions for China to emerge as the largest, fastest-growing automotive market in the world. But it came after seven long years of relatively flat production and sales.

At a micro level, most of the switch from gasoline to diesel engines had already been accomplished by 1997, so sales by the major diesel engine makers naturally began to slow. This had a direct impact on our business. By the end of 1996, year-on-year sales growth was virtually flat, and as we entered 1997 we actually began to contract as a company. (This was the period, as I still say, when I got all of my gray hair.)

Much of the sales growth we'd seen in late 1995 and early 1996 was illusory. Many of the general managers of our companies, those who came from state-owned, production-oriented backgrounds, had been producing products and shipping them to our customers before they actually had the orders in hand. This didn't just fill the pipeline and lead to an inventory overhang; it also con-tributed to the negative growth we later experienced, when customers starting returning products and many of these early sales ended up being reversed.

During this period, the distinction between "profits" and "cash" also became apparent. When a company in China shows profits, the question you always have to ask is "How are accounts receivable and inventories?" The good news is that state-owned managers in China can be profit oriented. The bad news is that they don't often attach the same importance to cash as a Western company might.

In a system where state-owned enterprises could always get more money from the large state-owned banks, and where every company and bank had effectively the same owner—the state—it didn't really matter where the cash was. In the bank, in the hands of a supplier, or with an end customer, it was all the same. If asked about a two-year-old account receivable, the manager of a state-owned enterprise would typically respond with confidence that the receivable will ultimately be collected. I know this, because I routinely got this response when I asked our first batch of Chinese managers this question. Although there is a greater appreciation for cash today, the legacy of the state-owned enterprises, where everybody eats out of the same rice bowl, is still apparent.

Tax policy in China doesn't permit companies to establish provisions against past due receivables or obsolete inventories. This encourages the overstatement of income statements and balance sheets. Under Chinese tax laws, you literally have to take your customer to court and lose before you can write off an overdue receivable. With respect to obsolete inventories, you have to physically destroy the product before you can take a charge against inventories. The state-owned mentality that still lingered from an earlier time in China, in combination with factors such as this, combined to overinflate asset values, and this became all too clear to us as we moved through 1997.

At the same time, it seemed like we were having management issues at just about all of our operations. Our fuel plant in Beijing is a good example. The general manager there kept buying more equipment, which led to overcapacity when the industry slowed and saddled the company with a high debt load that hampered it for years afterward. Obsessed with continuing high growth and "profits," he was also one of the biggest culprits in shipping products that hadn't even been ordered by the customer. As goods were returned, his sales slid by 24 percent in 1997.

At a joint venture that made gears for the motorcycle industry, the general manager had subcontracted machining to local factories in his area—many of which, we later discovered, were at least partially owned by employees and managers at our joint venture. As these factories developed, they began to compete with our joint venture to undercut our prices with customers. Result: sales down at that joint venture by 26 percent in 1997.

The general manager of another factory was determined to create a large aftermarket business. Without adequate credit controls in place, he shipped way too much product to aftermarket distributors, who were only too happy to take product that they didn't plan to pay for until sales were made to an end customer. When the goods didn't sell, we had a huge accounts receivable problem and stopped shipping. Result: sales up by 47 percent in 1996, down by 20 percent in 1997.

Even at our better companies, industry conditions and the general state of the Chinese economy made for some tough going. At our fuel pump business in Hengyang, sales growth was only 5 percent, and at our molded rubber business, which had always been a solid performer, sales were down 1 percent after having been up by 49 percent in 1996. Our piston ring business was the only one to show good growth, growing by 12 percent in 1997 following an increase of 22 percent in 1996.

On top of the operating problems, we were also the victims of fraud. The most blatant incident occurred at CAC, our brake pad company in Zhuhai, which is just a short ferry ride from Macau, one of the world's largest gambling centers.

CAC exported brake parts to the United States, so Liang Jinwei, the general manager, attended the after-market show in Las Vegas, Nevada, in November of 1996. When he didn't return to China on schedule, we all became a bit concerned. He had last been seen leaving the show and boarding a plane to New York City, so my first thought was that he'd ended up on the wrong side of the street in New York.

A subsequent inventory of the contents of his office safe, however, revealed that he had actually become involved with gambling interests in Macau and criminal elements in Hong Kong and China. The joint venture bank accounts were still intact, but we discovered four fraudulently issued letters of credit that would saddle the joint venture with obligations of almost $8 million once they were cashed. This set off one of the darker periods in the history of ASIMCO in China and also provided us with our first exposure to the Chinese courts. (See "gray hair" above.) As it turned out, the general manager had colluded with several members of the bank to commit the fraud.

Reasons for China's Management Gap

And so 1997 became the real turning point for us. It was the one time in all my years in China where I thought that maybe the whole thing had been a big mistake. In truth, the economic and industry conditions that we faced in China that year would have been difficult for any company, and in any economy—not just China's. There are always obstacles. The companies I'd financed at PaineWebber had to deal with the high inflation of the 1970s, raw materials shortages, and the first energy crisis. Equally difficult circumstances, I'd say.

The key difference was that managements in the United States quickly formulated corrective action plans to deal with the issues. This wasn't happening in China. Most of the general managers had no idea what to do. Worse than that, they seemed remarkably passive about the need even to confront the realities of the economic environment at that time. This fundamental difference leads us to two of the largest questions of this book: Why was the reaction to adverse economic and industry circumstances so different in China? And why is management in China such a difficult issue?

You can start by looking at history. In the aftermath of World War II, when the United States, Western Europe, and Japan used free markets and capitalism to rebuild their economies, China turned inward. State ownership and central planning, not market forces and entre-preneurialism, were the key elements in its model for economic development. Managers in the West had to face the markets and learn how to manage more effectively in order to compete for the customers and capital necessary for survival.

In China, managers were given the capital and the labor by the state and then simply told what products to make. Once they were manufactured, the products were then turned over to state-run companies for distribution. Under this kind of system, nobody ever had to face an actual marketplace, and so nobody ever changed. China's state-owned enterprises became stagnant, and the country's management pool came to consist almost entirely of managers who could only be described as "highly bureaucratic."

Meanwhile, in order to succeed in an increasingly competitive world, companies in the West (led by the United States) began to regard management as a science, and they invested heavily in management development programs to improve and broaden management expertise. Individuals interested in improving their career prospects also invested time and money in their own development, and getting an MBA became a must for advancement in many companies. The objective of management development and MBA programs is to take raw management talent and give it enough structure to run a large organization, without destroying the entrepreneurial spirit that moves a company forward. The West developed a growing pool of managers who combined the best of these features. Training future leaders for business was as important to some as training generals for the army, and the Harvard Business School came to be known as the "West Point of capitalism."

The capital markets in turn heralded good management. Companies like General Electric, which developed reputations for the depth and quality of their managements, were rewarded with high stock market valuations. When companies in the United States lost their way in the late 1970s, investors shunned their equities, making them vulnerable to hostile takeovers. Japanese companies, with innovative management systems developed by industry leaders like Toyota, entered the U.S. markets and lured away customers. Combined with the free market for capital, the free market for customers ultimately forced management reform throughout industry in the United States. This stands in pretty stark contrast to China's closed economy during that time.

In 1978, Deng Xiaoping began his economic reform program and effectively took the economic handcuffs off the Chinese people. As everybody knows, the Chinese are among the most entrepreneurial people in the world, and once liberated the entrepreneurial spirit in China flourished. But with no legal system or independent markets to serve as a check on this spirit, unbridled capitalism created a different set of problems. Where once you had only the highly bureaucratic managers in China, you now had a second category, one that can only be described as "highly entrepreneurial."

Historically, China hasn't recognized management as a science. It wasn't taught in the schools, so Chinese managers had no real opportunity to learn basic management concepts and tools. With the 1990s came a wave of foreign direct investment, just as government was decreasing its involvement in nonstrategic industry sectors and the country as a whole was shifting toward a market-driven approach. All of this created a growing demand for professional managers—precisely those who were in short supply. Even with the establishment of MBA programs, beginning in 1991 at Tsinghua University, and the introduction of management development programs by multinational corporations during the 1990s, the rapid growth of China's economy has created a demand for management talent that the country simply can't meet. What's more, it's a situation that's likely to persist for some time to come.

Practically speaking, what this means is that when companies from developed economies arrive in China, they immediately confront a "management gap." Unlike home, where there's a large universe of local professional managers to choose from, in China you're more often than not faced with a choice between the highly bureaucratic or the highly entrepreneurial. Neither type will take your business where you want it to go.

With the overly bureaucratic, nothing gets done. The inevitable reply to every suggestion for improvement is "This is China, and China is different." On the other hand, the overly entrepreneurial don't follow any rule books. You simply can't sleep at night, since you never know what these cowboy entrepreneurs will do.

At ASIMCO, our state-owned, highly bureaucratic managers kept producing goods the market didn't want. Our highly entrepreneurial managers, on the other hand, concocted deals with criminal elements or tried to set themselves up in competition with us. Our biggest challenge in 1997 is still the biggest challenge for any company operating in China today: filling that management gap.

McKinsey & Company, the famous consulting firm, did a study estimating that China has a shortage of more than seventy-five thousand "globally competent" managers. This is a staggering number. All projections are for China to continue to grow, and for more multinationals to come to China. The need for local managers is only going to increase.

Because the state-owned and private enterprises that make up the purely local companies in China are all run by Mainland Chinese, they have an inherent advantage in understanding the local market and how to do business here. Improving management is certainly becoming more important at these companies, but the issue hasn't been as acute as it has been with foreign-invested enterprises. Foreign companies have to please investors, senior managements, and customers, and they are expected to operate at the same level in China as they do in other parts of the world. China's entry into the WTO has led to increased competition from overseas companies, but many of the purely local companies in China haven't yet been compelled by market and capital forces to change in any dramatic way how they're managed.

Large enough segments exist in each industry in China where low price, rather than quality and level of technology, is paramount. Local companies can safely operate in this space, virtually immune from foreign competition. (This unique aspect of China is discussed more fully in the chapter on China's two markets.) State-owned enterprises and favored private companies can get whatever capital they need from state-owned banks, and many now have permission from the central government to list overseas to raise additional equity capital. With the state remaining as a controlling shareholder in most cases, pressure exerted by the capital markets doesn't have the same impact on performance and transparency as it does with a company whose shares are widely distributed.

But, in time, this will all change. As Chinese markets become more uniformly developed, as achieving global standards of quality and services becomes critical in all segments of the economy, and as local companies begin to execute global strategies (more on this later), they too are going to have to face the issue of management reform.

China's management gap is going to be the biggest problem with doing business in China for many, many years to come—for both foreign-invested and local companies alike.

As 1997 came to a close, we were learning some harsh lessons about the realities on the ground of running a competitive business in China. "Necessity is the mother of invention," and this was a period in which we had to do some inventing. The silver lining was that out of all of this difficulty would come a new management approach, our "New China" strategy, which would revitalize our company and prove to be a workable, reliable model for building our business here.

Chapter 7

Closing China's Management Gap

Confronted with China's management gap, the initial reaction of most overseas companies is to tap into the vast pool of home-based professional managers and send them to China. Managers with known track records and reputations are the easiest and most comfortable means by which to bring order to doing business in China. If a Mandarin-speaking manager fitting this description can be found, so much the better, but even this has not been a hard-and-fast requirement. Serious about building their businesses in China, multinationals now send their most trusted managers to figure out how to do business here.

This approach makes sense, if done selectively. It ensures that a company's well-established business systems, management philosophy, and know-how are transferred and adapted to the China market. But too heavy a reliance on expatriate managers also raises certain other questions. How do you know if a manager coming from a Western background and a completely different culture can be truly effective in China? What yardstick do you use? Expatriate managers are also a lot more expensive. Once you introduce them into your China operations, the cost structure changes significantly. In the extremely cost-competitive Chinese market, this can quickly undermine a company's competitiveness. Finally, is this the best long-term solution for China, given the rapidly growing size of the market and its unique requirements?

Because we didn't operate anywhere other than China, ASIMCO didn't have the luxury of tapping in to a proven management team from someplace else. Ultimately, this would prove to be a blessing in disguise, because it forced us to rely on the management resources available here. As it turns out, identifying, developing, and retaining a local management team would be the key to our development. But we didn't get there in a straight line, and we had to try and then discard two other approaches before we found the one that worked.

Plan A: Expatriates

ASIMCO's Plan A for dealing with China's management gap was to use foreign expatriates, which led to the hiring of Don St. Pierre and his team. Because we were a new company, we had to build from the ground up and look outside to find managers. Hiring off the street, so to speak, is risky in any economy, let alone in a difficult, emerging economy like China's. First, no matter how well a résumé reads or how impressive a person might be during the interview process, you never really know how effective somebody will be in your organization until he or she is actually onboard. Second, people can do well in one organization and fail miserably in another. And third, you never know the extent to which a person will be accepted by his or her peer group of managers. In a situation where everybody is doing something they've never done before and everybody is learning, having the support and help of other managers is crucial. Although I knew all of this from my hiring activities at PaineWebber, I would relearn this lesson again in China, the hard way.

Despite its years of operation in China, Beijing Jeep hadn't prepared Don and his team for the complexities and sensitivities of managing a broad range of operations across the entire country. Also, because they'd been out of the United States for so long, Don's people weren't in the mainstream of the global automotive industry and weren't familiar with the latest trends in manufacturing. Even for a very capable and accomplished manager, China's a challenge. For someone less qualified, it's nearly impossible to be effective in dealing with local managers.

The Chinese are hard markers. They all seem to be from Missouri and have a very strong "show me" attitude. I initially thought that the Chinese managers would automatically respect somebody who'd operated in a developed country, that they'd give somebody credit for credentials and past accomplishments. Not so. Managing in China is hard, and the Chinese general managers know it. There's a feeling on the part of Chinese managers that success in another country is one thing, but it certainly doesn't guarantee success in China.

One of our more cynical general managers once went so far as to tell me, matter-of-factly, that many Chinese had gone to the United States and developed successful businesses.

"How many Americans have come to China and been successful here?" he asked.

It's not an unfair question, and the lesson is simple. If you're going to pay considerably more for overseas experts, then they had better be at the top of their game. Don and his team were not in that category. Beijing Jeep is not considered a success in China, so running it or working there was not a particularly strong credential. Before coming to China, Don had worked as a midlevel purchasing executive with American Motors, a second-tier company in the auto industry that was eventually acquired by Chrysler. It was not General Motors, Ford, or General Electric, which are the American names that Chinese respect.

Most of the people Don hired were journeymen who had worked in different jobs in a variety of countries, including but not limited to China. There was no particularly strong set of skills or expertise that they had and could impart to the Chinese managers. They might know the words *just in time* or *lean manufacturing*, but they had no idea how to implement the programs, which was all our Chinese managers wanted.

One of Don's hires was assigned to review capital

expenditure plans at our Beijing fuel plant, despite the fact that he had no knowledge of the sophisticated equipment used in the diesel fuel injection business. As a result, he signed off on whatever new equipment the manager of the plant wanted to order. One day, I saw him reviewing reams of purchase orders. After looking at a few items, he concluded that the general manager "knew what he was doing" and moved on to other business. I doubt he ever read past the first few pages.

Most important, though, our operations team didn't have the "roll-up-your-sleeves" approach that is the only one that works in China. Chinese managers don't respect consultants or armchair quarterbacks telling them how to do things. What they want are people who have specific expertise and can work with them on the floor to fix a problem or improve a process.

Liu Hao, ASIMCO's first director of lean manufacturing, is a good example of this. He's about as strong conceptually in lean manufacturing as anybody inside or outside of China, and he could lecture on the topic for days. But he gained the respect of the general managers largely because he isn't afraid to roll up his sleeves and work alongside them. In one instance, one of our operating units had to prepare for an important audit by a large global assembler. At 10:00 P.M. the night before the audit, the assembler faxed over the list of items to be covered the next day, and our general manager was nervous that the factory wasn't quite ready. At midnight, he called in all of his deputy managers and put them back to work. Liu

Hao came, too, and he and the management team worked through the night until 5:00 A.M., when they knew they were ready. That experience created more mutual respect and increased Mr. Liu's effectiveness more than any number of weeks in the classroom.

Admittedly, we didn't do a good job putting together an effective operating team, but even if we had I believe I would have ultimately come to the same conclusion: if your business is in China and your opportunities and problems are in China, you'd better build your management team around a well-qualified staff of Mainland Chinese managers for long-term success. Over the years, I've come to appreciate what a general manager in China has to deal with on a daily basis. Few foreigners are equipped to do what they have to do to keep a plant running. Not being brought up in this country, how can they be?

Chinese managers aren't perfect, but because they have grown up here they instinctively know how to deal with the many issues that occur daily. They know how to work with Chinese customers to get their receivables paid before other suppliers, and how to sell the trucks they may get in barter trade. They know how to deal with a large Chinese workforce, and how to handle local government officials—politely and respectfully, but never allowing them to take advantage of the business. They also know how to get a piece of equipment out of customs that may be hopelessly tied up in red tape.

They might not have all the tools that Westerners do,

but the good ones are smart, hardworking, and anxious to improve. I've also found that they're generally very interested in learning from somebody whom they respect. My biggest mistakes in the early days occurred when I discounted the views of my Chinese managers. It's all too easy and familiar to go with the advice given by a Westerner instead.

After a while, I began to hear some serious grumbling from our Chinese general managers. They resented paying management fees to cover the high costs of expatriates who couldn't help them. On top of the expatriates' obviously higher salaries, the Chinese managers also disapproved of all the other costs associated with having these Westerners in China. One of Don's managers booked a room in a five-star hotel in Shanghai, and then insisted that the general manager make the seven- or eight-hour trip at the expatriate's convenience to discuss sales and marketing activities. Examples like this abounded and began to fray relationships with even our most cooperative managers.

As I listened to the complaints of the Chinese managers, I realized that they were legitimate, and I couldn't help but agree with them. After all, ASIMCO was also paying for the high costs associated with the team, and we were getting little in return. I eventually concluded in 1996 that they were causing me more problems than they were solving, and I sent the entire group of expatriate managers home. (After he left ASIMCO, Don went on to establish a company that has grown to be one of the largest importers of wine in China. No one doubts his business acumen and knowledge of China, but it just didn't work for ASIMCO.) While we would later learn how to use experienced Westerners more effectively to provide our Chinese managers with a global perspective, our Plan A was a complete failure as far as I was concerned.

Plan B: Trying to Convert "Old China" Managers

Plan B was to try to convert the "highly bureaucratic" and "highly entrepreneurial" managers whom we'd inherited with the joint ventures into professional managers who could run a business in a global economy. We had some limited success with this approach, but we found that most of these managers were simply too set in their ways to change. Creating transparency and insisting on global performance standards, which were both vitally important, ran counter to the prevailing vested interests in the operating units. Despite their obvious advantages in knowing how to operate in China, most of our "Old China" managers weren't about to change their ways and help me build a globally competitive company. It required too much change, and too much work. In 1997, as the company contracted and I began to wonder what I was doing in China, I concluded that Plan B wasn't going to work any better than Plan A. It was back to the drawing board.

Plan C: Taking a Page from Coach Noll's Playbook

As the head of the company, I found myself in a position that I liked to think of as similar to the position that Chuck Noll found himself in during the 1970s. Noll, who was the legendary head coach of the Pittsburgh Steelers and led them to four Super Bowl victories, didn't exactly inherit a winner when he took over the team in 1969. Like the Steelers, ASIMCO was losing on the playing field. Financial results were unacceptable, and fundamental disciplines like receivables collection and inventory management were lacking, to say the least.

Because we had majority ownership positions, like Chuck Noll I could put anybody on the field that I wanted to. But, also like Chuck Noll, when I turned around to look at my bench, there simply wasn't anybody there. Faced with this situation, Coach Noll had carefully defined the kind of athlete that he believed would lead to success on the football field, and then he used the draft to bring in players who fit that description. After several years of recruiting the likes of Mean Joe Greene, Franco Harris, Jack Lambert, and Terry Bradshaw, the Steelers were off to the Super Bowl. Unlike Buddy Parker before him, Noll built from the ground up and created a winner. Like Noll, the first thing I needed to do was define the type of manager we wanted to build our company around.

The answer came more or less by accident in late 1997. Getting the management right at our gear factory in Sichuan had become a serious issue. We had to remove the original general manager because of the incestuous relationships he had allowed to develop between certain of the company's employees and suppliers. The managers we had sent to replace him were unable to solve the problem, and the company's financials continued to deteriorate. At a loss as to whom we should appoint permanently, we decided to give the opportunity to Ding Zhiyuan.

Ding had come to us several years earlier from GE China and was assigned as ASIMCO's financial representative to our piston ring business in Yizheng. Due largely to the strong leadership of Cheng Dexing, the general manager there, Yizheng has been one of our best performing operating units year in and year out. I've always had a great deal of respect for Cheng's judgment, so I asked him what he thought.

"It's a good idea," he said to me, after a bit of deliberation. "Ding has what it takes to make a good general manager."

As an incentive to do a good job, Cheng told Ding that he would visit him when the operation in Sichuan was straightened out. Cheng had a surpassingly good reputation and was in high standing with our entire company. This was pretty strong encouragement for a young Chinese up-and-comer being given his first crack at general manager.

Ding went to work immediately. Instead of giving excuses about why changes couldn't be made, he quickly took a series of actions: he replaced underperforming managers; he renegotiated supply agreements to reduce costs by at least 10 percent and to improve payment and delivery terms; he reduced our head count; he reinvigorated our quality standards; he developed customer relationships; he began developing new products; and he began to develop standard costing to control manufacturing costs. In a short time, he completely transformed the company. Unlike the managers before him, Ding understood the importance of cash, and that's where he focused his efforts in 1998—reducing inventories and collecting accounts receivable.

All of a sudden, my headache started to clear. Ding was doing all of the right things, and it was working. By accident, we'd found the formula for what we would come to call our "New China" strategy. We were used to listening for hours on end as various general managers told us they couldn't reduce inventories and collect receivables because "This is China, and China is different." Now we had someone who simply went out there and started doing it.

Using Ding as an example, we embarked on Plan C: finding and empowering New China managers. As we thought about Ding's characteristics, we began to define what a New China manager looked like. First and foremost, a New China manager is a Mainland Chinese who is open-minded, and who recognizes the importance of being open to new ideas and concepts if the company—and China more generally—is ever going to reach its full potential. Many managers in China have engineering backgrounds, and this is certainly a plus in a manufacturing-oriented company. But on top of this, New China managers have had real experience managing in China and at least some exposure to modern management concepts and tools. They may not have an MBA, but through management training or development programs they've come to understand that management is indeed a science, and that the management tools and methods that have proven to be successful in other parts of the world may have an application in China.

Ding had been with GE China before joining ASIMCO. So, prior experience in another multinational corporation was vitally important for us when it came to hiring general managers. We had to jump-start our program, and we didn't have the time to develop these managers completely on our own. (Later on, we would begin ASIMCO Leadership and ASIMCO Management Programs to develop our own homegrown managers.) Because they are Chinese and have experience here, New China managers know how to operate in China, but they also know what companies in China need to do to compete in the global marketplace.

The "New China" Management Strategy

These traits—open-mindedness, experience in China, management education, and prior experience with a multinational—formed the profile for the candidates we began searching for in 1997.

Now, with a clear idea of what we wanted, we recruited about fifty New China managers into ASIMCO between 1997 and 1999. As they came onto our "bench," we began to use the leverage of our majority ownership positions to take true operating control of our joint ventures, removing the incumbent managements and replacing them with New China managers.

These weren't simple management changes. They were full frontal attacks on the strong vested interests, economic and otherwise, of the managers in power. In the three chapters that follow, I'll describe three different management changes that we undertook at three different companies, and more than any abstract description they'll show you what I mean.

Suffice it to say that changing managements at virtually all of our operating units was an extremely difficult program to implement. More than four years later, the question that had first been asked by astute investors when I was raising capital—"Does having majority ownership mean that you have hire and fire rights?"—was going to get answered. Could we really make these changes? Could we install somebody of our own choosing to run the company? We were about to find out.

In my twelve years in China, I've learned that there are only two rules:

RULE #1:   EVERYTHING IS POSSIBLE.
RULE #2:   NOTHING IS EASY.

Is it possible to build a completely local management team that can run a business or a factory in China according to the rules of the global marketplace? Absolutely. Is it easy? Absolutely not. Three hurdles typically stand in the way.

Hurdle #1: Finding New China Managers

One of the first questions people ask me is "How do you even find a 'New China' manager?"

In this sense, I was envious of Coach Noll. He had an easier time assembling his Pittsburgh Steelers team through the National Football League's well-organized draft. Each NFL team has a chance to select from among the best of the college seniors. Coaches can watch game films of potential choices and evaluate the physical abilities of each player in organized camps. Before a player is even considered for the draft, he's played organized football for at least eight years and has been coached by excellent coaching staffs at thousands of high school and college campuses across the country.

There's no such system to leverage in China. The first business school wasn't founded here until the early 1990s, and the multinationals, with their management development programs, didn't begin arriving in large numbers until about the same time. The resulting shortage in management talent made our job particularly difficult in the late 1990s, but I'm afraid that assembling a first-rate local management team hasn't gotten any easier since then. In spite of the proliferation of MBA and management development programs in China, there's still a long way to go.

We used every resource we could think of to find New China managers—executive search firms, Internet searches for candidates, advertising job opportunities in magazines and newspapers, accepting recommendations from our employees. In the end, we found word of mouth to be the most reliable source. If a valued employee thinks enough of a classmate or a friend to recommend him or her, the odds are good that the new hire will be successful and fit well within the organization. People don't recommend friends for jobs, no matter how close the relationship might be, if the qualifications are truly lacking. As our employees became more engaged with ASIMCO, they realized that a bad hire didn't just weaken the organization. It also reflected poorly on them.

Ultimately, we left no stone unturned to find people who fit our New China profile, and it was well worth the effort. The dramatic and sudden improvement in a given company's financial performance demonstrated almost immediately that we were on the right track. Within a month of installing a New China manager, inventories were reduced and receivables were collected. Plans for improvement that had previously fallen on deaf ears (or met with active and passive resistance) began to be implemented. Because these New China managers bought our vision for the future and saw the opportunity in it for them, they were ready to be proactive and to make the necessary improvements. Because they were Mainland Chinese, they also knew how to implement change within the context of a Chinese factory and the Chinese environment. Each new manager developed his own approach to implementing change, and we began to learn as an organization which techniques worked and which didn't. The managers we hired into ASIMCO during this period form the core group of managers in the company today.

Hurdle #2: Breaking Vested Interests

The second obstacle to overcome in implementing our New China strategy was the prevalence of vested interests in the joint ventures, people who sought only to perpetuate themselves and resisted any and all threats to the status quo.

The "work unit" played a unique role in post-1949 China. A person's job in a factory—or in some other type of work unit, such as a hospital or a university—was the way he or she was defined. The work unit was the person's entire universe. In addition to providing jobs to both husband and wife, the work unit provided housing, schooling, and medical and retirement benefits. In essence, the entire welfare system in China had devolved to the work unit.

Factory leaders reigned supreme. Favored employees got the best jobs and the best housing, and the reverse was true for people who were out of favor. The leaders were naturally able to save the best of everything for themselves, and they could take advantage of the system and of their power to create benefits well beyond what was available to an ordinary worker. Just as you'd find in any country, some of these factory leaders were fair-minded, balanced, and not inclined to abuse the system. And, just as you'd find anyplace, there were those who took maximum advantage.

Because cash flowed through the factory, the leaders found that they could use some of this cash to coddle favor with the local government officials and ensure their position—providing vehicles, buying meals, or paying for overseas trips. Employees were beholden to the leaders of their work unit for nearly every aspect of their lives. The factory leaders themselves had strong vested interests to protect, and the cultivation of local government officials was one means by which they protected them.

Before Motorola became one of the first companies to establish a significant "wholly owned foreign enterprise," or WOFE, in the mid-1990s, the only way a foreign company or investor could establish a presence in China was through a joint venture with an existing Chinese company. In the beginning, it was difficult to obtain a majority ownership interest, so many joint ventures were done as 50-50 splits, or as joint ventures where the foreign partner had a minority interest.

Today most foreign companies strongly prefer to establish WOFEs or have majority control, but this isn't possible in all industries. For example, foreign companies cannot set up WOFEs to assemble passenger cars in China. In fact, it's not even possible for a foreign company to have a majority ownership interest in an assembly plant in China. Central government policy prohibits foreign investors or companies from having more than a 50 percent ownership position in a car or truck assembly plant. Depending upon the industry, similar restrictions may apply.

Historically, there has been a strong conventional wisdom that a foreign investor or company needs to have a partner in China. I was told over and over again, on my initial trips here, that the secret to doing business in China is to "find a good partner." If you go to a conference on China, this is one piece of advice that you will still routinely hear.

That may have been true, but my best advice is to take the time to build a good local management team and become your own Chinese partner if at all possible. We've had good and bad partners in China. I agree that a good partner can be extremely helpful, but the reality is that there's no amount of work you can do ahead of time to determine whether your partner will be good or not. It comes down to individuals, and individual behavior is difficult to predict.

When you do a joint venture in China, even one that's majority owned, you step into a web of vested interests, and the joint venture itself creates a new set of conflicts of interest. Whether these end up being handled appropriately or not is almost entirely a function of the good intentions and actions of one or two key people.

If the factory leaders, or the head of the Chinese partner, set a good example in dealing with conflicts, the rest of the organization will follow. If they don't, there will be nothing but problems. Unless you're a much better psychologist than I am, I don't see how you can predict ahead of time how somebody from a completely different culture, in a country with a different set of values and notions of legality, will handle these conflicts.

Take purchasing. In any company, that's an area where those in power can abuse the system to gain personal advantage. If a completely transparent system isn't in place, purchasing managers can accept a higher price on behalf of the company for raw materials or purchased parts in exchange for personal kickbacks from the suppliers. When we took control of the joint ventures and installed purchasing managers of our own choosing— and instituted transparent bidding procedures—we began to challenge these vested interests.

At one factory, the new purchasing manager we had appointed found that, every morning, the keyhole in the lock to his office had been filled with a sticky substance; he had to disassemble the lock to get inside, every day. Worse, he constantly had to deal with people throwing rocks through his window from the street below as he worked at his desk late into the night.

It would be difficult, if not outright impossible, to determine beforehand whether the kind of abuses in purchasing that obviously precipitated this angry reaction were taking place at any given company. And it certainly would be nearly impossible to predict whether efforts to make the process transparent would be resisted in this way by those in power. If we'd had any inkling that this was going to happen, naturally we would never have entered into that particular joint venture in the first place.

The structure of the joint venture itself can also create its own set of conflicts of interest. Let's say that a Chinese company producing a certain kind of automotive component wants to do a joint venture with a foreign company to gain access to advanced technology. Depending on the circumstances, the shares of the Chinese partner might be owned by the local government, a group of individuals including managers and employees of the company, other companies (including Chinese investment companies), or some combination of all of these. Whatever the ownership structure, the factory's assets may include any number of different things—land, buildings, equipment, inventories, accounts receivable, dormitories, schools, hospitals, medical clinics, and myriad other assets. On top of all that, the Chinese partner might also be producing a variety of different products, and the foreign partner might want to include only a few of them in the joint venture itself.

Against this backdrop, the foreign partner begins to negotiate with the Chinese company to form a joint venture that will leverage the Chinese company's position in the marketplace and bring a higher-quality and higher-technology product to its customers. In general, the Chinese company will want to contribute assets to the joint venture, while the foreign partner contributes some combination of cash, equipment, and technology. Nonessential assets like dormitories or schools are often excluded from the joint venture, and the foreign partner often doesn't want to include all of the company's products or production assets. If the foreign partner doesn't include everything in the joint venture, the Chinese partner will continue to do business, making and selling the non-joint-venture products while still participating fully in the joint venture itself.

In this way, the joint venture process carries the seeds of its own destruction. Given that most, if not all, of the employees and managers of the joint venture were former employees of the Chinese partner, where do their loyalties really lie? With the Chinese partner, which might still employ an employee's spouse and provide housing and schooling to the family, or with the new "foreign bosses"? The answer is pretty clear.

And what's to prevent the Chinese partner from using some of the raw materials purchased by the joint venture for non-joint-venture business? Or technology from leaking from the joint venture to the Chinese partner— leading in turn to the Chinese partner becoming the joint venture's biggest competitor? If both companies sell to a certain customer in China, and the customer runs into financial difficulty and can't pay, what's to prevent the Chinese company from advising the customer to pay the Chinese partner's receivable and to forget about the amount owed to "the foreigners"?

The short answer to all of these questions is "Nothing." We've faced all of these problems and more in China, and there's not much more that can be said. You have to rely on the good intentions of everyone involved, a degree of fair-mindedness from the Chinese partner, a good, loyal local management that can discover inappropriate behavior and deal with it in a timely manner, and a reasonable set of controls. Building a trusting relationship with the Chinese partner and developing a capable, loyal local management team are the keys to success. But this cannot be accomplished overnight, and it takes a great deal of work.

Hurdle #3: Overcoming Unfavorable Contract Provisions

In retrospect, we could have done a better job at negotiating some of the earlier joint venture contracts.

In the early days, when a foreign company came to China, it had no prior experience dealing with the Chinese government, no manufacturing or marketing infrastructure, and no employees in China (or even, really, any idea how to hire them). It was quite natural to leave all of this, including the management of the joint venture, to the Chinese partner—hence the advice regarding the importance of finding the right one—and for the foreign partner to bring technology, advanced management practices, cash, and export channels to the joint venture.

For this reason, the standard contracts contained an innocuous-sounding provision that held that, regardless of the ownership structure, the Chinese partner would be responsible for "nominating" the general manager, while a majority of the board of directors would be required to approve the appointment of the general manager. If the foreign partner has a majority ownership position, it also has a majority of the board of directors—and, therefore, the sole ability to appoint the general manager. This also means that the majority shareholder has the ability, by a simple majority vote of the board of directors, to remove a general manager.

The rub, though, is that the Chinese partner has the sole ability to nominate the general manager. So, if you're the foreign partner, how do you get your candidate nominated for general manager and put to a vote by the board? The answer is that you can't, unless the Chinese partner agrees with you.

In the case of our brake venture in Langfang, which I'll describe in more detail in the examples of implementing management change that follow this chapter, we had to deal with this issue head-on and managed to find a solution. In other instances, we've had to be more creative. We've found, for example, that we could use a vote of the board to remove an incumbent general manager and to appoint an "acting general manager." This isn't a perfect solution, because the title conveys that the arrangement is temporary, and it doesn't remove some of the uncertainty from the minds of the employees. That said, this move allowed us to avoid stalemates and to move forward in cases where we've used it. It's also given us a certain amount of leverage in dealing with our Chinese partners.

DESPITE THESE THREE hurdles in implementing management changes in China, we've managed to figure out how to work the system and get what we want. Each case where we implemented change was different, and each management change presented a new set of challenges. In Anhui, we dealt with a strong set of vested interests and had to find the right general manager to replace a very powerful entrepreneur. In Langfang, we had to work around a less-than-ideal contract. And in Hengyang, we didn't have to deal with any of these issues. The outgoing general manager himself devised a novel— and, in China, I'd venture to say unprecedented—way to identify his successor.

Chapter 8

Guerrilla Warfare in Anhui

In Anhui Province in late 1998, we faced our most difficult challenge as a company. Fang Yuan, the general manager of our first joint venture, was one of China's successful entrepreneurs, and our joint venture making molded rubber products was profitable from day one. But Fang wouldn't follow the rules, and he decided to set up a competing company despite the fact that he had signed a noncompete agreement only months before. Allowing this to go on would have undermined our entire effort in China, so I only had one option—to remove him.

But that was easier said than done. Fang had built the company himself, high in the mountains of Anhui Province, and it had become the largest employer in his area, which meant that he was well entrenched in the local community and with the local government. On top of that, he was also a crafty street fighter. Removing him as general manager of our joint venture, while not destroying that joint venture in the process, was going to be nearly impossible. Fortunately—or unfortunately, depending on how you look at it—we had already had some experience in similar situations, so we knew what could go wrong and what we had to prepare for. This chapter describes how we successfully made the management transition at our Anhui plant and got the business under our control, proving once again that in China, "Everything is possible, but nothing is easy."

IT WAS 9:30 in the morning, and I was standing in the middle of our molded rubber facility in Anhui Province. Normally a beehive of activity, the factory on this day was eerily silent, dark and empty. Not knowing what else to do, I called in to the Beijing office and spoke with Carleen.

"Well," I said, "the good news is that we successfully replaced Fang as general manager. The bad news is that we have no employees and no electricity!"

So began one of the best-planned, best-executed, and most difficult management changes in our history. We had done everything we could to prepare ourselves, but from my vantage point on the darkened factory floor that morning our path to keeping the business in Anhui afloat was anything but clear. I had just replaced the incumbent manager and founder of a company that we owned 80 percent of, and now faced the prospect of figuring out how to manage a factory in one of the most remote areas in China. Fang had always said that he doubted whether we could ever run his factory in this inner province. That morning I was beginning to think he might be right. (In the interest of both parties, I thought it best not to use Mr. Fang's real name. This is the only exception I've made to using real names in the book.)

Of all my experiences in China, the episode in Anhui was the most tragic, only because of what might have been. Most of our joint ventures have been with state-owned enterprises, but our first, the joint venture with Mr. Fang and his company, was with one of China's early entrepreneurs. If both partners had found a way to cooperate long term, the combination of Fang's entre-preneurial instincts and knowledge of China with our access to capital, technology, global markets, and modern management practices would have created a very dynamic company. Instead, it ended in an ugly divorce.

Fang's factory was near the top of the list of potential partners that Dong Jianping of CNAIC had compiled for us, and at that time Fang and the factory that he ran were well entrenched in the city of Ningguo. Originally from the city of Wuxi in neighboring Jiangsu Province, Fang had come to Ningguo in the 1970s during the Cultural Revolution. As a part of Mao's program of "reform through labor," middle-school graduates like Fang were relocated from the cities to the countryside to work on the farms. Unable to return to Wuxi when the Cultural Revolution ended, Fang took advantage of Deng Xiaoping's new economic policies to establish a collective enterprise to make rubber parts. (In the transition to a market economy, thousands of collectives were formed throughout China after Deng started his reform program. Collectives were typically local enterprises with a diverse group of owners, which might include the local government, managers, workers, or other entities.) With the equivalent of about $100, Fang proceeded to build a respectable, profitable company; when Fang told this story to one of our investors in New York, the investor opened his wallet, threw $100 on the table, and suggested that they start a business together.

I was excited to meet Fang, because we had finally reached the end of our yearlong investigation phase and were now ready to begin building the business. He stood out, among all the people we'd met, as a real entrepreneur.

In December of 1993, Tim, Ai Jian, Dong, and I flew from Beijing to Hangzhou, in prosperous Zhejiang Province. From there, we drove a hard five hours along winding mountain roads to Ningguo. It was a long time to sit in a car, and it didn't help that a large part of the journey took us over dirt roads filled with potholes. Even in the bleak chill of Chinese winter, though, the scenery was spectacular. We swept past miles and miles of tea fields, bamboo forests, and mountains upon mountains that had been terraced over the years by many generations of Chinese farmers, trying to coax a bit more planting space from the unforgiving terrain. Sichuan and Anhui have become my favorite provinces, due to the sheer physical beauty of the mountain scenery.

When we arrived in Ningguo, we headed straight for Fang's factory, a clean and tidy facility right off the road and across the street from the village of Zhongxi's admin-istration building. Fang was waiting for us when we arrived, and since nobody in Ningguo—including Fang—spoke any English, Ai Jian translated for each side as we toured the factory grounds.

I was impressed with what I saw, and toward the end of the tour I turned to Fang and asked him, "What are your sales?"

"About 50 million RMB," he replied.

I was pretty surprised by his answer. The factory looked great, and Fang clearly ran a tight ship, but $9 million in sales wasn't a very encouraging number. (The exchange rate was still 5.5 yuan to the dollar at the time.) My spirits began to sink. It was going to take a long time to build a major company, I thought.

Sensing my concern, Fang started talking animatedly about the company's growth prospects. He pointed to the construction of a newer, much larger building on the other side of a small river that ran in back of the factory. "This is the future of the company," he said, gesturing with his arms, clearly trying to get me excited again.

We crossed over a bridge and entered the construction site, carefully stepping over the steel reinforcing bars that were laid out crisscross fashion in preparation for the pour-ing of the cement floor. The building was going to be large and modern and would certainly increase the scale of Fang's business. It was the future, to be sure, but it wasn't until much later that I realized just how much that future had already been determined before an ounce of concrete had been poured.

Breaking the Ice: Our First Joint Venture

After I closed the initial funding for our company on February 28, 1994, and ASIMCO Technologies was born, Fang's company was one of our first targets for a joint venture. Yet despite the interest Fang had shown when we met with him in Ningguo, the initial negotiations didn't go very well. Fang was reluctant to give up a majority interest, despite my best efforts at persuasion. To justify and protect our investment, I told him, we simply had to have majority ownership, and any other position was a complete nonstarter for us. When negotiations continued to stall around this point, I started to lose hope that we'd ever reach a deal.

And then, late one Friday afternoon in August of 1994, Fang showed up, unannounced and completely out of the blue, at my office on the sixth floor of the Hilton Hotel in Beijing. (In 1994, as I've mentioned before, there was a shortage of office space in the capital city. Hotels like the Hilton reserved space for offices, and it gave new meaning to the phrase "It's a small world." You could literally walk down the hall and look in on some of your competitors and customers, all working away at their desks.)

Fang hurriedly explained to me that he had had a change of heart and was prepared for us to take majority ownership.

"There's just one condition," he said. "The contract has to be completed by Sunday night." He wanted to be able to take all of the relevant documents back to Hefei, the capital city of Anhui Province, for approval on Monday.

This was the break we'd been waiting for, and I didn't think much about the reasons behind his desire to get things done so quickly. I gathered the staff and we worked through the weekend, negotiating late into the night on Friday and Saturday. I caught what sleep I could on the floor in my office, not even bothering to go to my home, only fifteen minutes away. By Sunday, the contracts were ready for translation, duplication, and signature, and by Monday morning Fang was off to Anhui. We'd taken care of the entire negotiation in one weekend.

Having heard that government approvals can take a long time in China, I was shocked when Fang called on Monday afternoon to tell me that the deal had already been approved. I hadn't been expecting it to happen nearly that fast, and it felt like great news. We funded thirty days later, and our first joint venture was complete. In China, I've learned, nothing succeeds like indifference. All those months pursuing Fang had only pushed him farther away. When we went on to looking at other deals, he unexpectedly fell into our lap.

I know now that Fang didn't reverse his position out of some newfound sincere desire to be our partner. He came around so quickly because he was backed into a corner and had no place else to turn. His ability to procure such rapid governmental approval of the joint venture was evidence of the strong support he enjoyed from the local government, and he clearly had never had much trouble securing bank loans to grow his business. But in 1994, his company was heavily leveraged, due largely to the expansion Fang had undertaken across the river. Our capital was just about the only thing that could bail him out. When Fang sold us 60 percent of his company, I optimistically expected that we would build a large business together. I had no way of knowing that all he really wanted was our capital, and that his real intention was to keep me and ASIMCO at arm's length.

Our joint venture with Fang got off to a solid start. His company had always been profitable, and it continued to grow and pay cash dividends. The new factory building and the molding presses bought with the proceeds from our equity contribution more than quadrupled the company's production capabilities.

I introduced export opportunities from companies like Bosch to Fang so that we might grow the business even further, but he resisted them. I couldn't figure this out at the time, but I've since come to realize that he didn't want us to control any part of his business, and least of all his market. Anything that might increase our control over the company would increase our control over him, and he didn't want it.

From the beginning, he made a big point about needing advanced oil seal technology, so I went out and found Chicago Rawhide, a subsidiary of SKF, the large Swedish bearing company, and concluded a joint venture with them.

Enamored as everybody was on first exposure to Fang and the factory that he ran, which always showed well, particularly in comparison to the other factories in China at that time, Chicago Rawhide insisted that Fang also serve as general manager for the new joint venture. Since Fang did not want "another tiger on the mountain," he was only too happy to agree. (When there is a conflict between two powerful individuals in a company or organization, the Chinese always explain by saying that you can't have two tigers on a mountain.)

I expressed my concerns to the higher-ups at Chicago Rawhide at a post-closing lunch, but to no avail. They were impressed with Fang and were set on having him serve as general manager. I was discreet when I raised the issue, but I suspected at the time that Fang, ever perceptive, calculating, and aware, knew by my body language that I wasn't in favor of installing him in both positions.

Over time, my concerns about Fang and his motives steadily deepened. We began to hear rumors that he was building a new plant, separate from the joint venture, that would eventually compete directly with our business. We had no real way of knowing if it was true. Trying to verify a rumor like that, without being accusatory and ending up completely at odds with your partner, is a difficult thing to do in any part of China. In the closely knit community of Ningguo, it was nearly impossible.

Partly because of these rumors and my general worry about Fang's intentions, but primarily because it was a profitable company, I decided to increase our ownership of the joint venture. In 1998, we upped our stake to 80 percent by acquiring an additional 20 percent from the Chinese partner. (Exactly how much control Fang had over the Chinese partner—or whether the Chinese partner was, in fact, simply Fang by another name—was impossible to determine. Whatever the ownership structure was, Fang had a pretty firm grip on the entire thing.) One of my conditions for purchasing the additional 20 percent was that Fang and the Chinese partner sign a noncompete agreement, which they did. It should have been case closed right there.

But, of course, it wasn't. As soon as the ink was dry on the contract and the additional equity from us had cleared, Fang apparently began building his new company in earnest, in blatant violation of the noncompete agreement. We began hearing more and more reports about the new factory Fang was building on the other side of town, and the growing chorus was hard to ignore. In hindsight, you could argue that the cash the Chinese partner received for its 20 percent stake enabled Fang to set up the competing factory, and under that view we should never have upped our shares and given them the money. Maybe that's true. But I think it was only a matter of time before the Chinese partner accumulated enough dividends for Fang to do it anyway. The specifics weren't the determining factor. Simply put, Fang had resolved to open up in competition with us, one way or another.

Once I had sufficient evidence that Fang had violated

the noncompete agreement, I confronted him and told him that something had to give. He responded by offering to run our joint venture under a management contract that would guarantee us a certain level of profit. This was completely unsatisfactory to me. Apart from the fact that our joint venture would never have any equity value under this type of arrangement, I also wasn't about to agree to any formal relationship with someone who had already proven to be untrustworthy. I made the decision then and there to replace him. He had crossed the line, and the die had been cast.

Preparing for Battle

Given some of our past experiences with management changes, and Fang's tight hold on the business, we knew that we had our work cut out for us. I called a meeting of our key managers at headquarters in Beijing to begin planning a course of action, and we agreed that all information about our plans in Anhui had to be kept entirely under wraps. If word got out ahead of time that we planned to replace Fang, we could be sure that he would steal or destroy our proprietary tooling and every valuable, portable piece of equipment in the factory before we ever got there. In all likelihood, he and his cronies would try to empty out the joint venture's bank accounts, too. We'd seen all of this happen before.

A week later, I informed the ASIMCO board of our plans. While all necessary precautions were being taken, I told them, I expected it to be a difficult transition. Our position, in legal terms, was about as cut-and-dried as you could get, but that didn't guarantee us anything. Everything, down to the last detail, had to be handled carefully, and perfectly, before we made our move.

Of uppermost importance in my mind was controlling the company's chop, the little round stamp issued by the government and used to certify the company's approval of a transaction. In China, nothing gets done in the name of the company without the chop. You can't pay bills, write checks, or execute any important documents. The chop was usually stored in a safe place in the general manager's office, and if we were going to be successful at all we had to figure out how to get our hands on it and keep it secure. When we changed the general manager at a different joint venture, we'd had a bad experience: I left to meet with the vice governor of the province to tell him about the switch we'd made, and in my absence the newly installed general manager gave up the chop to an unruly and threatening mob of workers organized by the ousted manager. It had been a costly lesson. Once the share-holders are in dispute, it's almost impossible to have a replacement chop issued, no matter how legitimate the claim.

We also had to immediately change all of the bank mandates by action of a majority of the board of directors, removing Fang as an authorized signatory. Otherwise, he might well have been able to convince a friendly bank officer to transfer funds with only his authorization, despite the fact that the bank was required to get authorization from us, too. This happens, even though it isn't supposed to; I've seen it any number of times.

Apart from the financial aspects of the joint venture, I also had to protect our physical assets. The molds and tooling for a molded rubber business are critical. They generally take a long time to make and aren't easily replaceable, and if you don't have them, you can't make parts. They're also easily transportable, so we needed to protect them physically. Likewise with key machinery, and certain of the more expensive (and portable) presses. Maintaining the integrity of the manufacturing work-shops was essential, and if we didn't guard them adequately, a few trucks could quickly have emptied out the factory.

If you had concerns like this in a developed country with a highly refined legal structure, of course, you could simply take the appropriate legal actions and enlist the support of the police to protect company assets. But given Fang's influence in the local community, I couldn't take the risk of allowing anybody in Ningguo, inside the factory or out, to become aware of what we were about to do. Naturally I would have preferred to sit down with the local government ahead of time and explain what we were doing, but this wasn't an option.

In trying to maintain his control over the joint venture, Fang had always played the card that he had a strong relationship with the local government. Anhui is one of China's most rural provinces, and a growing industrial business like Fang's was an exceptional asset for the area. For this reason alone, he would have been accorded special treatment. My suspicion, though, is that Fang provided some "economic benefits" to local officials—not necessarily illegal favors, but certainly the kinds of benefits, commonly found in China, that made the local officials eager to support him and keep him happy.

Over time we had made many efforts to establish our own direct relationship with the local government, meeting on numerous occasions with various deputy mayors, but Fang did all that he could to insulate us from the most senior officials. (In any government entity in China, the top official is the party secretary.) Whenever I visit one of our factories, I make it a point to meet with members of the local government, the more senior the better. In most cases, the general managers make certain that this happens, because they're well aware that encouraging a good relationship between me and the senior leadership of the city can lead to more support for our business. In Ningguo, though, I had never met with the top leader, and in retrospect that failure has Fang written all over it. I should have tried harder to break through, and the fact that I didn't most likely confirmed in the local government's eyes that ASIMCO was a provider of capital only, and nothing more—as I'm sure Fang had told them.

As a result, we were left pretty much to our own devices. The only real leverage I had in dealing with Fang was that I could have the board of directors resolve to remove him as general manager. But before I could do this, I wanted to have everything ready at the factory, so I needed to buy some time. I scheduled the board meeting in Hangzhou, the large city that we typically flew into and that was about five hours from Ningguo by car. It wouldn't seem unusual for us to have the meeting there, and the intervening period would give us valuable time to establish and implement our precautionary measures.

I also knew that we had to have a replacement general manager waiting in the wings, somebody loyal to ASIMCO to jump into the breach and fill the power vacuum immediately after Fang had been deposed. We were lucky enough to have somebody on hand, Zhang Hongwei. While he didn't exactly fit our description of a New China manager, Zhang was a seasoned fifty-five-year-old veteran. He had run the China Brilliance factory, which made vans under license from Toyota in the north of China. While general manager there, he had been responsible for a much larger factory and had handled some pretty tough labor issues. We had recruited him for another management position within ASIMCO, but when the need to replace Fang arose I asked him to take the Anhui assignment instead. He was as well prepared as anybody in China for the guerrilla warfare that we all feared was about to ensue.

HANGZHOU, ONE OF the Seven Ancient Capitals of China, is located on West Lake and is famous because a long line of emperors used it as a summer resort. Though not nearly as international a city as Beijing or Shanghai, Hangzhou does have a modern, resort-style hotel, the Shangri La, which I was thrilled to find the first time I visited in 1993. The hotel sits atop a small hill, surrounded by trees, and offers nice rooms and even a fairly decent Western restaurant and bar. All in all, it's a whole lot better than the normal fare I'd gotten used to on my trips around China. Since we usually stayed there on our way to and from the factory, it was natural to have the fateful board meeting there.

Under the pretense of other business, trusted members of the ASIMCO team had arrived in Anhui in the days ahead of the meeting to make sure we were ready on the ground. When informed of our plans, Gary LePon, head of Asia for Chicago Rawhide, and several other Chicago Rawhide and SKF representatives were there as well. In Hangzhou, everybody on our side knew what was about to take place, but I suspect that Fang thought we were going to seriously consider his idea of a management contract, having convinced himself that we could never run a factory in Anhui and would never even try. Unbeknownst to Fang, his replacement was waiting patiently outside the meeting room. Our managers were already in the factory, waiting for our signal.

Confronting Fang

You could pretty much feel the tension as we gathered in the meeting room at 9:00 A.M. I took my customary seat at the center of the table, with Tim on one side and Ai Jian on the other, while Fang sat directly across from me, alone. He always traveled and attended our meetings by himself, which was a good indication of how he saw things. There was no number two in his world.

We quickly got down to business, hashing out how the joint venture was going to be managed in the future.

"Mr. Fang," I said, looking directly across the table at him, "several weeks ago, you proposed that you'd manage the factory under a management contract and guarantee ASIMCO a certain profit. Can you please explain how that would work?"

As Ai Jian translated, I watched Fang carefully. We were never going to approve his idea, but the board needed to be on record as having formally considered every proposal made by a director. No matter how justified your position might be in China, it's important not to be perceived as having acted in an arbitrary or unilateral way. If you're not careful, the focus can easily shift from a serious transgression by Party A (the Chinese partner) to the insensitivity of Party B (the foreign partner) in dealing with the transgression. We hadn't been so careful in the past, and I'd had minutes or other records of meetings literally shoved in my face, leaving me scratching my head and wondering how we could possibly have allowed the tables to be turned on us in that way.

Fang gave a fairly predictable answer. Once he finished, I told him that we weren't going to accept his offer and that nothing he had said or would say could change our minds. He was now the general manager of our joint venture and also of another separate, competing entity, which was unacceptable to us and against China's company law.

"You can't be general manager of both," I told him firmly. "You're going to have to resign one of the positions. Which will it be?"

Fang's eyes darted from side to side as he evaluated his possible courses of action, the wheels in his mind spinning a mile a minute. After a brief period of consideration, Fang said he'd resign as general manager of the joint venture.

He agreed to put both his resignation and our formal nomination of a new general manager on the record, which I did as quickly as possible. We pulled out the letter and resolution we'd prepared beforehand and passed them to him so he could take a look.

His only comment was that there was certain compensation owed to him, and he would sign if we could reach agreement on when it would be paid. After huddling with Tim and Ai Jian, I made a suggestion that he accepted, and he signed.

Within two hours, the whole thing was finished. I was surprised, relieved, and a lot of other things, too. It hadn't gone at all like I'd anticipated. I fully expected Fang to contest the resolution to remove him, which is why we played it so carefully by the book. I didn't think he'd step down so willingly. I wasn't happy that he had violated the noncompete, but at least we were rid of him. All I wanted now was an orderly transition.

After all the documents were signed, I made one final suggestion. Eyeing him all the while, I said, "Mr. Fang, everyone at the factory will hear of this change and will be wondering what's going on. Why don't we meet at the factory tomorrow morning to make a joint announcement to the management team?"

I have learned that anytime a management change is made in China, you can expect the managers and work-force to become apprehensive. A stable, profitable business represents security for everyone, and shareholder disputes or leadership vacuums breed instability. I considered maintaining stability throughout this change a high priority, and I felt that a joint announcement by both parties would go a long way toward overcoming any concerns the folks at the factory might have.

Fang was genuinely surprised that we planned to go to the factory that afternoon, and he didn't try to hide it. But he was quick on his feet.

"I have some other business in Hangzhou later today," he said. "I can't get back to the factory until 3:00 P.M. tomorrow. Is that okay?"

I agreed, and we scheduled the meeting for 3:00 P.M. the next day. Given how events would play out, Fang probably hightailed it to Ningguo as soon as he left the meeting.

Guerrilla Warfare

We hurried to the factory after lunch, and the ASIMCO troops gathered in the guesthouse to go over the day's events. Everybody was relieved to learn that our plans had gone off without a hitch, on both ends. The careful planning that had gone into this was paying off. We had an uneventful dinner and went to bed, planning to tour the factory the next morning at 8:00 A.M.

We awoke to the first sign of trouble: the elevators in the guesthouse weren't working. A few of our more engineering-oriented managers were able to fix the problem, but as we started our factory tour the lights began going out, workshop by workshop. There were no managers or supervisors in sight, and the employees were standing idly by their workstations, talking among themselves and looking suspiciously like schoolkids at recess. And then, inexplicably, all of the workers started filing out of the factory, instructed by anonymous posted signs to take the next three days off. By 9:30 in the morning, the factory was completely empty and dark.

Eventually we gathered in the large bullpen area outside the general manager's office where the finance staff sat, to huddle and decide what to do. It was obvious to me now that we needed to go to the local government, tell them what had happened, and try to enlist their support. Our Chinese staff started calling the municipal building to speak with somebody in a position of authority, but nobody had any luck. We were going to have to go over there ourselves. There was no guarantee that we'd get anything out of it, but we had to try. I had been in China long enough to know that government officials avoid controversy at all costs, and stepping into the middle of a management and corporate governance conflict wasn't going to be an appealing proposition. Nonetheless, we piled into several cars and made our way to Ningguo.

The municipal government's offices were located in an older building, 1960s vintage. The lobby was situated at the bottom of a large set of stairs, which went up to a landing and then branched off in two directions. There was no reception desk of the sort that you might expect in a building like this, so the six of us stood haplessly in the lobby, stopping everybody who passed in an effort to get the attention of somebody who could help. One of the various people we stopped told us, somewhat ominously, that Fang had been seen going to lunch with one of the deputy mayors. So much for his prior commitments in Hangzhou.

Finally, we saw a tall, fortyish man walking down the stairs toward us, clearly a man of some importance in the government. When he reached the ground floor, he introduced himself as Wu Yi Jun, the party secretary and the number one official in the Ningguo government. He then invited us upstairs to a meeting room that was obviously reserved for important meetings.

Every government body in China has one or more of these rooms, and the layouts are generally the same from place to place. There are two basic arrangements. One is for the two leaders to sit side by side at the far end, facing the rest of the room and the entry, with the Chinese official on the left and the foreign leader on the right. The two main figures sit in the middle of a U-shaped grouping of club chairs, and their respective delegations fill out the chairs on their respective sides (sort of like at a wedding), in order of seniority. You'll typically see this arrangement when media are present, as when President Hu Jintao is meeting with a visiting head of state or with some other senior official. The other arrangement is to have two rows of cushiony chairs (with the inevitable white doilies on their backs) facing each other, and the two leaders in the center on either side. Since no media were present, this was how we met with Secretary Wu.

Leaders speak first, and others in the delegation only speak when spoken to. Facing Secretary Wu, I introduced myself and the rest of the delegation and then talked a bit about ASIMCO, the scope of our general activities in China, and our cooperation in Ningguo. Although I'm pretty sure he knew quite well who we were and what we were up to, I always assume that the person I'm meeting with doesn't have any background on us. That way, I can present the company in the way that I want it presented, highlighting the points that can help us the most in that particular situation.

After I was done, I asked Gary to introduce SKF and Chicago Rawhide and the separate joint venture we'd formed. As it turned out, SKF is a very large investor in Anhui Province, and Secretary Wu noted this with what seemed like a great deal of interest.

I then explained why we'd replaced Fang, to which there was surprisingly little reaction. Secretary Wu said only that internal management issues were to be dealt with by the shareholders and were not issues for the government to concern itself with.

At the time, I thought he was trying to distance himself from us, which worried me. But I've gotten to know Secretary Wu a bit since then, and I've realized that he was just trying to maintain an appropriate level of neutrality. Just as he wasn't for Fang and against us, he wasn't going to take our side against Fang on corporate governance issues, either. He wanted both companies to succeed and would use his authority, as best he could, to protect the rights of both parties. Of course, I would have liked it better if he'd just come out and said he was on our side, but given that he wasn't going to do that I started to see the logic of his position. And regardless of what he decided, I'd finally met him face-to-face. Fang couldn't keep me away any longer.

After our discussion was finished, Secretary Wu invited us to lunch in a dining room in his building, which we all took as a good sign. We had a pleasant banquet-style meal, featuring at least a dozen different dishes, and we never once discussed anything related to the joint venture. As the meal was drawing to a close, I decided to mention our power problem.

As I was standing up, I said as innocently as I could, "Oh, by the way . . . we seem to have lost our power," and asked if there was anything he could do to help.

Looking a bit surprised, which I'm sure he was, he said that he'd look in to it. I had always thought that turning the power off was the work of a lower-level employee, so

I took some comfort in what he said. We exchanged our good-byes and then returned to the factory.

For the rest of the afternoon, we sat around in the finance department, literally twiddling our thumbs. We had done all that we could, and now it was time to just sit and wait. I remember being impressed with Zhang's unflappability with respect to the workers. He was very matter-of-fact about it, saying without any shadow of doubt that he knew they'd be back.

"After all," he reasoned, "they have to work."

At about 4:00 P.M. we got a call from the local government, telling us that power would be restored within the hour, and at the stroke of 5:00 the power kicked in. We were beginning our climb back from the depths of that morning. Zhang's prediction ended up being accurate, and the employees began to filter back the next day. We were at full production within three days.

BUT IT WASN'T over yet. The next year was filled with skirmish after skirmish with Fang. He hired away our key managers and employees, promising higher wages and better living conditions. (He even went so far as to send a bus to our factory gates to transport those who wanted to take him up on his offer.) He stole our prints, collected receivables from our customers, sabotaged our shipments, created misinformation, and generally did whatever he could to cause us trouble. Whenever I met with Zhang afterward he would begin with a litany of complaints about what Fang had done in the past month. He was making Herculean efforts to deal with Fang's interference, so I indulged him at first and just listened patiently. But after about a year, it started to seem like Zhang was somewhat obsessed with fighting Fang, playing Captain Ahab to Fang's Moby Dick. It took him a while to realize that Fang was just our competitor now, and though we had to deal with his shenanigans, the focus needed to be on building our business, not fighting Fang at every turn.

In the meantime, with a very clear legal case supporting us, we took Fang to arbitration and won, hands down. There was no rejoicing, though. We'd won a case in arbitration before, and I knew that winning wasn't the hard part. The hard part is enforcing the award and having something tangible that you can go against as compensation. Instead of trying to enforce the award in court, I listened to the advice of one of the senior advisers we'd retained and asked Secretary Wu to assist in the negotiations. This was one of our better moves. With a clear legal ruling in his hand and a desire to see the feud end, Secretary Wu sat in on our negotiations with Fang and helped bring the matter to a sensible conclusion just by being there. We wanted a cancellation of any back dividends owed to the Chinese partner and its remaining 20 percent of the joint venture, and that's exactly what we got. Our rubber business in Anhui became a wholly owned company, and we were now, finally, completely rid of Fang.

Reflections on Anhui

The problems that plagued our relationship with Fang were there from the beginning; we just didn't realize the depth of his motives. Most important, he never really bought into our strategy. Others, Chinese and non-Chinese alike, have been skeptical about our chances for success, so I can't really blame him for that. But his main problem, as with many entrepreneurs, was that his focus was exclusively on the short term. His method of doing business was to take everything off the table as quickly as possible. The less his customer or partner received, the more there was for him. You could never understand what we were trying to do in China if this was your predominant attitude. You had to have a bit of vision, and patience, too. We were a young organization then, prone to making mistakes and not always receiving the best advice. But a long list of successful Chinese businessmen, including Wang Jianming, chairman of Yuchai, and An Qing Heng, chairman of Beijing Auto Industry Corporation, understood what we were doing and gave us credit for what we were trying to create in China. Fang could never see past our immediate shortcomings to grasp the entirety of the vision, and things played out the way they did in large part because of that.

Fang's new company is one of our biggest local competitors, but his lack of a long-term view won't allow him to become a true competitor globally. Over the years, I've heard one global company after another complain about the way Fang treated them and swear never to do business with him again. A short-term outlook leads to shortcuts and other behavior, some of it unethical, that prevents you from being able to build long-term relationships, and this has been Fang's pattern. It might work in certain sectors within China, but it doesn't fit the China of tomorrow and has no place in the global economy.

Don't try telling that to Fang, though. He's always had a terminally high opinion of himself, and he isn't one to take advice, let alone ask for it. He never thought much of the other general managers in ASIMCO, completely overlooking people like Li Jienan and Cheng Dexing, whom I will discuss later and who were every bit his equals. (In partnership with ASIMCO, Li and Cheng have built substantial businesses with leadership positions in China that are now establishing strong positions in the global market as well.) In Fang's jaded view, there was nothing for him to learn and nobody in our company who could teach him anything. To be fair, the talented staff that we have at ASIMCO today is a far cry from the team that we fielded in 1994 when we were just getting started, and I can understand why he might have had some doubts. But his arrogance and general lack of regard for other people doomed our partnership from the start.

Fang also had a low opinion of foreigners—which, unfortunately, some of the actions of our own people reinforced. Once, when Don St. Pierre, Fang, and I were touring the factory, Don, a chain smoker, put out a cigarette butt on the ground. Understanding the irony of it all, Fang, who always maintained an immaculate plant, delighted in giving Don a nudge and asking him to please pick it up. In those days, factories in China were often dirty, and you might expect to see Chinese workers putting out cigarettes on the ground. But for a Westerner to do it—a Westerner who was supposed to teach Chinese companies to be world class, no less—was pretty unexpected, and Fang took a good deal of pleasure in pointing out Don's mistake.

Fang still takes the occasional shot at us (every once in a while a shipment is sabotaged with bad parts mixed in with our good), but we've continued to build the business since then. Our factory in Anhui is one of our largest exporters, to the likes of Bosch, Tenneco, and Honeywell. We've built a new facility in Wuhu, another city in Anhui Province where top engineering is more readily available, and we're moving the company up the technology ladder to designing and manufacturing sophisticated NVH (noise, vibration, and harshness) products that improve the ride quality of vehicles.

Our experience with Fang in Anhui was about as bad as it gets in China, but we weren't alone in our troubles. If you travel around China, or talk to those who've done business here, you won't have to go very far to hear of similar episodes at other joint ventures. It's an unfortunate part of the development process for a major country like China, where circumstances and deeply rooted vested interests are changing daily. But having gone through it, I no longer lose any sleep over what might happen in China. If we can handle Fang, we can handle anything.

We took a couple of positive lessons from what happened in Anhui. First, patience, perseverance, and careful planning *can* prevail, even against strong vested interests. Second, the local government can be an ally, but you have to work hard to develop the relationship. (After Anhui, I redoubled our efforts to expand our network of relationships with local governments in China, and we brought on several local advisers to make sure we never let up.) Third, learning to operate the Chinese way— leveraging relationships and playing to your strengths—will most likely lead you to the best result. In the case of Anhui, we had no real relationship with the local government before the change in management. One year later, they were our biggest ally in putting the matter to rest.

MANY BOOKS ON China fall into the "glass is half-empty" category, choosing to focus only on the negative aspects of experiences like ours in Anhui. There is no discussion of how you can deal with the adversity successfully, and only rare mention of the positive and affirming experiences you can have in China. The negative needs to be seen and understood, to be sure, but so does the positive. In the next two chapters, you'll see the other, brighter side of China firsthand.

Chapter 9

A Peaceful Transition in Langfang

At our brake joint venture in Langfang, we faced an entirely different problem. Despite our 66 percent ownership interest, the joint venture contract didn't give us the unilateral right to nominate and appoint the general manager. In a throwback to earlier days, when only the Chinese partner realistically had access to Chinese managers, our Chinese partner had the sole authority to nominate the candidate, while we as the majority interest had the authority only to appoint or remove the general manager. It was a seemingly harmless provision, but it ultimately prevented us from even getting our candidate on the ticket, so to speak.

The other problem was that, when we first faced these issues at Langfang, we had not yet implemented our New China manager program. As a result, I didn't have anyone on my bench to put on the field, and I had to accept a compromise candidate instead until I could find a suitable replacement.

Despite these difficulties, we managed to get what we

wanted through friendly negotiations, but only after a near divorce and reconciliation with our Chinese partner. Many in the West say that signing a contract with a Chinese partner is only the beginning of the negotiations, but this story shows that it can work the other way. We've gotten to the point with many of our partners in China where we can work around unfavorable provisions in a contract, simply because we've created trust and good faith, and both parties realize that full cooperation benefits us both.

IN LATE 1995, we were having problems at the Langfang joint venture. Relations with our Chinese partner had deteriorated badly, and we were trying to figure out why.

At the recommendation of Don St. Pierre and his on-site representative at the factory, I had decided to force out Mr. Liu, the incumbent general manager. Unfortunately for us, the contract contained that seemingly innocuous language giving the Chinese partner power to nominate replacement candidates and the board power only to approve. We were in a bit of a bind.

I decided to call a board meeting, thinking that it would be the best way to resolve our differences. I had known Xue Yixiu, the head of the Langfang Heavy Industry Bureau and our Chinese partner in the venture, since we first began to look at making an investment in Langfang. We'd always gotten along well.

But at the board meeting we called to discuss the problems, Xue moved to nominate a replacement for the general manager of the company, as he was entitled to do under the contract. His first choice was somebody whose sole management experience was with a state-owned enterprise.

I wasn't happy about it, at all. "I won't support that candidate," I told him, point-blank. "We've talked about this before. I want somebody who has experience with a foreign enterprise and ideally somebody who can speak some English and has export experience, too."

Xue didn't like my answer and became visibly agitated. He told me that if I vetoed his first suggestion, he would immediately nominate another person from the Chinese partner. Knowing that the second candidate would also have a "state-owned" mentality and none of the experience that I had asked for, I became frustrated because I wasn't getting through, and Xue wasn't listening.

Trying to keep my cool, I said, "Mr. Xue, you're welcome to do that." I leaned closer to him over the top of the table. "But you should understand that I will keep rejecting your nominee until I see someone who meets my requirements, even if it takes the entire fifty years of the joint venture's life."

I think that Xue had expected me to give in on this point, but my answer made it pretty clear that things weren't going to go his way. Recognizing that we were at an unanticipated stalemate, Xue's temper flared and the meeting degenerated into a shouting match. Waving a copy of the contract in front of him, Xue and his colleagues began yelling across the table at us in heated and rapid-fire Chinese, way too fast for Ai Jian to translate with any degree of accuracy. That the meeting had finally broken down became pretty clear to everybody there when Xue turned on his heels and led his team out the door in a huff.

Later, reflecting on the meeting, I thought I might have unknowingly been set up by my own staff. Ninety percent of the problems that occur in China are due to miscommunication and misunderstanding, and the meeting had gone badly enough that it seemed like there had to be something deeper going on. I'd been goaded into picking a fight with our Chinese partner by the reports I'd been receiving from our American expatriate managers who were at the scene in Langfang. Removing Liu seemed like a good idea while I was doing it, but in the aftermath of the meeting I wasn't so sure. Here we were at a stalemate, and now we either had to dissolve the joint venture or make peace and move forward.

Playing the role of an "honest broker," Ai Jian volunteered to spend a week at the factory to get to the bottom of the issue. After interviewing a dozen of the top and middle managers, Ai returned to my office a week later and tried to explain what had caused the falling-out. The tangled web of intrigue that he described was classic "he said/she said" and was completely incomprehensible to me as a foreigner, even though I'd been operating in China for almost three years at that point.

Things like this occur more than I'd like to admit, and when they do I'm always reminded of two of my children,

Sara and Douglas. They're less than two years apart, and as siblings often do, they had their occasional quarrels growing up. Trying to referee or understand what really happened when both were in tears, I found, was nearly impossible. Sara would have a perfectly reasonable-sounding complaint about what Douglas had done, but then Douglas's story of how he'd been provoked by his sister would be just as believable. The situation in Langfang was pretty similar, with everybody airing their complaints and feeling sorry for themselves—with the additional complication of a different set of cultural over-tones that made it all that much more difficult to decipher.

As Ai Jian told story after convoluted story about what was going on, I reached a state of complete exasperation and interrupted him. "Mr. Ai," I said wearily, "I simply don't understand a word of what you're saying!"

Looking at first surprised and then confused, Ai confessed, "I'm Chinese and I don't understand!"

Off to a Bad Start

Completed just a year earlier, in December of 1994, the joint venture in Langfang with the Meilian Brake Company had been stillborn, if truth be told. The products were good, but we'd agreed to some provisions in the contract up front that would severely limit our ability to take a state-owned enterprise and reform it so that it could compete in an increasingly global economy.

Over the course of that first year, we would discover just how much we had hurt our prospects before we'd even spent dollar one on the business.

Langfang is a vibrant city of about four million people, located approximately forty kilometers south of Beijing, halfway between Beijing and Tianjin. Although it's close to two major cities, labor costs there are no higher than at any of our other factories in more remote provinces, and it's only about an hour from headquarters by car. Tianjin, just sixty kilometers farther south, is one of China's major port cities, with ships leaving every day for the States. The area is a logical and convenient place from which to export and to build an export business. (We've since built two additional factories in Langfang, largely for these reasons.)

The local government has also been on the ball about selling the advantages of the city, establishing an economic development zone and attracting large global companies like TRW and Sandvik. On top of the commercial incentives, Langfang's city fathers have also paid a great deal of attention to beautifying the city over the years, and it has paid off. Newly planted trees, flowers, and gardens line the streets, and the city is clean and open.

Meilian had two product lines when we did the joint venture: air compressors and brake components. Air compressors essentially generate air for the air brake systems used primarily in trucks and buses. The compressors are assembled and then sold to the diesel engine manufacturer, which fits them onto the engines before the engines are in turn sold to the vehicle assembler. Because Meilian had obtained technology under license from Munich-based Knorr-Bremse, one of the two major producers of compressors worldwide, our Langfang venture has dominated the original equipment market in China. Today our market share is still over 65 percent, and we manufacture more than 650,000 compressors annually for the commercial vehicle market. This is significant, because the entire U.S. and European markets are approximately 500,000 units each. Knorr-Bremse, which now also owns Bendix in the United States, and WABCO, the old Westinghouse Air Brake Company, more or less split the U.S. and European markets. The second product line at Meilian was brake components for the passenger car market, sold primarily to First Auto Works Volkswagen in the north of China.

When we began the negotiations to start a joint venture, Don and his group of Beijing Jeep alums took the lead. Don was confident that he and the factory rats he'd brought with him—whom he referred to, in his own inimitable way, as "us guys"—could do a better job negotiating joint ventures than Tim Clissold and Michael Cronin. There was clearly no love lost between these two parts of the company. Don regarded Tim and Michael as "bean counters," and accused Tim of having an "unnatural love" for China, while Tim and Michael had no use for Don and the team he'd brought with him. In lobbying me to hire Kerry Ivan, his chief financial officer at Beijing Jeep, Don had made a special point of telling me that

Kerry really knew how to decipher the Chinese books, something that he didn't think Tim or Michael could ever do. And since Don and his guys were the ones who'd found the opportunity for the joint venture in the first place, I decided to let them carry the ball all the way to the finish. It was a mistake I would never make again.

To say that Don was bested in the negotiations by the Chinese is a severe understatement. The assets that the Chinese partners infused were seriously overvalued, there were limitations on our ability to lay off workers, and the contract, despite our majority position, was one-sided in favor of the Chinese partner. We had shot ourselves in the foot right at the start.

We then proceeded to shoot ourselves in the other foot when Don sent Earl Hicks to Langfang to be his on-site representative. A gruff, burly guy who'd been in China on a number of assignments, Earl had the kind of no-nonsense approach that holds a surface appeal for foreigners who view the Chinese as adversaries. Due largely to his attitude, however, he made no friends among the Chinese managers at Langfang, and we would only later discover that he'd actually generated a high level of enmity against our company. His tough-guy antics had hurt our business. One small example of the insensitivity of Don and his crew: they canceled, at the last minute, a trip to the United States that Liu, the general manager, had spent a lot of time and energy planning. Trips overseas are commonplace today, but they were a pretty big deal in 1995. To have his trip canceled, and by the foreigners, no less, was an enormous loss of face for Liu and was the kind of thing that really could and should have been avoided. (We later learned that Earl's recommendation to replace Liu was based largely on innuendo that he had been fed by a deputy general manager who wanted to be promoted. Unwittingly, we had fallen right into Chinese corporate intrigue.)

A little over a year into the joint operation, with mistrust and miscommunication in full bloom, we had ended up at the board meeting stalemate in 1995 with Xue walking out in anger. After another visit to the factory, Ai Jian had eventually confirmed that certain members of Don's group were to blame for the way things had deteriorated so rapidly. All things considered, he concluded, the Chinese partner was actually behaving quite rationally when faced with the relatively irrational actions of our own Western staff.

All along I had taken what my Western employees were saying at face value, but that had gotten us nowhere and I was ready to be a bit more open-minded. As I thought about what Ai Jian had told me, it started to make sense. I couldn't think of any other reason why the Chinese partner and Xue were acting the way they were, and I began to question my own decision to change the general manager. Should I have left Liu in place and tried to work with him? After all, it didn't look like we were going to get anybody better. This is yet another case where a calm, deliberate analysis by a broader group of people would have served us well.

Liu, by the way, went off and started his own compressor company. His company isn't very big and isn't a threat to us, but it's a respectable enterprise and I give him a great deal of credit for taking the initiative and the entrepreneurial road.

The Road to Recovery

The more I thought about it, the more I was convinced that I'd made a mistake. Most important in my mind was the fact that the leadership vacuum that had been created while the shareholders were fighting threatened to destabilize the joint venture. I decided to meet with Xue and try to work things out.

"Mr. Xue," I said when we met, "Ai Jian has done some investigation, and I have come to the conclusion that our people were at fault. I realize that we've had a serious dispute, but if you'll accept my apology for what happened, I'd like to resolve the current situation and let bygones be bygones."

Xue was so relieved to hear me say all of this that his face lit up with a smile and he took my outstretched hand and went into a deep bow. I thought he was going to kiss me! The Chinese have a saying that you can't have a good partnership until you've had a fight, and that's the way it worked. We ended up having a good cooperation for years afterward.

But because we hadn't yet developed our New China management strategy, I didn't have anybody on the

ASIMCO bench whom I could put on the field to replace Liu as general manager. About a week later, Xue called Ai Jian to tell him that he had come up with another candidate for the position of general manager, and he wanted me to meet him. A day or so later, Xue came to our office accompanied by Mr. Zhang, who was then the general manager of a smaller factory in Langfang. Along with Ai Jian, I interviewed Zhang in our conference room at Parkview Center. A quiet man with a reddish complexion and thick-rimmed glasses not unlike Jiang Zemin's, China's president at the time, Zhang didn't meet any of my requirements. All of his experience was with state-owned enterprises, he didn't speak English, and he had no export experience. But he did seem to be cooperative, and I had made my point and was anxious to get the conflict behind us. Zhang would have to do. Besides, I rationalized, Zhang had to know that he was only getting this opportunity because of me, and that would make him easier to deal with. Round One in the effort to convert our majority ownership position into management control had been long and drawn out, and ended in a draw.

AFTER I HAD made peace with Xue and appointed Zhang as general manager, things calmed down at the joint venture and we tried to work with Zhang to improve operations. While there were no real problems and no glaring vested interests that were being served other than those of the joint venture, we made frustratingly little progress. Zhang was a nice-enough guy, but he had the kind of state-owned mentality that meant that nothing would ever change.

In 1997, for example, I began a major drive at ASIMCO to establish an export business. I felt that this would diversify our markets and also provide valuable experience selling to demanding global customers. Although quality standards were improving in China, customers were still much more forgiving than companies in the United States in terms of quality. If we could sell to the best companies in the global industry, I reasoned, we would know that we had a future. If we continued selling only to companies in China, we could never be certain of that.

There also seemed to be a genuine interest on the part of U.S. companies to source from China. Companies began calling and visiting more frequently, and Langfang's casting and machining capabilities were in great demand. But despite my best efforts, I could never get Zhang to embrace the export idea. The passenger car industry was in an early stage of development in China, and it was insulated from competition by regulation and local protectionism. As a result, passenger car prices were approximately double what they were in more developed countries. With the central government strictly controlling the number of models being produced in China, there was little competition from new entrants. The foreign-invested enterprises that already had assembly licenses could afford to continue to import components from their factories back home, at high cost, without fear of losing market share due to the high price of their cars. Naturally, component prices in the passenger car industry in China were approximately double global prices, and the brake components that the Langfang joint venture was supplying to First Auto Works Volkswagen were well above the global market.

Given this situation, Zhang simply could not understand why he should export products at global prices when he could sell inferior products at fatter prices in China. This would be a valid point if you could be certain that the situation would never change, but Zhang's view, like Fang's in Anhui, was myopically focused on the short term. China was already in negotiations to join the WTO, and I knew that once that happened pricing would drop to world prices, or below, very quickly. We'd be ill-prepared to compete in the global market unless we developed export customers to help us become globally competitive in price and quality in these products. Zhang didn't understand any of this. But until I figured out how to assemble a team of more farsighted managers, I was stuck with him.

Even though it was a peaceful period at the joint venture, this was a very frustrating time for me. Because the company was a joint venture, not a wholly owned subsidiary of ASIMCO, Zhang reported to a board of directors and not to me personally. As a result, we had to manage Zhang through meetings of the board of directors, which we began having quite frequently. As we've installed our New China managers and ASIMCO has developed as an organization, this formality has gone by the wayside at all of our joint ventures, including Langfang. All of our operating units today, joint ventures and wholly owned companies alike, are managed as though they are subsidiaries of the company. But in 1997, Ai Jian, Tim, Michael, and I would very regularly make the one and one-half hour trip from our Beijing office, and we'd spend the day at Langfang, trying to get Zhang and the joint venture moving along.

Although I was optimistic at first about our ability to force change through this mechanism, I began to dread going to these board meetings. By the time we'd driven to Langfang, toured the factory, eaten lunch, finished the meeting, and driven back to Beijing, the entire day was shot. If we had been able to accomplish a great deal at these meetings, I might have felt differently. But instead I dreaded going, only because I knew ahead of time that it would be a nonproductive, exasperating, wasted day.

No one at the joint venture spoke English, so all discussion was carried on through translation—which, by itself, doubles the time needed to conduct a meeting. In dealing with Zhang at Langfang, bridging the language gap was particularly painful. If you're on the same page as the person you're speaking to, translation can work reasonably well. But if you're on completely different pages, as Zhang and I were, it can try your patience.

A simple question about accounts receivable, for example, would be translated in five seconds from English to Chinese, and back would come a five-minute answer from Zhang in Chinese, which would then be condensed into a one-minute English translation that didn't even address the question I had asked. (After these experiences, believe me, I can identify with Bill Murray in the movie *Lost in Translation*.) Maybe we should have had better translators, but at least half of the problem was that Zhang was using the language gap to obfuscate the real issues, so that he could avoid having to take any action.

Despite my strong desire to stay calm in these meetings, my impatience and agitation would sometimes come through, and it would be clear from my tone that I was getting angry and frustrated with Zhang. (My kids can always tell when I have hit my limit and get like this, and they know to back off.) With his naturally reddish complexion, I could never tell whether Zhang was angry that I was challenging him, or if he even understood what I was saying. Xue would just look on and let it play out.

Enter New China

When we first started implementing the New China management strategy, we were forced to hire people off the street, so to speak, to fill immediate management needs. This is risky for a number of reasons. But as we developed our bench strength, we began to "inventory" managers, hiring them but not putting them into management positions right away. This gave them a chance to learn the organization and gain credibility with the other managers while we waited for the ideal position to become available. We used this approach to solve the problem in Langfang, and the story of Peter Wang, whom I eventually installed as general manager, is an example of the way in which we put this strategy into practice.

Peter, a highly likable guy with an easy, outgoing personality, joined us in August of 1998, right in the middle of the 1997–1999 period when we brought more than fifty New China managers into the organization. He was born in Tianjin, the large port city two hours south of Beijing by highway. His father was a government official there, so Peter expected to have access to higher education and a ready entry into a respectable job. What he didn't expect was the Cultural Revolution, which closed all of the schools from 1967 to 1976 and interrupted his formal education. When Mao finally passed away and the Cultural Revolution ended, Peter was among the first group of students to take the test to enter university, something that hadn't happened for anybody in a decade. He enrolled at Tianjin University and majored in the internal combustion engine.

(At the risk of being politically incorrect, I have to say that one of the things that absolutely floored me when I first came to China was how many students, men and women alike, had studied some aspect of engineering. I can remember interviewing young Chinese women and being stunned when they would tell me, very matter-of-factly, that their major was the internal combustion engine. They had no sense that I might find this at all unusual and said it in the same way that the American women I was used to might say that they'd majored in English literature or art history. I've since learned, as has much of the rest of the world, that China is a highly engineering-oriented society, with over 26 percent of undergraduates studying science or engineering.)

When Peter graduated, he worked briefly for a state-owned company, which he then left to take a position with an American company. One evening over beers, Peter told me about the early days of China's growing economic freedom, and how that period had changed his perspective and his life.

When he left the state-owned enterprise and went to work for the American company in the 1980s, Peter told me that he was being paid at the rate of 100 yuan per month. In those days, coming from a state-owned enterprise, I'm pretty sure he considered it a princely sum. He discovered that everything is relative, though, the first time he had dinner with his American boss in Beijing.

Peter's boss was staying at the Great Wall Sheraton, one of the first joint venture hotels in China. He invited Peter to dinner at the hotel's Western restaurant, for what would be Peter's first Western meal (he was in his late twenties at the time). That was the first part of the surprise. Another surprise came when Peter's boss ordered a steak, listed on the menu for more than 100 yuan—an entire month's wage. Even more startling was when the meal ended and Peter's boss, seemingly without even thinking about it, tipped the waitress another 100 yuan just for serving one meal.

Then and there, Peter decided that he had to improve his English and find his way to North America, which he eventually did. He landed in Canada and attended Western Ontario University, where he picked up a master's degree. From there, he went on to work seven years with General Motors in Canada. After his first year, he said, his English improved and he began to feel increasingly at home and comfortable in his new surroundings. As the years went on, though, he realized that facility with the English language provided only a superficial level of comfort. The longer he was in North America, the more he realized that there were parts of the culture that he would never understand. He was better off, for the long term, in China.

When he moved back to China, Peter picked up a job as general manager for Karcher, a German appliance company. This is where we found him. He fit the profile of our New China managers to a tee—Mainland Chinese, had management training (MBA at Western Ontario), experience managing in China, and experience with multinationals (General Motors and Karcher). Peter joined us in 1998 with no particular position in mind, as just another member of ASIMCO's growing bench of experienced managers.

It just so happened that Peter's first day on the job was a Monday that was also my first day back from New York, after a board meeting the previous week. I had told our directors that we would mount a special campaign to reduce accounts receivable, which had become a particular problem in the aftermath of the Asian crisis of 1997 and was tying up a great deal of the company's cash.

When I arrive at the office in the morning, I am usually preoccupied, deep in thought about all of the things I need to do that day. Carleen always chides me for not saying "Good morning" to the receptionist, an accusation that I strongly deny. But as I got off the elevator on the fourth floor of our building on that particular Monday and walked toward my office at the far side of the floor, I spotted Peter sitting at a desk outside one of the offices near mine. It was early, and the office was nearly empty, so Peter was the first person I saw.

"Good morning, Peter," I said as I came up to the desk where he was sitting, "and welcome to ASIMCO."

Peter looked up, a big smile on his face, and replied: "Hi, Jack."

Then I had an idea. I invited him into my office and sprang it on him: "How would you like to be ASIMCO's accounts receivable czar?"

It was a daunting task. When looking at the financials of Chinese companies, Westerners are often shocked at the high level of accounts receivable. When a company in the West ships products to a customer, it can normally expect payment within thirty days. In China, a good, well-financed customer *might* pay within ninety days, and if you receive payment within six months you think you're doing just fine.

On top of that, our operating units that sell to the local market often receive barter trade as payment.

Instead of collecting cash payments, our companies that sell fuel systems to local diesel engine makers (or our company that sells compressors to the same customers) might receive trucks for up to 40 percent of the amounts owed to them. The diesel engine maker has received a truck in payment for the engines it has sold to the truck maker, so it merely passes the truck along to its suppliers. And yes, oftentimes we pass that same truck along to suppliers of our own. If we don't pass the truck along, the unit receiving the truck as payment has to sell it to an end user in order to convert the asset to cash. (Just in case doing business in China is ever feeling a bit too easy, you can think about that one for a second. I have nothing but the utmost respect for our general managers, who deal with problems like this on a daily basis.)

When setting up in China, multinationals often insist on payment within thirty days and are not equipped (and usually refuse) to accept barter trade. That's understandable, and it helps assure headquarters that the business will be run in China the same way it is run elsewhere. But the effect is to subject a growing, underdeveloped market to the rules of a much more highly developed economy in the United States, Europe, or Japan. In China's truck and diesel engine market, for example, nearly all of the major producers are local Chinese companies. Therefore, the best and most desirable customers in this market have liquidity issues from time to time, and they may have no choice but to stretch payments or make them with bartered goods. If you refuse to work with them, you won't be able to penetrate the China market, the largest portion of which may be purely local and governed by a whole different set of rules.

Why are high receivables and bartered trade the norm in China? The answer is simple: China's capital markets, such as they are, lack the ability to distribute capital efficiently. In the early 1990s, when China had less than $25 billion in foreign currency reserves, liquidity was much tighter, and the "triangle debt" described in Jim Mann's book *Beijing Jeep* was commonplace. Company A doesn't pay its supplier, Company B, so Company B can't pay its supplier, Company C. Even with more than $1 trillion in foreign currency reserves today, the distribution of capital is still pretty inefficient in China. Long receivable delays and barter trade remain part of the business landscape in many industries.

As our newly appointed "accounts receivable czar," Peter's job was to work with each of our general managers to analyze receivables, formulate a plan for reducing them, and help come up with strategies for collecting any receivables that were more than six months old. In this capacity, Peter traveled around to all of our factories and got to know the different managers in the role of somebody who could help them. It was a good deal for both of us: he formed a solid network with the other managers, and we got to see him in action. This was a much more sensible way for us to fill our management slots, instead of hiring people, putting them in a management position right away, and hoping for the best.

With all of this experience behind him, and because Peter was from the same general area of China as Langfang, I convinced Xue to agree to let Peter serve as executive deputy general manager at Langfang in February 1999. It was a first step toward having Peter take over as general manager the following year, when Zhang's term ended, and in the end this is precisely what happened. We got around the contract provision by having our Chinese partner nominate *our* candidate. (This happened in Peter's case in 2000, and it happened again in early 2004, when the Chinese partner nominated Chi Kemin, Peter's successor and a Six Sigma black belt in his own right.)

Under Peter Wang, the Langfang joint venture began to make progress. Sales increased and the company turned profitable. We became more aggressive with regard to export opportunities, and we created a third product line, brake slack adjusters used in heavy-duty trucks, that we began exporting to Bendix in the United States. Peter also improved the factory's actual physical environment by repainting buildings, inside and out, and landscaping. This had obvious benefits for the employees and also impressed our customers, who are well aware that cleanliness and orderliness are the first steps to good quality. The improvements were so powerful that I held one of our quarterly general managers meetings in Langfang, so that the other general managers could see what Peter had done. This in turn touched off similar cleanup campaigns at our other factories, as each general manager competed to make his factory the cleanest and best within the ASIMCO group.

Another of Peter's smarter moves was his decision to empower the local managers and to encourage them to advance within the organization. At the Anhui operation, I filled nearly every management position with individuals from headquarters after removing Fang. Sometimes this has to be done, but the message it sends to the local staff is that all of the key positions in the company will go to nonlocal Chinese. In the case of Langfang, Peter didn't want anybody else from headquarters, preferring instead to promote from within. This creates a climate of loyalty, sends the right message to the local managers, and is the method we prefer to employ today.

Leveraging Our Business in Langfang

In the end, despite all of our changes in management and export focus, the Langfang joint venture will probably never be a big moneymaker for ASIMCO by itself. But because of the strong relationship we've built with our Chinese partner there, we've since spawned two wholly owned businesses.

In 2004, I began discussions with Haldex, a Swedish company that makes brake systems for commercial vehicles, and we teamed up to design a new, more powerful twin-cylinder compressor for Caterpillar. Instead of setting up production for this new line within the joint venture, I was able to convince Xue's successor to allow us to set up a wholly owned ASIMCO facility at another site in Langfang, even though we borrowed people and expertise from the joint venture to establish the business. (Ironically, we did exactly what Fang had done in Anhui, except we did it with full transparency, and with the full agreement of our partner.) He went along with this because he trusts me, and he trusts ASIMCO. That trust has allowed our Chinese partner to see that, even though he isn't involved as a shareholder in the new venture, the arrangement is good for the city of Langfang and for the old joint venture.

In 2005, we created ASIMCO Braking, and we've now completed a state-of-the-art, world-class manufacturing facility, complete with clean room assembly capability. (An absolutely clean environment is essential for assembling products that are meant to have a long working life. A clean room, among other things, is pressurized in a way that keeps dust and dirt away from the assembly area.) I tell people that you can measure ASIMCO's progress in moving up the value chain by the number of clean rooms that we have. Before ASIMCO Braking, we had none. Since then we have added two more: one in our fuel injection business in Hengyang, and another in our compound mixing operation in Anhui. Although ASIMCO Braking's a wholly owned company under ASIMCO, we couldn't have established this business if it weren't for the experience, market position, and engineering and manufacturing capability that we've found through our joint venture in Langfang.

A second wholly owned business that has grown out of the Langfang joint venture is the ductile, or nodular, iron casting business we established in Gu'an County, a part of the greater city of Langfang. While the Langfang joint venture has its own foundry, it can't make the higher-strength ductile castings required in many brake components. Again, with the complete support of the Langfang government and our Chinese partner, we established ASIMCO Gu'an, which is dedicated to making and machining the ductile iron castings used in brake parts. Eventually, the Gu'an operation may form the cornerstone of a higher-value-added business to manufacture and sell brake modules and assemblies.

LANGFANG AS A whole has been a success story for us. Once I overcame the bad advice that I'd been given by my own foreign staff, I developed a strong working relationship with our Chinese partner and was able to overcome the provisions of the poorly negotiated contract. The relationship has worked well enough that I've been able to convince the Chinese partner to support our candidates for general manager, even though they aren't required to do so by the contract. The only lasting difficulty was just finding the right management talent for the job there. If I'd had my New China management team in place in early 1996, I wouldn't have had to agree on a compromise candidate, and progress could have come sooner.

I also learned a great many other lessons from Langfang. First, not to react too quickly. You can't always believe the people you're most familiar with. Just because

Don and his team were Westerners didn't mean that they were right, and I needed to learn to make more of an effort to understand what the "other side" was really saying. As I've said before, 90 percent of the mistakes made in China are due to misunderstanding and miscommunication.

Second, I learned how strongly and favorably the Chinese react when they realize that you trust them. When I admitted our mistakes to Xue, and said that I believed him, our relationship underwent a visible and long-lasting change for the better. The fact that I could set up a wholly owned facility to manufacture higher-technology compressors—which, on some level, competes with our own joint venture—would never have been possible if a certain amount of trust didn't exist between the two shareholders. But because of this trust, our Langfang joint venture markets, our new compressor in the China market, and our wholly owned facility focuses on exports. Everybody feels involved, like we're all part of the same family.

Third and last, we were able in Langfang to further refine our approach to implementing management changes. We learned, or at least understood more clearly, that you have to preserve opportunities for everybody, not just folks from headquarters. This includes the local managers who may not have the language capabilities or the more extensive educations of their counterparts in Beijing or Shanghai.

Chapter 10

An Election in Mao's Backyard

Year in and year out, our diesel fuel injection business in the city of Hengyang, in Hunan Province, has been one of our best-performing units. Under Li Jienan, the general manager who built the business and supported the joint venture with ASIMCO, the company has a strong legacy of good management. In terms of training and developing Chinese managers, it is truly a "mini GE." A man of the highest integrity, Li always thought first of the welfare of the joint venture, so we had none of the disputes or issues about vested interests that we had elsewhere. And when it came time to select a successor, we never even consulted the contract. Li proposed a novel method that would ensure stability for the new management team, and I readily agreed.

Despite the health of our relationship, all of us in Beijing were a bit confused, as you'll see, about what was actually going to happen. It proves once again that, even under the most favorable circumstances, China isn't always transparent, and if you're not careful, disagreements can still occur. Instead of overreacting or leaping to conclusions, the best policy is to take the time to listen and to understand.

THE LETTER CAME as a complete surprise.

Two years earlier, in 2001, Li Jienan had hinted to me that he wanted to retire. This was not good news. Li had helped engineer the joint venture with us and had been the general manager of the factory since 1984, turning a small country manufacturer of pistons, piston rings, and other components into one of the best diesel fuel pump factories in China. His company was one of our strongest performers, and I would have been happy if he never retired. I did my best to convince him to stay on for two more years, which, thankfully, he did. I hadn't heard anything since.

Now, out of the blue, came a letter from Chen Youhai, Li's partner and the party secretary for the factory. It was addressed to me, in Chinese, with no one else copied, and suggested in no uncertain terms that it was time for Li to retire and for the shareholders to name a successor.

I was confused, and a bit apprehensive. I couldn't figure out what was actually going on behind the scenes, and I was concerned that it pointed to some type of power struggle in one of our top units. I called Henry Huang and a few other members of my staff together, and we gathered in my office to discuss what it might mean.

Everybody else was just as confused as I was. Taken

literally, Chen's communiqué seemed like a classic end around, a knife driven into the back of an old friend and longtime partner. Was Chen, just one year younger than Li, on the prowl and angling for his boss's job? It certainly seemed that way, particularly to somebody like me who was used to U.S.-style power struggles. Henry and the experienced Chinese in our office couldn't rule it out as a possibility, either. The fact that Li hadn't given us a heads-up that the letter was coming gave the impression that he knew nothing about it.

After a number of carefully worded phone calls to Chen and Li and some discreet calls to knowledgeable insiders, we concluded that nothing particularly unusual was afoot. Thankfully, we'd been worrying about nothing. (That said, I'm not sure we ever got a real answer about the genesis of the letter, just another example of how the inner workings of the Communist Party and the government are opaque, even to the Chinese themselves.) It seemed that Chen, as the head of personnel for the joint venture, had written purely to inform me that Li had reached retirement age and that we needed to discuss the process for finding a replacement.

Now we had to call Li to arrange a meeting to sort out the end of his tenure, and I really didn't want to pick up the phone. I didn't want to see him go. I was genuinely sad to be starting a process that would lead to separation from an old friend.

When you meet someone for the first time in China, you're a "new friend," but the next time you meet you're considered (and said) to be an "old friend." It's the Chinese way of breaking down barriers and creating a mood of familiarity, and it's a bit overused for my taste. But to me, Li is a real old friend. A class act through and through, he's quiet, unassuming, hardworking, and as honest as the day is long. I consider it a great honor to have been able to work with him for more than ten years.

I always considered Li a New China manager, because of his genuine openness to new ideas, but he's from the old school of management in the sense that he was hands-on and not at all afraid to roll up his sleeves. Every morning, rain or shine, he gathered his managers at 7:30 A.M. in front of the factory gates to go over the key activities for the day, and he prided himself on the fact that he always walked through the entire factory at least two or three times each day. Nothing went on in that factory without Li knowing it. In 2001, we began the ASIMCO Leadership Development Program, and from day one a mandatory part of the program was a lengthy session with Li. There was simply no better way to give the young leaders of ASIMCO practical advice on how to run a business in China.

Knowing what a special individual he is, I should have known that the process of his retirement, and the appointment of a successor, was going to be a real eye-opener.

Hunan Spicy

Our fuel pump factory is located in the city of Hengyang in Hunan Province, approximately two hundred kilometers south of Changsha, the capital city of the province. When we visit the factory today, we fly two and a half hours from Beijing to Changsha and then drive another two hours on a four-lane expressway to Hengyang. Ten years ago, before the highway was built, it was a much different trip. If you look on a map, find Hong Kong and then draw a line north through the city of Guangzhou (formerly known as Canton), it'll take you to Hengyang and Changsha in Hunan Province. Until the new highway was built, the road following this general path, the one that we used to take to and from the factory, was the major connection between the south of China and the northern cities like Beijing.

At any time on any day of the week, the old two-lane road was filled with trucks carrying manufactured goods from Hong Kong, Guangzhou, and the south of China to consumers in the north. Headed the other way was truck after truck loaded with live pigs, chickens, or ducks from the farms in China's interior, headed for the cities of Guangdong Province and Hong Kong. Chinese shippers have a propensity to overload their trucks; when you combine this with the rather loose maintenance procedures common in China, you end up with a lot of breakdowns and accidents. When these happened, as they did inevitably and often, you were in for a long day. You might wait for hours, literally at a dead stop, while a truck was repaired, hauled away, or moved to the side. With a seemingly end-less line of trucks in both directions, it could take anywhere from eight to twelve hours to travel the two hundred kilo-meters from the airport to our factory.

The combination of crowded, truck-filled roads and erratic Chinese driving habits forms a toxic recipe. When people ask me whether I drive in China, I immediately say, "No way. Life is too short as it is." Anybody who has trav-eled even a little bit in China has a favorite car story. Carleen and I went to a comedy show in Beijing once, and the comedian, who had only been in China for a few days, opened up his act by saying, "Now tell me, I just want to know one thing: What the fuck are the lines in the middle of the road for?" He'd gotten right to the heart of it in just a couple of days. There is a common joke that median lines and red lights are merely "suggestions" in China.

I still can't decide whether Chinese drivers are extremely good or extremely bad at what they do. Driving like a maniac can have its merits in China. Passing on the right (by going onto the bike path) or passing on the left (playing chicken with oncoming trucks and then ducking back in line just in the nick of time) does have the advantage of getting you to your destination faster. Staying passively in your lane and within the rules, how-ever safe it might seem, could add two or three hours to your average trip to Hengyang.

Being a driver or a passenger in China is not for the faint of heart. One of my worst white-knuckle rides came on a nighttime trip along the old road from Hengyang to the Changsha Airport. There were three of us traveling back to Beijing, and my colleagues suggested that I take the front seat next to the driver so I could have more legroom. The driver was one of the regulars, and the people in Hengyang are very considerate, so I was confident that he would drive in a prudent way.

It turns out that his definition of prudence was significantly different from mine. He darted from side to side—at night, mind you, and at speeds of fifty to sixty miles per hour on a slow-moving road—and he seemed determined to keep the nose of the car as close as possible to the back bumpers of the trucks in front of us. He would stay just slightly to the left, so he could see oncoming traffic more clearly, and quickly zip out and pass if he saw an opening.

With my heart pounding, I decided to try to sleep, figuring that what I didn't see couldn't hurt me. Leaning my head against the window, my coat rolled up as a pillow, I dozed off. But every time I awakened and opened the corner of my left eye to see how we were doing, I was staring at the back corner of a truck's tailgate hovering only a few feet away from the windshield and from me. If the truck in front made a sudden stop, or even slowed down a bit, and our driver didn't react fast enough, I would have been history.

I've been able to roll with most of the punches in China, but that ride absolutely terrified me. After that trip I sent a memo to our managers, telling them to remind their drivers that safety comes first and mandating that trips at night be avoided at all costs. Driving like that is scary enough in broad daylight, and there's no need whatsoever to add darkness into the mix unless you absolutely have to. (In general, in an emerging market like China's, safety awareness is low and standards for what's acceptable are quite different from what they are in the States. Chinese often don't understand why foreigners are so concerned with the way they drive, or why we insist that safety glasses and ear protection be worn in factory environments. It's all part of an economy going through its development period.)

Hunan Province itself is known for a lot of things, though perhaps it's most famous for being the home of Mao Zedong, who was born in Xiangtan, a midsized city on the way from Changsha to Hengyang. The locals will tell you that the town is famous for its production of *baijiu*, but over the years I've heard so many provinces and cities lay claim to that honor that I've come to doubt them all.

One product that I can't recall any city or province laying claim to, however, are "1,000-year-old eggs." Dark inside and out and commonly served as a side dish at all meals, these eggs aren't really that old—though, I must say, they look it. They get their dark color not from age but from being coated in a plaster of clay, garden lime, salt, wood ash, and tea for one hundred days. The name and appearance put me off the first time I saw them, and I didn't want them anywhere near my mouth. But after trying them, I have to admit that I like their salty taste and always look for them when I sit down to a Chinese meal. At one of our dinners with the local officials of a small city under the jurisdiction of Hengyang, the party secretary told me that his city was famous for its production of 1,000-year-old eggs and claimed to be the largest producer in China, cranking out more than 100 million each year.

Hunan Province is also one of the two places in China known for hot, spicy food, the other being Sichuan Province. I've asked my Chinese colleagues which version is spicier, but I have yet to get a consensus. Whichever it is, I can tell you that the food in Hunan is plenty spicy. Whenever we have lunch or dinner anywhere in the province, the host will always ask, "Do you like spicy food?" Unsuspecting foreigners will answer yes but not think to qualify their answer, believing that nothing can be spicier than that Mexican restaurant back home with a "five-pepper" rating.

In 2005, we had the representatives from a company in Ohio come to visit our Hengyang plant. At the evening meal, they were asked the inevitable question. Although they answered yes, I'm pretty sure that the host didn't give them the full treatment, letting them off relatively easy with the three-pepper version of Hunan spicy. Even still, they had to have known they were in trouble when that first dish, with its thick topping of red peppers, came out. I wasn't there, but I'm told that they took one taste and then began reaching desperately for water or beer, whichever was closest. This company is now part of the folklore in Hengyang, and every time I've been there since somebody always brings up that story with a laugh.

The House That Li Built

Our factory in Hengyang was founded in 1950. It started off making pistons and piston rings before focusing on fuel pumps, a part of the system that injects diesel fuel into the combustion chamber of a diesel engine. Diesel fuel, because it's cheaper and more fuel-efficient than gasoline, is used heavily in China's countryside. For many years, tractors and "agricultural vehicles" were the only mechanized means by which China's farmers could get their goods to the marketplace. The only other way was the old-fashioned way, by foot.

Agricultural vehicles are a unique invention of China's rural population. By combining what looks like the front end of a motorcycle with a one-cylinder diesel engine, some type of a cab, and a truck bed to carry goods, you end up with an agricultural vehicle. They come in all shapes and sizes, depending on the ingenuity of the inventor. Many in China call these vehicles and their permutations "inkfish," because of the large amounts of thick, black smoke that spew from their exhaust.

The joint venture in Hengyang, our second after Anhui, ran smoothly from September of 1994 until 2003. But after receiving Chen's letter, we now had to figure out how to replace departing general manager Li.

Back in Beijing, Henry and I made the official call to Li. I told him I'd received the letter from Chen, that I wanted him to stay on as a consultant for three years despite his retirement as general manager, and that I would come to Hengyang the next week to discuss a successor.

As always, all of this was through a translator—Henry, in this case. Only rarely do I get to speak English with people when I am outside Beijing, and that certainly wasn't going to happen with anybody in Hengyang. Our factory there is in a remote location, and we're still one of the few foreign investors in the 7.2-million-person city, so English capability isn't very widespread. On top of that, Li's accent is so thick that even many of our Chinese managers have a tough time understanding him. I can remember one meeting in particular when Li gave a presentation and whoever was translating had to stop, get further clarification from Li, and then get help from random people in the audience just to be able to translate what Li was saying into English.

The next week, with no idea what to expect, Henry and I went to Hengyang as promised. Since there are no hotels near the factory, we generally stay at one of the hotels in Hengyang City. Whichever one we select always appreciates our business. When we decided to hold one of our quarterly general managers meetings in Hengyang in 2006, the hotel manager greeted me when I arrived at the front door, gave me a bouquet of flowers, swept me past forty uniformed and clapping hotel employees (twenty to a side), and then escorted me to a large suite on one of the upper floors. Utterly overwhelmed and slightly embarrassed, I told Carleen what had happened as soon as I saw her; it turned out she'd been given the same treatment several minutes earlier. Touched by the genuine and warm welcome, we both immediately began to feel guilty that we hadn't taken the time to shake the hand of each and every staff member who had lined our path to the elevator.

Our factory in Hengyang is located at the edge of the city. To get there, our vehicle had to crawl for several kilometers on a road with outdoor markets and shopping stalls on the right, and the Xiang River, which cuts through Hunan Province running from south to north, on the left. As you turn into the factory's entrance, you travel about one hundred yards with tall walls and buildings on either side, almost as if you're going through a tunnel. When you emerge, the administration building is off to the left, and the factory is straight ahead. Though many of the factory buildings themselves date back to the 1980s, all of our buildings in Hengyang have been redone and we've paid close attention to the landscaping. It's a good-looking and clean factory, well-kept and positive, and it creates a very good impression when you pull in.

"Electing" a General Manager in China

When we arrived, Henry and I went straight to the large conference room that had been home to so many of our meetings over the years. For as long as I can remember, the administrative staff in Hengyang have been anxious to please. When we first walk in, without fail, somebody will immediately offer us coffee, made from small packets containing a powder mix of instant coffee, sweetener, and cream. (When we visit, we are probably the only coffee drinkers in Hengyang.) No sooner do I sit down than a hot cup of sweet and light coffee is put in front of me. If I'm not careful, the enthusiastic staff will ply me with more sweetened coffee in one meeting than I would normally drink in a year. There's usually an ample supply of pistachios and bananas on the conference table, too. You can always tell when we've been there for a while by the piles of banana peels and empty pistachio shells that cover most every part of the table.

While we were settling in, Chen and Li came into the room, Li with a big smile on his face, as always. Li is perhaps the easiest person whom I have ever dealt with in China. Even with Chinese who are friends or allies, having to carry on a discussion through translators can be cumbersome and difficult, robbing the situation of the easy banter that makes establishing relationships that much easier. With Zhang in Langfang, the need for translation had made a difficult situation worse. With Li, it was never that way. He was always upbeat and positive, which needed no translation whatsoever. He lit up the room with his presence and never made me feel that he wanted anything from me, even when he did. Chen, with his ruddy complexion, was pleasant and always smiling, but he was quiet and didn't wear his heart on his sleeve like Li did, so it was sometimes a bit more difficult to understand exactly where he was coming from. Chen and Li had been partners for ages and had a great deal of respect for each other, but it was clear in this matter that Chen was acting on behalf of the Chinese partner and the local government, implementing the personnel policies of the Communist Party.

After Chen and Li sat down, we got right to the matter at hand. Taking the lead, I opened up the conversation, with Henry translating. I told them that I wished Li would stay, but that I understood he was of retirement age and that it was time for him to step down.

"I've asked Mr. Li to stay on for an additional three years as a consultant to the company, which he has agreed to do," I told Chen. I looked over at Li, who was nodding in agreement. Then I looked back at Chen. "If this is acceptable to the local government and the Chinese partner," I said, "then I will agree to his retirement as general manager."

Chen indicated that this was acceptable and mentioned as an aside that he, too, would retire the following year. (So much for our earlier worries of intrigue.) Very quickly, that part of the conversation was closed.

On to the real question. "Now," I said, "we have to turn to the issue of naming a successor." This was the million-dollar moment. Looking around the room and trying to convey my open-mindedness (and not my apprehension), I asked calmly, "How do you suggest we go about this, Mr. Li?"

Several years before, when he'd first mentioned

retiring, Li had told me that he had two candidates in mind to succeed him. I knew both and would have been happy with either. Under Li's leadership, there seemed to be an endless supply of qualified managers, one better than the next. But we had never discussed which of the two candidates he actually preferred for the job, so I was pretty curious to hear what Li had to say.

Li stepped in, but he didn't name either of the two candidates as his preference. Instead, he said something that absolutely shocked me. "I suggest," he said matter-of-factly, "that we put the matter to a vote."

What? I wasn't sure that Henry had translated correctly, or that I had heard him quite right. The management team was going to *elect* a general manager? In all my years in both the United States and China, I had never heard of such a thing. And even beyond the astonishing novelty of the concept, I started to worry that doing something so unprecedented would result in just the kind of long, drawn-out process that I'd hoped to avoid.

Li then shocked me for a second time. "Do you want to do it now?" he asked.

A bit at a loss for words, all I could muster at this point was an amused "Sure." What else was there to say?

"Then let's go into the meeting room," Li said. "The management team is waiting."

As we entered the room, all of the one-hundred-plus managers were already at their places, sitting in absolute dead silence. (I have no idea how long they'd been there waiting for us.) We entered and took our seats at a long, raised table in front, with Chen on my left, Li on my right, and Henry at the end. When we were all settled in, Chen got up, went to the podium, and announced that Li was retiring and that we were there today to select a successor.

"The names of the deputy general managers have been placed on the ballots that you have in front of you," he said. "At the end of the meeting, you will make your selection and drop the ballot in the box at the front of the room.

"But first," Chen continued, "I would like to ask Mr. Jack to say a few words."

(In China, the first name is the surname, just the opposite of the United States, so that's the one people use. I am known throughout China either as "Chairman Jack," a reference to my position with ASIMCO and all of our companies in China, or as "Mr. Jack." This makes everybody's life a bit easier. Every Chinese person I have met who has attempted to pronounce "Perkowski" has as much trouble with that one as I have with many Chinese surnames.)

With Henry translating through a separate microphone, I provided a brief update on ASIMCO, discussed how the Hengyang fuel operations were vital to our business, and spoke of Li's great achievements during his long tenure as general manager. As I was speaking, I looked around the room and recognized many of the managers present. I also saw many I didn't know, because the management group was a good mix of seasoned managers in their forties and young up-and-comers in their late twenties and thirties. I also noticed a small group of about a half-dozen senior citizens, both men and women. I later learned that they were retired members of the management team who had been invited to witness the meeting. Leave it to Li to make sure that all interested parties were included, in what seemed more like a large family gathering than a meeting of top-level management.

Li then addressed the group, touching on the challenges facing the business, and talked about how much he'd enjoyed being the general manager. He closed by saying that he was going to enjoy having more time to spend with his grandson, a sentiment that was met by a warm round of applause from his audience.

Once the speeches were finished, the managers filled out their ballots and deposited them in the box at the front of the room. After about ten minutes it was over and the room was empty. Li suggested that we go back to the conference room and await the results.

As we sat there, Li explained his reasoning. "If we had just selected a general manager," he said, "there would be others in the organization who believed there was a more deserving candidate. The new person would need to spend a certain amount of time reuniting the factory behind his leadership. By including all of the key managers in the selection process, the new general manager can begin with a united factory."

As I listened, I couldn't help but marvel at his wisdom. More had happened in twenty minutes than I could have imagined possible. I doubt that Li had ever read a text-book on modern management, but he instinctively recognized that if you trust people and involve them in the decision making, they'll not only be more likely to make the right decision but they'll also own whatever decision is made.

After about twenty minutes, a manager came in with the results. Fan Jiang, one of the two potential successors Li had named several years before, was the clear winner. He had received more than 60 percent of the votes, with the runner-up getting only a bit more than 20 percent. Li said he wasn't surprised. Fan's father had worked in the factory, and Fan had started working there at the age of seventeen. He had moved up steadily in the organization, had headed up both the sales and manufacturing divisions, and was generally well liked. (Li had established a practice of rotating his key managers among different departments to give them experience in all key areas of the business, a practice that Fan has continued.)

I turned to Li and asked, "Mr. Li, tell me. Did you know that Fan would get the most votes?"

Li just looked at me and smiled.

Fan's name was submitted to the company's board of directors as the nominee for general manager, and the board unanimously approved his appointment. It was the right choice. Fan has performed brilliantly, not missing a beat when he took over—just as Li had predicted. Our fuel business in Hengyang remains one of our best performers. At a time when China is searching for new, more affordable answers to the question of how to meet emission requirements, Fan has promoted a spirit of innovation in the company. Working closely with our team at the Beijing headquarters, Fan has been able to keep up a steady supply of new products to meet the ever-changing needs of our customers.

Keys to Success

As I look back on the management changes at the other ASIMCO operating units, the effortless and harmonious way that we achieved change at Hengyang stands out in sharp contrast to our efforts elsewhere. While I would like to think that this was the result of the brilliant way in which we developed the relationship with our Chinese partner and the local government, I know this isn't true. As has been the case in all of our joint ventures, we had some rocky moments in Hengyang, many due to our own inexperience in China and to the naïveté of some of our senior managers. The reason these rocky moments didn't cause permanent damage to the relationship was because of Li. Once we formed the joint venture, he decided that he was going to do everything in his power to make it work. With Li, there was never a doubt that the good of the joint venture came first.

The three hurdles that we had to clear to make management changes at the other joint ventures never came into play at Hengyang. Li developed a succession plan, so finding a suitable successor was never an issue.

Because the joint venture always came first, there were no vested interests to overcome. And it didn't matter what the contract said about who nominated the general manager: mutual recognition by both shareholders that each only wanted the best for the joint venture meant that the question was never even raised.

Perhaps Li had such an enlightened attitude because he had personally built the company and wanted to see it succeed and prosper after he left. Perhaps he knew how much the local area and the employees of the factory and their families depended on the future growth of the business for their well-being. Only Li knows the real reason. But to me, it all went so well because Li is an individual with the highest level of integrity. He took his responsibilities to those who depended on his leadership seriously. I was very fortunate to have him as part of our company.

Chapter 11

Building for the Long Term

China Is a Marathon, Not a Sprint

"May you live in exciting times" is an ancient Chinese blessing that can also be a curse, depending on the context. The challenges we faced when starting our company certainly made the first part of our trip an exciting one. Once we got Chinese managers onboard who would follow our lead, though, we no longer had to operate in daily "crisis management" mode. After five long years of development, we could finally take a harder look at what was happening around us and begin to make some sense of where China and the automotive industry were headed. The challenges ahead, as we position ASIMCO to compete both in China and in the global marketplace, will be somewhat different, but the ride promises to be no less exciting.

From a strictly personal point of view, Beijing during the late 1990s really began to develop into an international city, complete with cultural and sports events, restaurants, and nightlife. Creature comforts improved, making daily life less of a grind, and the tremendous investments that China made in its infrastructure were clearly visible. Getting around became easier day by day. After more than twenty years of rapid development, much of it with China's economy growing at 10 percent or more each year, the outward appearance of the country and its people began to change. In both professional and personal terms, the idea of truly building a long-term business in China—of actually running and finishing that marathon—became a real possibility.

Giving Everyone an ASIMCO T-shirt

The process we went through between 1997 and 1999, when we brought fifty or more New China managers onto our bench, was a necessary first step to get the company on track. But for the longer term, we needed to unite all of the new managers, plus our existing managers, behind a common goal. To stand on our own globally, we also needed to implement all of the tools of modern management: performance management, leadership development, lean manufacturing, Six Sigma, quality management, and so on. The next steps of our development toward these goals began in 1999.

While we had our core management group in place by then, we didn't have a common culture. Most of our existing managers came from backgrounds with state-owned companies, and our newer hires brought with them the views, management approaches, and corporate cultures of their previous employers. As I liked to put it at the time, the players on our team were each wearing a different-color T-shirt. Some had a Delphi T-shirt, others had a General Motors T-shirt, and still others had a GE T-shirt. I wanted to give them all an ASIMCO T-shirt. This meant we had to define ASIMCO's culture by articulating our vision, our core values, and our long-term goal.

During the last six months of 1999, we undertook a process to do just that. To be truly effective, a company's managers have to be empowered to make decisions. This is only possible if they identify with and buy in to the goals of the entire organization, and if they can put their individual effort into the context of the company's overall strategy. I wanted to be able to lead our Chinese managers, not manage them, which meant that we had to be able to agree on and articulate what the company was all about. Beyond being a collection of individuals and factories, what were we as an organization trying to accomplish?

We thought this task was so important that we hired Hewitt Associates, a well-known consulting company, to help. I'd never been through an exercise like this before, and I have to admit that I was somewhat skeptical at the start.

In our initial meeting, Marybeth Robb, Hewitt's lead facilitator, explained that a company's "vision, values, and goal" wasn't something that I should push down as the chairman and CEO of the company. If I wanted the entire organization to genuinely embrace our mission, she counseled, everybody had to own it, and that meant it had to come from the bottom up. She seemed to know what she was talking about, so I went along.

The goal with Hewitt was to try to define our culture.

As Marybeth explained, we were going to do that through a process of discovery. We could start by looking at why our key people had left good careers at large, successful companies to come to join this struggling upstart called ASIMCO. What did they see in the company? Was there a common thread in their thinking? What, if any, common values did they share?

The first step would be to hold a series of meetings and discussions with our key managers, beginning with Tim, Ai Jian, Michael, and me. (At the time, this constituted the top leadership of the company.) The four of us set aside an entire week for this exercise, and on the appointed Monday morning we all gathered in a conference room at Hewitt's offices in Beijing.

Marybeth spoke first and outlined the schedule for the week. We would start with each of us telling the group why we had come to China and joined ASIMCO. We'd then move on to various role-playing exercises, and at the end of the week we would each be asked to give our retirement speech, describing our accomplishments and what ASIMCO would look like in ten or twenty years.

My heart sank. I couldn't think of anything more corny. It was hard for me to relate to such touchy-feely human resource practices. I'm generally uncomfortable discussing my personal feelings and thoughts and doing things like role-playing in an artificial setting. Giving a retirement speech to Tim, Michael, Ai Jian, Marybeth, and her assistant at the end of a week in a conference room seemed utterly absurd.

I went along. But when I led off with my story of how I'd gotten to China, and Marybeth started diagramming what I was saying on big sheets of white paper that she then taped onto the walls of the conference room, I nearly lost it.

By the end of the week, though, I have to confess that I was converted. Despite my initial skepticism, it was easily the most important week that we had spent at the company. Encouraged by what had happened, we rolled out the process to the rest of the organization. In the following weeks and months, we had a three-day meeting with a wider group of key managers, and then a one-day meeting for an even larger group. We wanted as many of our managers as possible to participate.

Overall, the meetings gave us a common way to think about ASIMCO and created a framework through which we could understand the kind of person who stood the best chance to succeed with us. Participants were asked to describe why they joined ASIMCO and what they liked and disliked about the company. They were asked to tell a success story, but then also to tell a story about an event at the company that didn't end quite so well. Like us, the other participants were asked to give their retirement speech, forcing them to envision what the company might look like in twenty or thirty years.

From all of these discussions, we determined that ASIMCO's managers actually liked the idea that we weren't a well-established organization, and that what we were doing was "creating" something. Moreover, they liked that what we were creating was a "truly global company," not just one that aspired to be the best in China. They also liked the fact that ASIMCO was "unique"—we didn't accept everything as it was in China, but we also didn't say that everything in China was bad and then seek to impose some solution that had worked well in another part of the world. What we were doing instead was picking and choosing, "combining the best in China with the best from the rest of the world." From this came our Core Purpose:

> *To create a truly global company which is unique because of its ability to combine the best in China with the best from the rest of the world.*

When our vision was articulated in this way, the reaction from our managers was immediate. "Aha," you could almost hear them say. "This is why I get up every morning and come to work for ASIMCO." It truly excited them, and I believe it's one of the reasons our management turnover is so low. Our managers and employees believe that the company is doing something unique and important. It's not just a job. In China or anywhere else, people don't simply work for money. They want to feel that the organization they work for has some higher purpose, a mission that they can identify with.

From the stories of success and failure at the company, we began to identify the core values that most people shared, what worked and didn't work. We determined that the managers who were most successful at ASIMCO were those who believed in *teamwork*; accepted *personal responsibility*; understood the need for *continuous improvement*; had joined ASIMCO because of the *opportunity*; and were attracted by *significant goals*. These five values then formed ASIMCO's Core Values, which, along with the Core Purpose, began to define our culture. Now we knew what to look for when hiring or promoting our employees.

Finally, a group of our managers, after several days of discussion, determined that the company's long-term goal should be *To be recognized as the global leader in all of our products*. Over a two-day period, we wrestled over every word in that sentence. We discarded a "number one" or "number two" kind of goal, because it's quite possible, given the size of the China market, to be the biggest but not the best. We said that we wanted to be recognized as the best by industry experts, our customers, you name it— a much higher standard. We wanted to be *the* leader, not just *a* leader, and we wanted our leadership to be global, not merely in China. And last, this statement meant that we wanted to be the leader in all of our products—not some, not most, but all.

Long-term goals like this are meant to be difficult and nearly unattainable. They're meant to drive an organization over a twenty- to thirty-year period of time. Even I would admit, though, that in the context of a large, well-developed, mature global industry like automotive components, accomplishing that kind of objective across a broad range of products as an industry newcomer is an almost impossible task. I don't know whether we're going to make it, but we're going to try.

What makes it all possible is that the future growth of the Chinese automotive industry, with its cost, market, and technological benefits, adds a new set of variables and realities to the global equation. Given China's potential to become the largest automotive market in the world and the substantial presence in China that ASIMCO has already established, this goal, while still lofty, becomes achievable. The relentless pursuit of the goal of global leadership is now a key motivating factor and driving force for the entire organization.

In order to get everybody behind us, we then communicated what we'd done to all levels of the company. We handed out cards with our "vision, values, and goal" printed in both Chinese and English, and we put signs up at all of our factories and offices with the same message. No matter which ASIMCO factory you visit, or whether you're in our offices in the United States, the United Kingdom, or Japan, the first thing you will see is the plaque with our vision, values, and goal proudly stated.

With the right people on the team and everybody united behind a common vision, we were then able to implement the third step in the process of building a local management team: introducing modern management tools and concepts like performance management, leadership development, incentive systems based on value creation, quality systems, and lean manufacturing and Six

Sigma programs. In many of the books and articles written on reforming Chinese managements, there's often much discussion about installing stock option and other incentive schemes, or about the importance of implementing lean management systems and robust quality programs. In our experience, this last step becomes much easier to take once the right people are onboard and united. We tried to install some of these programs early on in our development, but only had limited success; we didn't have the right people. There's always going to be some resistance to change, but we've found that the implementation of key initiatives across the company runs a lot more smoothly now that we've taken the first and second steps. Trying to implement step three before steps one and two are complete is a lot like putting the cart before the horse.

Mutual Trust

Through all of this, I learned a number of things. First, it was refreshing to discover that our Chinese employees could become truly loyal to the company, beyond what loyalty could be bought with money. Given the strong nationalistic tendencies and inherent suspicion of foreigners in China, I wondered whether we'd ever accomplish that here. Though we're foreign-owned and have made a lot of typical foreigner mistakes, our managers and employees have given us the benefit of the doubt. Once they were empowered and knew that we valued their input, they began to think of ASIMCO as their company.

I also learned that, in China, trust is the most important thing that you can give to an employee. If they believe that you trust them, their loyalty to the company skyrockets. Many companies here will tell you that they employ local managers, and that might be true. The key question, though, is "What are the local managers empowered to do?" In other words, "How much do you trust them?"

The analogy that I use is of a parent whose son or daughter first gets his or her driver's license. Inevitably, that first Saturday night rolls around and they ask for the keys to the car. As you reach into your pocket for the keys, you really don't want to hand them over. A million concerns race through your head. Will they drive carefully? How do I know they won't drink? And even if they don't, how can I know that their friends won't? The answer is that you don't.

But you realize that you're never going to get anywhere if you can't trust your kid. You have to think logically, not emotionally. After all, you've raised your child to be a responsible adult and to exercise good judgment, so why not trust him or her? You hold your breath, but you hand over the keys.

With your Chinese managers, you have to do the same. You literally have to hand over the keys, and trust them. If you can do that, your trust will be returned ten times over.

One of the best programs we've instituted is the ASIMCO Leadership Development Program (ALDP). Every year, each general manager nominates one or two up-and-comers from each operating unit, and we select up to thirty Future Leaders of ASIMCO to participate in a one-year program during which they're taught various leadership skills. Activities include Outward Bound–style teamwork-building exercises, lectures and classes by both inside and outside experts, meetings with the more experienced general managers, and projects that draw upon their leadership skills. It's not an expensive program to run, but it tells our key managers that we think highly of them, that we're willing to invest in their future, and that we trust them.

Truth be told, I also had my doubts about the Outward Bound–type exercises. I wasn't sure how that kind of thing would translate in China. In fact, it's probably the most popular part of the curriculum. The highlight of every program is when the pictures of our employees doing "trust falls," climbing vertical walls, or helping a colleague over a barrier are displayed on the screen with everyone watching.

One of the real benefits of ALDP, which we've since supplemented with an ASIMCO Management Development Program for promising managers who are still early in their careers, is that it has enabled us to fill new management needs internally. We no longer have to take the risky step of recruiting from the outside to fill vacancies. In mid-2006, we completed a joint venture with

Phillips & Temro to make air intake heaters in China. When it came time to pick a general manager for the joint venture, we posted the position internally and seven managers applied. Gary Edwards, the CEO of Phillips & Temro, and Ted Winterrowd, head of our fuel systems business unit, then interviewed each candidate and selected one. The fact that we first look internally to fill new management positions makes it clear that there is an opportunity for everybody to grow at ASIMCO—which, in our experience, is the best way to retain employees.

Building a Hybrid Organization

If ASIMCO's first ten years was about learning how to do business in China, then our next ten years will be about building on our base here to create the truly global company that is a vital part of our vision. As we move forward, we'll be forming alliances that provide technology and help us to attain global leadership in all of our products, and we'll be adding individuals who can bring a global perspective to all of our businesses. We will truly be combining the best in China with the best from the rest of the world. And, as we do so, we'll be creating a true "hybrid organization": the local managers will play the leading role in managing the company's operations in China, adapting Western management practices to the unique circumstances here, while the Western managers will determine how best to integrate our China operations with the global economy. Having gone through the

1994–1997 period with Don and his team of expatriates, we've got a good understanding of what does and doesn't work on both fronts.

A good example of the hybrid approach is Ted Winterrowd. One of our core businesses is diesel fuel injection systems, so we've always had some of our best managers in that business. As China raises its emissions standards and existing technologies become obsolete, we know that we need to develop a long-term business and technology strategy—which, by definition, has to be a global strategy. Ted had previously served as the head of manufacturing engineering for the diesel fuel system unit at Cummins, one of the world's largest diesel engine companies, and he'd been exposed to ASIMCO and our fuel business in China through his work there. When Ted suggested to me that he might be willing to consider taking early retirement in order to work with us in this area, I was thrilled. The decision to bring Ted's thirty-seven years of experience onboard was an easy one to make.

Ted and his wife, Cindy, joined us and moved to China in August 2004. It has been quite an adventure for both of them. Cindy quickly made many friends in Beijing, and Ted has been thrilled to have the opportunity to pass along his years of experience and knowledge to a group of managers who are eager to learn. From ASIMCO's point of view, Ted has made an important contribution to the company. He is a great teacher who has helped our fuel managers to improve their operations and think through their global strategy. He is hardworking and has a roll-up-your-sleeves attitude that has earned him a great deal of respect from everyone at the company. He promotes teamwork and is a consummate professional, and nobody doubts his knowledge of the diesel fuel injection business. In short, Ted is the type of expatriate manager that works in China: knowledgeable, hardworking, patient, and professional.

GIVEN THE LARGE gap between manufacturing practices and technology levels in China and the West, I thought initially that our Chinese managers would more easily accept advice from a foreign expert, as opposed to someone from China. My instinct was that they might not feel that they could learn as much from someone whose only experience had been in their own country. I couldn't have been more wrong. Whether Chinese or foreign, anyone who hopes to lead or teach Chinese managers had better be at the top of their game, because they'll be held to a high standard. I've found that Chinese managers respect specific expertise and somebody who can show them how to do it on the shop floor. While foreign experts may be knowledgeable, oftentimes they don't understand that circumstances are different in China, and their advice isn't viewed as sufficiently practical. The advantage of Chinese experts is that they understand the way it works in China and can offer very practical, usable suggestions. (The fact that these experts can communicate more easily is also a benefit.) We're always interested in professionals like Ted who can bring the global perspective to our Chinese managers, but we also hire as many good Chinese experts as we can.

Over the years, I've learned that, with Chinese and foreign experts alike, it's a big mistake to promote their credentials up front. In the beginning, when we would bring on a particularly well-qualified person, I would make a bigger deal than I should have in announcing them and describing their qualifications and accomplishments. I feel sorry for the people I did this to, because I had just made their job that much harder. Given the "show me" attitude in China, I had just raised everybody's expectations, and now the bar was even higher. Today when we bring new people in, we do it in a very low-key way. To set them up for success, we find some way for them to help one or more of our Chinese managers. Once they do, word gets around quickly and their credibility within the organization builds.

APART FROM DAY-TO-DAY operating management, a good board of directors, or an understanding boss back home, can be extremely important to success here. In early 1998, the General Electric Pension Trust (GEPT) became a shareholder of the ASIMCO management company, and I benefited greatly from the experience they brought to the table. Before GEPT joined as a shareholder, I had no one at the board level who even had the capacity and patience to listen—let alone offer advice—as I struggled through the operating issues in China.

When GEPT became a shareholder, Jim Mara, the investment officer, promised me that he would find two experienced retired GE executives to serve on our board of advisers. True to his word, he brought Jack Pfeiffer and Paul Dawson to our board. Jack was a very experienced manager who had come up through the finance ranks and played a major role in succession planning at GE corporate before retiring as a vice president; Paul had run GE plastics in Europe and had also been a senior manager in the aircraft business.

Though GEPT didn't participate in the restructuring of the ASIMCO entities in early 2004, they were a proponent of the transformation of the company from an investment to an operating company structure. In structuring our board of directors with the new shareholder group led by Key Principal Partners in February of that year, we were careful to include both financial and operating experience. Rudy Schlais, a longtime member of the General Motors management team who established Shanghai GM and ran GM Asia, is a key director. Rudy's experience in the industry generally, and in Asia and China in particular, is invaluable to me and the rest of the management team as we build our business.

I would be the very last one to tell you that we have all the answers with respect to building a good local management team in China. Every day brings new challenges, and every day we learn something new. We've been through a great deal, though, and because we're a Chinese company based in China, we've had to rely primarily on the resources available to us here. In general, we have low turnover, at both the top management and operating levels, and our employees exhibit a high degree of engagement with the company. It was precisely this high level of engagement that enabled us to be named one of the ten best employers in China in both 2001 and 2005, the two years in which we participated.

In the end, any organization, no matter where it is located, is only as good as its people. China has an abundance of human capital, waiting to be tapped. The companies that do the best job in developing this talent will be the ones who enjoy long-term success in China.

Chapter 12

Decentralization and China's Local Governments

The Mountains Are High and the Emperor Is Far Away

In September of 2003, a group of senior marketing executives from Microsoft spent a week in China, trying to learn everything they could about the country and where it's headed. They asked me to speak at their executive luncheon in Beijing and to pass along whatever insights I could about doing business here.

Their schedule was tight and I only had twenty minutes, so I thought about the two or three things I could tell them that they might not have heard before and that would have the biggest impact. As always, I spoke about the importance of developing a local management team, and also about the different cost perspective in China. (This will be discussed in the next chapter.) The third topic I decided to cover was decentralization.

When I started in China, my instinct was to try to find a central government organization that could open up the whole country to us. I gradually, painstakingly learned that this isn't the way China works. Most things get done at the local level. Nobody likes it if you go above them to exert pressure, and local government officials in China are no different. They tend to react negatively to pressure or guidance from Beijing or the provincial authorities. I had made this mistake often enough and hadn't fully appreciated how decentralized China actually is until I had been here awhile. I thought this was important to pass along to the Microsoft execs.

At the end of the luncheon, the senior person in the delegation summed up his reaction.

"In our industry," he said, "intellectual property considerations are so important that we tend to spend all of our time working with officials in Beijing. If I understand your point, Jack, we should spend more time developing solid relationships at the regional and local levels."

That was precisely my point, and it's as true today as ever.

Due to its size, and a host of natural barriers such as rivers, mountains, and deserts, China has always had strong regional influences. The warlords of old and the local government officials of today have historically enjoyed a great deal of autonomy. "The mountains are high and the emperor is far away" is an ancient Chinese saying that sums up the way in which the country has been governed over the years.

The Reason China Creates Overcapacity

Understanding the decentralized nature of China's economy and government can provide some important clues about the way the country works, as I found several years ago when trying to make some sense of the expansion of China's steel industry. In the spring of 2004, I received a phone call from Keith Bradsher, a reporter at the *New York Times*, who wanted my input on a story he was writing about the rapid rise in global steel prices and what it might mean for the industry's future. I told him what I thought, and in the final version of the story, he quoted me as saying that the world would soon be "swimming in steel."

My view was at odds with the other predictions he'd been getting, so Keith was only too happy to include it. The commonly held view at the time was that demand in China—already one of the major consumers of steel—was expected to remain strong, so the world could count on tight supply and high prices for a long time to come.

Steel prices had begun to rise dramatically in 2003, as had the prices of almost every other commodity. This was due in large part to the strong demand in China, but also to strong and growing economies around the world. Steel and commodity analysts were talking about the "perfect storm" that had been brewing in the preceding years, resulting in the unprecedented high prices. The last time this had happened was the 1970s, when strong growth in Japan added to global demand and increased competition for commodities. Because China is so much bigger than Japan, the fear was that the addition of Chinese demand would have an even larger, longer-term impact. Stable prices since the 1980s had resulted in low levels of capacity expansion in the major commodities, and with the U.S., European, and Japanese economies all going strong, the common wisdom was that something would have to give.

I didn't think that any of the steel analysts had taken into account China's tendency to create overcapacity, so I developed a bit of a contrarian view. I'd seen firsthand how quickly overcapacity had developed in other industries—notably motorcycles, cement, and beer—and believed it would happen once again in steel. Despite the higher level of demand in China, I believed that the forces at work would eventually cause the amount of steel produced in China to flood not only the China market but the global markets as well.

My views were further confirmed in the fall of 2004, when I was invited by the mayor of Hengyang to see some of the projects that were springing to life in his city.

One of the companies we visited was a steel tube factory that had begun an aggressive capacity expansion earlier that year. The manager giving us the tour confidently predicted that, once the expansion was completed, his company would be the largest producer of steel tube in all of Asia. When I asked him when the plant would be in full operation, he told me mid-2005.

With only the steel frames in place, this was pretty hard to imagine. In any other country in the world, there'd be no way to meet this deadline. But this was

China, and having seen how quickly factories get built, I didn't doubt his prediction for a minute.

My analysis of what would happen to the steel industry in China turned out to be correct. China's steel production, which was almost 130 million tons a year in 2000, had grown to 270 million tons by 2004. According to my sources, China's steelmaking capacity was expected to grow to 350 million tons by the end of 2005. Ultimately, steel capacity in China exceeded all previous forecasts, ending up at almost 530 million tons before all was said and done.

With my dissenting opinion about steel supply now out there in the *Times*, I started to receive a great number of inquiries about why I'd made the prediction I did. After all, industry analysts saw the same increase in China's steelmaking capacity, but their conclusion generally was that China's efforts to rein in the economy through restrictions on lending would put a brake on all of these new projects. From a pure, national-industrial-political point of view, it made no sense for China to continue to invest so much capital in additional steel capacity. But China doesn't work like that.

Due to China's legacy of central planning and state ownership of production facilities, the perception that China's economy is tightly controlled by Beijing is quite common. In fact, though, the reality is quite different, and China's economy, government, legal system, banking system—you name it—are actually highly decentralized. Beijing is engaged in a constant struggle to exert some measure of control over what happens at the local level.

With regard to steel, the reality is that the decisions to increase capacity were being made individually, at the local level, by hundreds of governments across the country. Capacity was not being created as a result of some edict from Beijing. To the contrary, the central government was alarmed at what was being done and stepped in from time to time to stop particularly flagrant abuses of authority, like it did when it shut down a huge steel project in Jiangsu Province. Trying to exert that kind of control throughout China, however, is a bit like the legendary Dutch boy putting his finger in a hole in the dike.

The dynamics of decentralization in China work like this:

In the mid-1990s, China had a problem raising enough money to fund the daily operating needs of its government. This was true at the central government level, but it was particularly acute at the provincial and local levels. The state-owned enterprises required more and more capital and couldn't be counted on for cash. Though China did have a corporate income tax, the lack of profits from these enterprises, and also of a strong enforcement mechanism, meant that funding from this source was also unreliable.

To solve this issue, China instituted a 17 percent value-added tax (VAT) on most manufactured products in 1994. Under this system, VAT is levied on goods as they move from the raw material stage through the various processing stages and then on to the consumer. At

ASIMCO, for example, we buy raw materials like steel and aluminum. When we convert them into a finished product, which we then sell to our customer, we take the difference between our sales price and all of the costs incurred to make the product—the "value" we've "added"—and add 17 percent of it to our sales price. In this way, 17 percent of the value added at every step of the way is collected continually throughout China, providing a steady stream of revenues for the government to use to pay its bills.

The VAT system solved the government's revenue problem beautifully. But it also created a strong local development incentive, because local governments typically keep 25 percent of the VAT collected from companies in their areas. With this system in place, local governments are indifferent about whether a company is a wholly foreign-owned entity, a joint venture, a state-owned enterprise, or a private company. Any company that invests in the city generates sales and VAT and provides revenue to the local government.

The development incentive created by VAT is one of the reasons why China is probably one of the easiest places in the world to start a business. In any one of the more than eight thousand economic development zones across the country, all you have to do is meet with the head of the zone and deliver a feasibility study for a wholly owned enterprise; within thirty days, you'll get formal government approval to establish your business. The head of the zone will also be more than happy to put you in touch with a developer who'll buy the land and build the building to your specifications, and then lease it to you.

In general, having local governments highly incentivized to develop their economies is a good thing. But when you combine those powerful incentives with the overall lack of separation of power in China, the dynamic for creating overcapacity begins to emerge. Local officials don't have absolute control over the local bank, or even the local branches of the big state-owned banks, but they do have tremendous influence on what companies receive loans. When a commodity like steel is in high demand, any local company or entrepreneur interested in building a steel plant could expect to get favorable treatment from the local government, including bank financing. Over the past ten years, it has been this precise dynamic that has led to the overcapacity in motorcycles, cement, and beer that I mentioned earlier. As demand for these products increased, every city and town in China wanted to get into the act and have its own factory. Similarly, when demand for steel, and steel price levels, began rising in 2003, the stage was set for China's unprecedented capacity expansion.

As the demand in China started to create supply pressures around the world, I began to receive invitations to attend breakfasts, lunches, and other meetings with analysts from Wall Street who were visiting China. They wanted to determine the sustainability of the country's high demand firsthand.

On September 16, 2003, I had breakfast in Beijing

with a dozen investors and analysts organized by CLSA, a Hong Kong–based securities firm. This particular group, which consisted of about twelve analysts representing various investment funds, was looking at all commodities, including steel, and they'd already had a number of meetings in China by the time I met with them.

One analyst told me they'd spoken to a number of different companies in China that were claiming to be making one- to two-year paybacks on their investments in steel production.

"Could this possibly be true?" he asked. "Or did we just lose something in translation?"

As I listened to their questions and stories, I knew two things. First, while I'm no steel expert, I did grow up in Pittsburgh. Steelmaking is not a one- to two-year payback industry. Second, having been in China for a while, though, I could understand how this might happen. In the face of increasing demand and a sure profit in steel, a local company decides to build a mill and commits a certain amount of equity, which amounts to a relatively small percentage of the required capital. Because the local government wants the mill and the VAT it will generate, it arranges for the local bank to provide the bulk of the financing through bank loans. The factory goes up quickly and begins producing steel in a market where prices are still high and climbing. On a relatively small amount of equity, the returns on equity are high.

But, of course, this scenario leads to more capacity, and ultimately to overcapacity. As more supply comes on stream, or demand weakens—or both—prices peak, and then tumble. In more-developed markets, this would lead to an industry shakeout, capacity would be closed down, and demand/supply would reach some kind of equilibrium. Not in China. With little enforcement of creditor rights, and with everyone incentivized to keep producing (and generating VAT), this capacity never closes.

Instead, the plant churns out product at ever diminishing prices. As long as it can sell at a price equal to the variable costs of production, it keeps producing. Even if the mill can't cover these variable costs, the bank may well keep lending in order to help the company cover its operating losses.

As a result of the process that began in 2003, China now has 530 million tons of steel capacity, almost one-third the total steelmaking capacity in the world. China's estimated excess capacity of 100 million tons is as large as any single country's capacity. In a January 29, 2007, article entitled "China's Steel Woes," the *Wall Street Journal* pointed out that there are somewhere between three hundred and one thousand steel companies in China; nobody knows precisely how many there really are. Decentralization, and the inefficient use of capital, has led to yet another fragmented industry with over-capacity in China. The *Journal* reported that Baosteel, China's largest steel company, has just 5 percent of the market, and the top ten companies account for just 14 percent of total production. The central government is now trying to slow investment in the industry and to consolidate production. If the past is any guide, local resistance will continue to frustrate its efforts.

What does it all mean? Knowing that this is the way China works can provide insights into other industries besides steel. It means that you have to be careful when planning new capacity additions and determining which products to manufacture here. If you pick an industry where the barriers to entry are low, and where capacity can be added cheaply and quickly, it'll be impossible to attain adequate pricing. Rather than producing these products, it may be smarter to take advantage of the overcapacity and low prices and source these products from China. The trick in China is to make products that can't be easily made by others, for whatever reason. Generally, these will be products with a higher technology content that are difficult to manufacture and can't be easily duplicated. While it may seem difficult, it's surprising how many products there actually are that fit this description. It just takes a bit of analysis to identify the right ones.

Local Governments: Who Are They?

Since much of a company's fate can rest in the hands of local government officials, it's important to know as much as you can about them and how to deal with them.

I often amuse my government hosts by telling them how much has changed in China over the past fifteen years. "When I first came here," I say, "I was always younger than the mayors and party secretaries I would meet as I traveled around the country. Now, I'm always older."

Granted, I've gotten older since my first trip to China, but the more important point is that the local government officials are now younger and better educated than they were when I first arrived. China has implemented its own version of the New China management strategy with a good deal of success.

The central government continues to battle issues of personal greed, corruption, and abuse of power at the local level, but the local government officials I've met and done business with over the years have generally impressed me. Nearly all have traveled to other parts of the world, and many have studied (or at least attended some type of training) in the United States or other Western countries. The up-and-comers tend to move to different assignments every three or four years. The more officials move around, the more varied their experience and the less likely it is that they become entrenched in their positions or develop strong vested interests.

One of the biggest lessons we learned, as I explained about our run-in with Mr. Fang in Chapter 8, is that maintaining good relationships with the local government is absolutely vital. Local officials can help you smooth over many of the daily difficulties encountered in running a business, but they can also bring tax and other benefits to your company.

While it may seem like hard work, developing relationships with the local officials can be a lot of fun.

Some of the best times I've had in China are the dinners I've shared with them. I don't know where the government finds its talent, but I've rarely come across a mayor or party secretary who isn't outgoing and doesn't have a great sense of humor. Beyond the funny stories, though, is a true seriousness of purpose—to promote the economic development of their particular city. At the drop of a hat, local government officials can rattle off statistics and give you a litany of reasons to invest in their city.

One of our best relationships is with the government of Yizheng in prosperous Jiangsu Province. A city of approximately six hundred thousand, Yizheng is under the overall jurisdiction of Yangzhou, a famous city in China that is also the hometown of Jiang Zemin, the former president of China.

In 1996, we completed a joint venture with a local company in Yizheng, an entity owned by the local government, which was making piston rings. As at our diesel fuel injection plant in Hengyang, we were blessed from the start with an excellent general manager who built a good business, and a strong and deep management team in the process. Like Li Jienan, Cheng Dexing had taken over as general manager in the early 1980s and had built his company into China's leading piston ring producer by the time we signed the joint venture in 1996.

Though simple-looking in design, piston rings, which are made from either cast iron or steel, are critical to enhancing fuel economy and controlling emissions in an internal combustion engine. They fit into a groove on the outer diameter of a piston, and their primary purpose is to seal the combustion chamber. If they aren't manufactured to precise specifications, your car will produce smoke, you will get less gas mileage, and your engine will under-perform. Every year we make more than 120 million piston rings for the domestic market in China, and we are now beginning to grow our exports to the international market.

In 2006, I was invited to attend the twentieth anniversary celebration of Yizheng's status as a city. At the celebration, I was seated at a very long head table with all of the former mayors, deputy mayors, and party secretaries of Yizheng. Henry was with me, and he joked that I wasn't just the only foreigner at the table; I was also the only person who wasn't a member of the Communist Party.

But my presence at that table was of great symbolic importance to me and to ASIMCO. Since the completion of our piston ring joint venture, the Yizheng government has been extremely supportive. That support, along with the strong leadership shown by Cheng Dexing, has encouraged us to locate even more of our operations in the city. The comments about Cheng might seem gratuitous, but it happens to be true: Cheng and the local government of Yizheng represent all of the positive things China has to offer.

Over the past several years, we've expanded our piston ring business by building a new foundry; we've built a new camshaft operation in the Yangzhou (Yizheng) Automobile Industrial Park; and we also set up our joint venture with Phillips & Temro there. We've encouraged other companies, like Nippon Piston Ring and Alpha Sintered Metals, to move there as well. I always recommend that any company looking to do business in China give Yizheng a good hard look.

Over the years, we've dealt with all manner of officials in Yizheng, but one constant has been Deputy Mayor Zhou Nong Sheng, who signed our original joint venture contract and now heads up the Yangzhou (Yizheng) Automobile Industrial Park. Deputy Mayor Zhou has a background in factory management and industry and has always been sensitive to our needs. He is someone who can be counted on to come through for us when we've needed to deal with particular regulations or issues.

Another constant has been Bu Yu, the party secretary of Yizheng. He's personable, funny, quick-witted, and sincere—and as good a salesman for the city of Yizheng as you can possibly have. One evening with Secretary Bu lingers on in my mind, where he managed to demonstrate his good humor but also his seriousness of purpose at the same time.

A bit of quick background: Beginning in 2003, we were starting to develop plans to build a camshaft manufacturing facility in China. Deputy Mayor Zhou knew of our plans and gave a heads-up to Secretary Bu, who made it a point to have dinner with me on my next trip to Yizheng. During the course of our dinner, Secretary Bu made a strong pitch for the camshaft plant.

"If you decide to locate the plant in Yizheng," he

told me, "I'll sell you the land at an 'unbelievable' price."

I was naturally curious what "unbelievable" meant, particularly when he mentioned it three or four more times that evening. But every time I asked, he would just look at me and smile.

"You'll learn soon enough" was all that he would say.

I later found that "unbelievable" meant "free": the Yizheng government was planning an auto development zone, and he wanted to get new projects in as quickly as possible. (In 2005 and 2006, the central government instituted a number of new land policies that, among other things, designated minimum price levels for land transfers. This was done to slow the development of economic zones, which were taking increasing amounts of land out of agricultural production. As a result, it's no longer possible to obtain free land.)

And so, in October of 2003, with our plans to put more of our resources into Yizheng still taking shape, I accompanied representatives of our major shareholders on a weeklong trip through China that ended in Yizheng. We flew to Nanjing, drove to Yizheng to tour the piston ring factory, and then headed over to dinner with Secretary Bu and the local government.

After the perfunctory exchange of business cards, Secretary Bu welcomed my shareholders and proposed the first toast of the evening—made, of course, with the infamous *baijiu*.

With Henry translating, Secretary Bu started off by giving me "face."

"Mr. Jack and I are old friends," he said, "and we've developed a close relationship over the years." He went on to praise my leadership, and the success of our business in Yizheng. He also didn't miss the opportunity to make a pitch for additional investment directly to my shareholders. "Because of our relationship," he told the assembled group, "if you decide to locate additional facilities here in Yizheng, I told Jack that I will give him an unbelievable price for the land."

Everybody nodded and took note.

I stood up and said that none of our success would have been possible without the support of Secretary Bu and the local government, thanked Cheng Dexing for his support and leadership, and then asked one representative from each investor present to give a short introduction to his company. I wanted Secretary Bu to realize that we were once again introducing him and Yizheng to new friends who might bring additional investment to his city.

John Sinnenberg, head of Key Principal Partners, gave an outline of the types of companies they invested in. After a few exchanges about Cleveland, where John is based, Secretary Bu gave a welcoming toast to John and his colleagues with the customary *ganbei*.

Next up was Scott Foushee, who pointed out that AIG, his company, was one of the world's largest insurance companies—and had, in fact, been founded in Shanghai in 1919.

With everyone nodding knowingly, Scott continued, "But we had to leave China in 1949." He looked at

Secretary Bu, as if expecting a comment, or at least some reaction, but Secretary Bu's expression was completely deadpan.

"But," Scott went on after a short pause, "I'm happy to say that we have recently reopened our office in our original building in Shanghai."

Before Henry even finished translating, I could see a slight smile start to come across Secretary Bu's face. He lifted his glass of *baijiu* and said, without hesitation, "Welcome back!" It was the perfect response.

Then it was Randy Damstra's turn. The DeVos family, which Randy represents, is one of two shareholders in Amway, one of the most successful U.S. companies in China, with China sales growing from virtually nothing in the late 1990s to more than $1 billion by the time of this dinner. Though many people in China buy the products, I would never have guessed that Secretary Bu would know much about the company or its offerings.

But when Randy started explaining that his company was the investment arm of a family that owned 50 percent of Amway, Secretary Bu immediately cut him off: "Yes, I know An Li," he said. ("An Li" is the Chinese name for Amway.)

Then, with a smile on his face, he suggested that they play a game.

"I'll give you two suggestions about how to improve Amway's business in China, if you give me two suggestions about how to improve the investment environment in Yizheng," he said.

Randy nodded in agreement.

"For every one of my suggestions that you agree with, you should drink one cup"—*baijiu*, of course—"and for every suggestion of yours that I agree with, I'll drink one cup."

"Fair enough," Randy said.

"If the suggestion is not accepted," Secretary Bu went on, "then the person making the suggestion should drink one cup."

With the taste of *baijiu* fresh in his mouth, and his antennae now fully up after this last statement, Randy hesitated a bit. But with everybody there and closely following the exchange, he agreed that it sounded fair and square.

Secretary Bu started off. "I use both the Amway shampoo and the Amway conditioner. Amway should consider putting the two together in one bottle."

Silence around the table. Everybody looked at Randy, knowing he'd be hard-pressed to say that this was a bad suggestion.

One glass of *baijiu*, bottoms up. Secretary Bu 1, Randy 0.

On a roll and clearly enjoying himself a great deal, Secretary Bu continued. "Amway's shampoo is only sold in one, very large bottle. Amyway should consider packaging in a smaller bottle."

Again, everybody looked at Randy. Hard to argue with that one. Another glass of *baijiu*, bottoms up. Secretary Bu 2, Randy 0.

Now it was Randy's turn. Randy thought hard, and then said, "On the way to Yizheng from the airport, the road was under repair and very bumpy. If you want to attract more investment, you should repair the road more quickly."

It seemed like a reasonable suggestion, but Secretary Bu requested a clarification: "Was the bumpy part of the road before or after the bridge over the Yangtze?"

Randy thought for a second, and then answered, "Before the bridge."

"That's Nanjing's responsibility," Secretary Bu said, with as big a smile as I've ever seen.

Another glass of *baijiu*, bottoms up, Secretary Bu the hands-down winner at three–zip!

To this day, everyone remembers the dinner and the fun we had. But apart from the jokes and the drinking, my shareholders were impressed with the strong support that we receive from the Yizheng government, and the very tangible benefits that this can provide to our company.

Forming Strong Local Relationships

We obviously have a good relationship with the Yizheng government, but this is true wherever we operate in China. Developing these local relationships is one of the things that we have learned how to do over the years, and I am frequently asked for some words of advice in this area.

First, what we are doing is good for the cities in which we operate, and this message has to be constantly reinforced. Our investment, employment practices, and emphasis on developing local managements and building the business are all positive, and we make sure to provide the local officials with periodic updates on our activities. In the early days, we didn't do this very effectively. As a result, the local governments didn't know much about us and were not as proactive in helping us solve our problems.

Second, if you have a joint venture, your Chinese partner can be very helpful in enhancing your relationship with the local government, just as Cheng Dexing does with the city of Yizheng. (Cheng has been the head of the Chinese partner from the very beginning of our relationship, even when he served as general manager.) Again, we did not take enough time in the early days to better understand our joint venture partners. As a result, most did not actively promote our cause with the local officials.

Whether you have a joint venture or a wholly owned company, one of the prime responsibilities of the general manager is to develop the relationship with the local government. This can help the general manager to deal with the many daily issues that can arise when running a company, but it also paves the way for more senior members of management to address the bigger issues as they come along. Our general managers do a very good job in this regard, and I am always well prepared whenever we need to ask for a favorable policy or treatment. Having local managers who instinctively understand the importance of having a good relationship with the local government is the best way to ensure that this happens.

Finally, it helps to make someone who has the ear of top management specifically responsible for dealing with both your Chinese partners and the local government officials. Henry Huang does a very effective job for me in this area. He's personable, has a great sense of humor, and gets along well with just about everybody—so people enjoy being around him. Bob Iwata, a top executive from Nippon Piston Ring who joined ASIMCO in August 2006 to set up our office in Japan, refers to Henry as "ASIMCO's foreign ambassador." It's impossible not to like him.

In China, Henry knows how to deal with the younger members of government, but he also knows how to interact with the more traditional, older officials. Everyone knows that he is close to me and that they can always get a message to me through Henry. Since most of the government officials I deal with do not speak English, this is important for language reasons as well as convenience and efficiency. Henry is also always alert to remind me of the small things that I might do to further develop my relationships—a message of best wishes at Spring Festival, a small gift to commemorate a special event, sometimes just a word or two of thanks in recognition of some special favor that the government has done. In China, I have found that showing respect through these seemingly small gestures goes a long way. Nowhere is this more true than in dealing with the local governments.

Chapter 13

China's Different Cost Perspective

The question I'm most frequently asked is "How can China make things so cheaply?" The "China Price" has become such an issue for American manufacturers that the cover for BusinessWeek's December 6, 2004, issue carried the headline "The Three Scariest Words in U.S. Industry: 'The China Price'." Everybody wants to know how the China Price works, and why it's so low.

In September of 2006, I was asked to speak about China to the American Foundry Society conference in Napa Valley. After my formal presentation, a hand shot up and a gentleman off to my left asked the following question:

"Jack," he said, "at our foundry in Mexico, our cost of manufacturing a ductile iron casting is forty cents a pound. But we're constantly getting e-mails from China foundries that say they can deliver them to us in the United States at that price or lower.

"My understanding," he went on, "is that raw material

prices are generally the same the world over, so how can they do it?" He looked at me with wide anticipation, clearly very interested in whatever answer I could give him due to its effect on his business. "Is the Chinese government subsidizing its foundry operations so that they can flood the market with castings? Or is it because the Chinese currency is undervalued?"

There's no simple answer to these questions, but there are some preliminary comments that can be made before moving on to a more complicated discussion.

First, it's legitimate to question whether the Chinese company promising a lower-cost product can even do what it claims. There are twenty-four thousand foundries in China, many hungry for more business, and it's highly possible that the Chinese company is throwing out a low quote just to get the order, the classic bait and switch. It's also possible that the company doesn't really understand the complexity of the part in question—and cannot, in fact, manufacture it to the specifications required. The Chinese company may not fully understand that the part is more difficult and expensive to produce than it appears.

Second, raw material pricing generally *is* the same the world over, adjusting for transportation differences. So if the Chinese are quoting you a lower price, it might be because they're using a lower, and cheaper, grade of material. In that case, you're actually comparing apples and oranges.

But there is the larger question: does the Chinese central government have a policy of subsidizing certain industries in order to flood world markets with low-priced goods from China? In fact, I've seen quite the opposite behavior. In the last chapter, I discussed how China is more decentralized than most people think—and that it's this decentralization, not some policy on the part of the central government, that leads to overcapacity in China. In automotive industry policy, Beijing has always acted as a brake on the creation of additional capacity. When China acceded to the WTO and demand for passenger cars began to skyrocket, everybody from appliance manufacturers to alcohol producers wanted to throw their hats in the ring and enter the automobile industry. Instead of making it easy for them to do so, the central government raised the bar for new entrants considerably by passing rules that require minimum levels of capital.

The same thing happened in the steel industry. As China's steel capacity increased from more than 125 million tons in 2000 to 530 million tons by the end of 2006, the central government tried to check the increases by warning against projects that didn't receive the proper approvals, going so far as to stop some projects in mid-stream. In 2006, the Chinese government also eliminated or reduced rebates of VAT on lower-value-added goods such as steel that were being exported from China. This effectively increased the China price of these products in world markets. (When a company exports from China, it is entitled to a rebate of the VAT it has paid in most cases. Critics of China's trade policy claim that this amounts to an export subsidy, a charge that I don't fully understand.)

Taken together, these actions by the central government suggest that the overcapacity we see in industry after industry in China is not due to central government policy. The central government recognizes the waste and duplication of effort that overcapacity creates, and it wants Chinese companies to begin moving up the value chain, producing higher-value-added products. It's actually *decentralization* and the lack of enforcement of national policy that create the problem.

The impact of China's currency level on the price of its manufactured goods is more difficult to address, only because large, sophisticated economies are complicated. If you change one variable, how do all of the others change? If China's currency appreciates, its labor costs will be more expensive in terms of world markets. But, with a more valuable currency, what China pays for its raw materials would theoretically be less. In a case where the cost of a product is 50 percent material and 50 percent labor, you could argue that the net effect of the currency fluctuation would be zero. Since the bulk of China's exports to date have been lower-value-added products, the raw material component is high. Those who advocate increasing the value of China's currency to affect China's global price competitiveness should be careful what they ask for; it might not make any difference at all, and it might even work to the advantage of the China-based manufacturers.

The Real Reason for the China Price

Short of running a complicated econometric model to analyze the net impact of making adjustments to China's currency, I believe there is a more fundamental explanation for China's price competitiveness: the Chinese have a fundamentally different cost perspective. They think about money differently. The effect of this different cost perspective is that Chinese managers instinctively and relentlessly search for manufacturing solutions that fit into China's framework of affordability. What they consider affordable or appropriately priced is radically different (and less expensive) from what might be acceptable outside of China.

I had been in China for at least five years before this realization hit home. The penny dropped for me when I took an American friend of mine to see our piston ring factory. Although our business is quite important to Yizheng, we're not the largest taxpayer in the city. The largest is a state-owned company, Yizheng Chemical, one of the largest polyester fiber companies in all of Asia.

In 1994, Yizheng Chemical went public in Hong Kong and raised a substantial amount of capital. It then took a small part of the proceeds to build a nice twenty-story hotel, largely to house its foreign visitors. At ASIMCO, of course, we were thrilled, because now we could rely on getting a nice room at a relatively cheap price whenever we visited Yizheng. Naturally, this is where my American friend and I stayed.

When we checked out the next morning, the bill was

240 yuan. When he saw his bill, my friend did what every American does, and what I still do after being in China for fifteen years: he divided 240 by 8 (the approximate exchange rate to the U.S. dollar) and came up with roughly $30 U.S.

"Wow," he said to me, obviously very excited. "Thirty dollars for this room! Now I understand why overhead costs in China are so low."

By that time, we had completely localized our management, and all of our factories were being run by Mainland Chinese. I didn't say anything to my friend, but it finally dawned on me.

"If any of our managers traveled to Yizheng," I thought to myself, "they wouldn't even dream of staying in a place like this. It costs too much." They would consider it too expensive and would look for a room that cost something closer to 150 yuan. In fact, if two of my managers were traveling together, they'd double up and stay in the same room for one-half the price.

My American friend looked at 240 yuan, saw $30, and concluded that the room was cheap. My Chinese managers would see the same 240 yuan and come to the opposite conclusion, that the room was too expensive. Same amount, different cost perspective.

Upon thinking a bit more about the price consciousness of our local managers, I was reminded of Wu Yingxue, the thirty-eight-year-old general manager of our piston ring business, who took over from Cheng Dexing in 2005 and has carried on the tradition of good management in Yizheng. When Wu travels to Beijing, instead of taking the 1,160 yuan ($152) economy flight from Nanjing, he'll take the overnight train from the nearby city of Yangzhou. The train only costs 429 yuan ($56), and it puts him in Beijing early in the morning, maximizing the hours he can work in the day and eliminating the need to spend money for a hotel in Beijing. He also saves himself money on the ground: the Yangzhou train station is minutes away from our factory, while the Nanjing airport is an hour and a half away by car.

(As in the case of Li Jienan at our factory in Hengyang, I would have been happy to have Cheng stay on for several more years as general manager. But he decided that he had brought the company as far as he could, and that it was time to turn over the keys to the next generation of managers. Cheng had tapped Wu Yingxue several years earlier to be his successor when the time came, and we'd gotten to know him quite well. I couldn't think of a better candidate. In his farewell speech, Cheng said that Wu and the new generation of managers were better equipped to take the next step into the international marketplace. He reminisced that when he took over as general manager, at roughly Wu's age, he could hardly sleep because he worked so hard. He was certain, he said with a wry smile, that Wu would bring the same energy to the position. I remind Wu of Cheng's speech every time I see him.)

$100 Versus RMB 100

I learned a valuable lesson that day in Yizheng. Since then I always carry two bills with me—an RMB 100 bill and a $100 bill—to convey this lesson to others. The point I make is that these two bills are treated in exactly the same way in their respective countries. Just as the $100 bill is the highest unit of currency that you can get in the United States, an RMB 100 bill is the highest unit of currency you can get in China. You can't get an RMB 500 bill, just like you can't get a $500 bill. If I go to the Wegman's supermarket near my farm in New Jersey and try to pay for my groceries with a $100 bill, the cashier will take the bill and run it under a light to confirm that it isn't counterfeit. If I go to the supermarket in the basement of Pacific Century Plaza across the street from my apartment in Beijing and attempt to pay for my groceries with an RMB 100 bill, the Chinese cashier will do the same.

To make my point with audiences when I'm giving a speech, I'll pull both bills out of my pocket and hold them up. When Americans look at an RMB 100 bill, I say, they divide by 8 and see $12.50. But when Mainland Chinese look at that same bill—and I don't care how wealthy they are—they see what Americans see when we look at our own $100 bill.

How does this make a difference? In more ways than you might think, but here's a simple example. An overseas company wants to set up a factory making a certain product in China. It has a Chinese competitor that wants to set up a similar factory making the same product in the same city.

The foreign company gets Joe Smith, its facility planner, to come to China to oversee the project. The Chinese company gets its Mr. Joe—only this person's name is spelled "Z-h-o-u"—to do the same thing.

When Joe Smith looks at the first input, priced at RMB 100, he mentally divides by 8 and says, "$12.50. That's 30 percent cheaper than back home. Buy it."

Mr. Zhou looks at the same input, sees the equivalent of $100, and says, "RMB 100—that's too expensive." He then proceeds to negotiate the price down by 30 percent.

The result is two companies making the same product in the same city in China, and one factory has significantly higher construction costs than another. And that's before you get to all of the other inputs that go into making a product. That is why foreign companies tend to build factories in China that are lower cost than their factories back home, but high cost for China. The only thing that allows this to work is the technology difference that often exists between foreign and local products. But as I'll explain in a later chapter, these technology differences will soon disappear. That is why understanding that there is a difference in cost perspective in China is so vitally important.

Even when Americans negotiate hard, it's difficult to overcome the different cost perspective—and nearly impossible to get the true China price. When I wanted to buy Carleen a string of pearls for Christmas one year, I took Henry and Leona Zhang, Carleen's assistant, to the pearl market in Beijing to negotiate on my behalf, and I allowed three hours for the event. I just knew that my foreign face and time pressure would result in a much higher price.

If you travel to China, you can test this yourself when you go to the Great Wall. As you walk down the steps, you'll be overwhelmed by vendors who want to sell you an "I Climbed the Great Wall" T-shirt.

After four or five minutes of negotiating, I guarantee that you'll give in and think to yourself, "Okay, I'll pay 25 yuan. What's three bucks anyway?" But a local Chinese would never pay that much. Their bottom line will always be different.

An amusing illustration of China's different cost perspective occurred in the early days of ASIMCO and involved Andrew MacDonald and Pete Groves, two young Americans who worked for us as interns. As you can imagine, they always had funny stories to tell about their adventures and exploits in China, but this one had us all in stitches.

Andrew and Pete shared an apartment near the Beijing office. One Saturday afternoon they went vegetable shopping in one of the many street markets you'd find in any Chinese city, where they decided they wanted to buy some green beans.

When they found the stall selling green beans, they tried, in their best attempt at Mandarin with a Beijing accent (Beijingers put an "er" at the end of every word), to ask the lady, "How much?"

She held up four fingers.

In China, everything is a negotiation, and Andrew and Pete had been around for a few months. They weren't about to be had. So they held up two fingers.

After much back-and-forth, walking away to the next stall and pretending not to be interested and all of the rest, they came back and settled on a price of three.

When they dug into their wallets and pulled out three 1-yuan bills and handed them over, the green bean lady's eyes lit up. She pulled out four huge plastic bags—each larger than the bag they were expecting to see—and started filling them up with more green beans than they could possibly eat in their entire stay with ASIMCO.

It turns out that while Andrew and Pete believed the negotiation was all about whether they were going to pay 4 yuan (50 cents), 2 yuan (25 cents), or something in between for a bag of beans, the green bean lady had been negotiating in fen. Like a cent in the United States, one fen is equal to one-hundredth of a yuan. When they handed the lady 3 yuan, she couldn't believe her eyes. She then proceeded to give them one hundred times more beans than they expected to buy.

I can't help but smile every time I think of our two young heroes walking back to their apartment, each with two large bags of green beans slung over his shoulder. It never occurred to them that they were negotiating over less than a penny. Not a lot to them, but meaningful enough to the green bean lady.

Niche Market for High-Priced Goods

China's different cost perspective works the same way in determining what Chinese consumers are willing to pay for a product or service.

With our wide range of capabilities, ASIMCO tends to be the largest single supplier to our key customers. In 2004, we began to consolidate our sales efforts to key existing and potential customers and established a key account management program.

To kick off the effort, Wilson Ni, our head of global sales and marketing, began organizing a series of group-wide sales calls to our large customers. On a typical visit, we might have as many as a dozen ASIMCO managers, including headquarters personnel and seven or eight of our general managers, travel to our customer. The group sales efforts have worked well for us, and, because I typically lead the delegation, we usually meet with the senior-most management of our customers. It builds a sense of teamwork among our managers and with the customers, but it also builds camaraderie within ASIMCO and often ends up being a lot of fun.

On one such visit in 2005 to Weifang Diesel, one of the largest diesel engine manufacturers in China, we had all arrived by 5:00 P.M. the day before the meetings. We decided to have an internal group dinner in a private room in the hotel where we were staying.

Henry was traveling with the group as he always does, and we put him in charge of the food for the evening. We often refer to Henry as ASIMCO's CFO—"chief food officer"—because, no matter where we are in China, we can always count on him to order up a nice meal that features the local cuisine. Since we didn't have any major business that we needed to cover, we kicked back, had a few beers, and enjoyed Henry's selections.

I don't know what possessed me to do it, but out of the blue I decided to ask Wilson what he paid for a haircut.

A graduate of Tsinghua University, Wilson visibly straightened in his chair. "I still get my hair cut at Tsinghua," he said proudly. "And I only pay 10 yuan!"

Wilson waited for the rest of the room to congratulate him on his frugality, but instead his answer was greeted with howls of disbelief from around the table. Nobody could believe that he could possibly pay so much.

This piqued my interest, so I asked Wu Yingxue what he paid. Yizheng is much smaller than Beijing, so I figured his price would be lower than Wilson's.

Sure enough, it was. "I only pay 8 yuan," Wu said.

A buck a haircut is cheap anywhere in the world, especially when you consider that a haircut in China isn't just a haircut. The twenty-minute cutting of hair is preceded and followed by a thirty-minute head and shoulder massage. (I've known foreigners who would get a haircut, even when they didn't need one, just to get the one-hour head and neck massage.) But because Beijing and Yizheng are pretty affluent cities, I had a feeling I could find an even lower price in one of the inner provinces.

In partnership with Caterpillar, ASIMCO has a foundry in rural Shanxi Province, about a thousand kilometers west and south of Beijing. Our foundry is located in the mountains in an ancient part of China, not far from the city of Xian, in neighboring Shaanxi Province, home to the famous terra-cotta warriors. Many people here still live in caves.

Jack Pfeiffer and Paul Dawson, the two GE executives who served on our board, visited our Shanxi foundry one year. They had heard me talk about the cave homes and said they wanted to see one. Ron Martin, a good friend and the general manager assigned by Caterpillar to the foundry at that time, arranged a visit to a cave dwelling near the factory that belongs to an elderly woman. She makes a nice additional income giving tours to our guests.

As we were standing in the doorway, listening to the owner describe her pictures and furnishings, we all noticed a long wooden box against the back wall.

"What's the box for?" we asked through our interpreter.

"That's my coffin," the woman said, ever so matter-of-factly. "It's a custom in this part of China," she explained, "to build your own coffin when you reach the age of sixty, so as not to be a bother to those you leave behind."

Hearing this, Jack and Paul, both into their sixties, turned to each other and said at the same time, "I guess we better get started."

With this knowledge about Shanxi as background, I turned to Steven Cao, general manager of ASIMCO Shanxi, and asked what he paid for his haircut.

As expected, he came in even lower. "Six yuan," he said proudly.

At this point, the only province more rural than Shanxi with an ASIMCO factory was Anhui. (Our factory in Zhongxi is the same one that was the subject of the dispute with Mr. Fang described in Chapter 8.)

Alongside our factory is a street lined with small shops where you can get shoes or clothes made, or get just about anything repaired—all at bargain-basement prices. A foreign visitor to our factory happened to spend the weekend there, and on his way back to the States stopped by my office to see me in Beijing.

"How was the weekend?" I asked him, knowing that he had been in Zhongxi and half expecting a horror story or two.

"It wasn't bad," he said, and he then proceeded to tell me that he'd stopped into one of the shops by the factory and had ordered a tailor-made suit for less than 100 yuan.

"What does it look like?" I couldn't help but ask.

"I don't know!" he said. "I haven't seen it yet. They're going to send it. But how can you go wrong for twelve bucks?"

Zhou Zhijin, our general manager in Zhongxi at the time, was at the dinner with us, so I turned to him next.

"What do you pay for a haircut?" I asked, fully anticipating that he would walk away with the "lowest price for a haircut" prize.

"Seven yuan," he said, shaking his head.

The rest of the Chinese in the room were shocked. "Is

that with or without the massage?" nearly all asked in unison.

They then turned to me and asked what I paid. Too embarrassed to answer, I replied with a "No comment."

I won't tell you what they make, but the people around that table were some of our most senior managers, and they all have incomes that would be considered good in any country. They would have been absolutely shocked to hear that I pay 240 yuan for a haircut, even though they could easily afford to do the same. (Of course, looking at my hair, they might have a reason to question what I'm getting for my money.) Given what they are used to paying, they just couldn't imagine why anybody would pay that much.

Importing a Higher Cost Perspective into China

With every passing day, the fundamentally different cost perspective in Mainland China is reinforced. If we need to buy a $100,000 machine in the United States to perform a particular function, more often than not we can buy a machine in China to perform a similar function for RMB 100,000. When one of our Chinese managers insisted on keeping the air-conditioning system for the new factory we were building at ground level, rather than putting it on the roof at an additional cost of RMB 250,000, a representative of our Western partner commented: "In my world, $30,000 is not a lot of money, but in theirs it is." What an apt description of China's different cost perspective!

As a Western company doing business in China, it's easy to import a higher cost perspective into China—thereby destroying the cost competitiveness of your China operations in the process.

When we held our first general managers meeting, we decided to hold it in a nice hotel in Beijing as a way of telling our managers that we thought highly of them. Because we had always stayed at the Kempinski Hotel, we had a good relationship with the management and got what I considered to be an attractive corporate rate of about $75 a night for our managers.

During the first day of the meeting, the deputy general manager of our fuel pump business in Hengyang pulled Michael Cronin aside and said that he had a problem. His daily allowance while traveling was 80 yuan, and he was wondering how he could possibly stay in a hotel that cost eight times that amount. (Seventy-five dollars versus 80 yuan. It's amazing to me how frequently that cost comparison occurs.) We recognized the problem we were creating and started holding our meetings in local Chinese hotels, where the rates are cheaper and more in line with the cost structures of our companies in China.

After being effectively closed from 1949 to 1978, China emerged after those thirty years in a different place than the rest of the world. Per capita income levels have been so much lower in China over these years that managers and consumers are operating according to completely different standards of affordability. In many ways, price levels in China for daily goods are similar to price levels that existed in the United States in the 1950s.

I got anecdotal evidence of this from an unexpected source when Carleen and I were unpacking a box of books over the Christmas holiday in 2006. Carleen's grandfather collected first edition hardbacks, most of which were printed in the late 1940s or early 1950s, and many of which were signed by the author and have beautifully illustrated jackets. One, in particular, caught my attention, *Last Chance in China* by Freda Utley, published in 1947. Knowing that a book on average sells for 25 to 30 yuan ($3 to $4) in a Beijing bookstore, I looked to see if I could find a price. Sure enough, there it was on the inside flap, $3.50, the same price I might pay in China today for a similar book!

The different cost perspective that exists today will certainly exist for another generation, and it may well extend beyond that for several generations more. Extrapolating from the current growth rates of both countries, many experts predict that China's economy will be as large as that of the United States by the middle of this century. Even if that's true, the size of China's population means that per capita income even then will only be one-fifth that of the United States.

To me, China's different cost perspective is the most fundamental explanation of why Chinese manufacturers can make things so cheaply. It's also why products that seem reasonably priced to Westerners are considered prohibitively high-priced in China, and why products that Western companies think will appeal to the mass market in China instead succeed only in a niche market.

To be competitive in the China market, it's essential that a company's managers have the same cost perspective as its customers and competitors. This is the most compelling argument for developing and empowering a good local management team, and why the lessons of Chapters 6 through 11 are so important. The following chapter will explain how this different cost perspective has given rise to two distinct markets in China, and how the ultimate merger of these markets may create some interesting dynamics for all industries globally.

Chapter 14

China's Two Markets

Every year, China puts on a major auto show where assemblers and component suppliers exhibit their wares, alternating each year between Beijing and Shanghai. Over a ten-day period in November 2006, six hundred thousand people visited the show in Beijing. Autos are now a very big business in China. A record 572 vehicles were on display, two-thirds brought by foreign assemblers, the rest by local companies. There were so many new models being shown that there was hardly any exhibit space available for the components companies in the China International Exhibition Center, the main display hall. A few of us—ASIMCO, Bosch, and Siemens—managed to get booths there, but most other components companies, including some major international suppliers, had to take booths in the National Agricultural Exhibition Center, a few kilometers away.

Wilson and a group of our managers made it a point to spend an afternoon at the other site to scout the competition, and the news they came back with was startling.

Although there was only room for a thousand exhibitors, six thousand local Chinese companies had applied for booths! That number in itself is amazing. In a speech at the Automotive News World Congress in Detroit in January 2007, Richard E. Dauch, the CEO of American Axle & Manufacturing Holdings Inc., noted that since 1990 the global supply base has consolidated from thirty thousand suppliers to ten thousand. That means that there are most likely more automotive component suppliers in China alone than in the entire world. (As I will discuss later, we put the number at well over twenty thousand.)

This phenomenon is not limited to automotive components. In late 2005, Ted Fishman, author of *China, Inc.*, and I were on a panel together in Florida. Ted said something during his remarks that has stuck with me to this day: there are now 85 million private companies in China, more than three times the 25 million private enterprises in the United States. That statistic, more than any other, demonstrates the sheer scale of the capitalism and entrepreneurialism that exists in China. It also suggests that the China market is much bigger, and the level of competition much greater, than anyone has imagined.

While the Western media focus on the vast amounts of foreign direct investment flowing into China and the international companies that are setting up or expanding operations here, little attention is paid to the purely local companies who are also competing in their own way for a share of the China market. Like the foreign companies who come to China with the glint of world domination in their eyes, these local companies also dream of conquering overseas markets. Despite their obvious shortcomings, they also have some unique advantages.

WHERE DO THESE local Chinese competitors come from? New entrants sometimes seem to appear out of thin air, but they actually emerge from a purely local market—a market that's beneath the radar of most foreign observers, and in most cases is much larger than Western competitors would ever expect. This is the indigenous China market that has been there all along, and that continues to grow and develop in line with the general growth of the China economy.

When Deng opened China up in 1978, more expensive and higher-technology goods were permitted to flow into China. As the country's economic growth accelerated, and as more companies and individuals could afford these higher-priced products, a second market was layered on top of China's indigenous market. The country's local market did not go away or shrink in the face of competition with goods from abroad as many expected. Instead, the vast disparity of income levels in China has perpetuated this market segmentation, and the local market has continued to grow in size and importance throughout the past thirty years.

As a result, the China market is actually two distinct markets. For virtually every product, there's a "foreign/local" market, characterized by higher technology and higher price, and a second purely "local" market, which is characterized by lower technology and lower price. The foreign/local market isn't necessarily dominated by foreign companies; rather, it's simply the segment of the China market with price and technology levels that are most familiar to them. In this segment of the market, foreign-invested enterprises compete with other foreign-invested companies and the best of the local Chinese companies.

Most foreign companies, if they consider it at all, don't believe the local market is a battleground on which they can be successful—the price levels are too low. The general manager of one of Dongfeng Motors' components companies told me that he once described the local market for his product to a German company he was negotiating with to do a joint venture.

"Oh, we don't want to sell to that market," the German representative said. "We only want to sell higher-technology, higher-priced products."

Dong Yang, the former general manager of BAIC, the Chinese partner in our Beijing fuel pump operation, analyzed it best: "People who wear shoes shouldn't try and fight with people who wear sandals." Non-Chinese companies instinctively appreciate the wisdom of this comment, and stay away from the purely local market.

China's Local Market: A Breeding Ground for Future Competition

My long experience in China tells me that understanding this local market—and perhaps even making a serious effort to tap in to it—is important, for several reasons.

First, it's big. The local market is where the ultimate economies of scale in China will come from. Opting out of this market forsakes those economies.

Second, as income levels rise over time, the local market will merge up technologically. Price levels between the two markets will also merge, but will settle somewhere in between the two—at levels lower than most companies would accept in markets outside of China. This creates an interesting dilemma: Should a company maintain global price levels, give up the China opportunity, and risk losing out to lower-priced Chinese competitors down the road? Or should it compete in China, recognizing that with global pricing mechanisms in place, the "China Price" may soon be the "global price"? I would argue that the latter is really the only option if you have any hopes of long-term global competitiveness, not to mention competitiveness within China itself.

Last, the local market is a breeding ground for future global competitors. Due to vast income disparities, the total China market tolerates all levels of technology and quality. (Average incomes in large cities like Beijing and Shanghai are $2,500 per year, while average incomes in the countryside, where 750 million people live, are approximately $500.) Any company, no matter how low its quality or level of technology, can find a market for its products in China—if its price is cheap enough. Where a company with inferior technology or quality would likely fail in developed markets, it may live to compete another day in China. In a familiar environment where they can compete the Chinese way, local companies have opportunities to gain scale in the large, local market. They can then move up to the higher-technology segment of the market as they gain expertise, and eventually may start to explore global markets.

Depending on the industry and the level of technology required to participate in it, the market share split between foreign-invested enterprises and the purely local companies in China varies. But make no mistake: the battles for market share being waged in China today will ultimately determine the fate of just about every global industry.

China's Two Markets: The Restaurant Industry

Perhaps the best way to illustrate China's two markets is to take an example from an industry that everyone can relate to: the restaurant industry.

In October of 2006, my younger daughter, Libby, came to visit Carleen and me in Beijing. This was a very special treat, because her birthday fell during her trip, giving us the rare opportunity to celebrate in person. (Normally, we'd be singing "Happy Birthday" into the telephone and wishing we could be together.) As it so happened, Carleen had an "important" birthday that year, and Franklin and Alex McCann, longtime friends from New York, decided to take that occasion to make their first trip to China. With my daughter and the McCanns in town, we booked a table at the Courtyard, one of our favorite restaurants in Beijing, for a Thursday night.

The Courtyard's setting couldn't be any more spectacular. It's located just opposite the East Gate of the Forbidden City, which the city fathers light up to spectacular effect each weekend night. The principal owner of the restaurant, Handel Lee, was our law firm's Beijing representative when I first came to China, and he was one of the first people I met. While still practicing law, Handel has managed to develop other famous restaurant and retail properties—including Legation and Three on the Bund in Shanghai—and has become something of a celebrity in the restaurant and art world.

The restaurant itself is located in a converted "courtyard house." There's an art gallery on the first floor, and a cozy cigar lounge upstairs; the dining area, draped with white curtains and with modern Chinese art on the walls, can safely be described as "upscale." When we arrived, the maître d' escorted us to a corner table in the back, where we had a large window to our right that placed the East Gate and the moat surrounding the Forbidden City squarely in our view. I'm not sure I've ever sat in a more picturesque location.

Apart from the allure of the restaurant's decor and setting, the food at the Courtyard is excellent. Rey Lim, the chef, worked at Bouley in New York and is a good friend. Whenever we're in for a meal, he always makes a point of coming to our table to say hello and to greet our guests. He also never fails to send out a complement of desserts. This time, he arranged a chocolate cake, complete with sparklers, in honor of Libby's birthday.

If it weren't for the view out the window, we could have been anywhere. Libby told me afterward that she considers the Courtyard to be one of her favorite restaurants in the world, not just in Beijing. The McCanns rated it with the best they'd been to in New York City. Prices at the Courtyard, naturally, are also what you'd expect to pay at a fine restaurant in New York or any other major international city. With a nice bottle of wine or two, the bill came to about $100 per person. That's one side of China.

The next day, we showed the McCanns the other side. In the morning, Libby took them to the Hongqiao market, where they loaded up on pearls and jewelry and learned the fine art of negotiating, Chinese style.

"You say, you say!" the vendor demanded as she typed her price into the calculator.

"Cheaper, cheaper," came the inevitable response from Franklin.

After a tough but successful three hours of this, the negotiating team arrived at our office. They looked a bit worn, and they were famished, so we decided to take them across the street to San Yuan You He, a local dumpling restaurant that our staff loves. (It would be a favorite of mine, too, if only dumplings didn't have so many carbs.) With the menu in his head, Henry offered to write out an order in both Chinese and English. He handed it to Carleen, and off we went.

For six people, Henry had ordered five plates of dumplings: fried dumplings, dumplings stuffed with pork and cabbage, pork and coriander dumplings, tomato and egg dumplings, and dumplings stuffed with pork and beans. He also included two cold dishes as starters, as well as a tomato and egg dish, an eggplant dish, and a spicy bean dish to eat with the dumplings. To wash it all down, we ordered five Diet Cokes and one bottle of water. Each plate contained about fifteen dumplings, and we had more than enough to eat. (In fact, we took at least a third of it home with us as leftovers.)

Henry's selections were excellent, as usual. As we all patted our gently stuffed stomachs, we agreed that between the dinner the night before and the lunch we'd just finished, we'd had two back-to-back excellent meals in China.

As we waited for the check, I decided to play the traditional "How much will the bill be?" game.

"Eight hundred yuan," said Franklin. He was roundly ridiculed immediately after he said it, because everyone at the table knew that was way too high.

"Two hundred yuan," said Libby, who has spent a fair amount of time in China.

Given the two extremes, no one else chose to play, and even I figured that Libby had hit it about dead-on.

When the bill came, we were shocked: 137 yuan, barely $3.00 a person! Even after being in China for more than fifteen years, I was still surprised. Franklin and Alex couldn't believe that such a great meal could cost so little. They were starting to understand a bit more about China's two markets.

But their lessons weren't over. In the middle of the afternoon of that same day, Carleen got a call from Vlad Reyes, the general manager of the Hilton Hotel in Beijing. Vlad and his wife had just returned from a vacation in Thailand, and he was organizing an impromptu Beijing duck dinner at the Li Qun Roast Duck restaurant that evening.

"Would you and Jack and your guests like to join us?" he asked. "The van leaves from the Hilton at seven."

Never one to turn down a party, Carleen immediately said yes, and we were off for Beijing duck that evening.

Li Qun sits just south of the Forbidden City in the center of Beijing and is impossible to get to by car. The van dropped us off at a spot about ten minutes away on foot, and our party of ten began the slow journey through dark, narrow, winding alleyways, or *hutongs*. Though once fully occupied, most of the buildings and courtyard houses we passed were vacant and scheduled to be demolished (which has since been done). The occasional arrow painted on a building wall directing us to "Li's Restaurant" was the only way we knew we were still on the right track.

During the van ride over, Vlad had described Li Qun

as a "hole in the wall," and he was right. Just like the Courtyard, Li Qun is in an old courtyard house that has been covered over to create additional indoor space. But that's where the comparison stops.

We came in through a small entry lined with pictures of ambassadors and other important people who've eaten there over the years, and we walked past a long line of people waiting to be seated. (Vlad knows the owners well and had reserved a room.) At the end of the long hallway, we entered a room at the center of the restaurant that had once been the courtyard. Surrounded by other smaller rooms, including the kitchen, this was clearly the restaurant's central nervous system. Customers filled its three battered tables.

Although Vlad had called ahead, our room was still occupied. So we just stood there, hovering over the seated customers, trying to stay out of the way of the waiters, waiting for the room to open up. The place was absolutely jammed. Kitchen workers walked by carrying ducks to the kitchen to be cooked. (On a good night, Li's goes through sixty ducks.) Half-eaten duck carcasses were tossed into a large tray at one end of the room—where, inexplicably, a kitchen worker would periodically come out to take one back into the kitchen. We all wondered aloud what he did with those carcasses.

On the basis of a favorable write-up in *Lonely Planet*, a feature in *That's Beijing*, and winning the designation of Best Peking Duck in Beijing in *Time* magazine in 2004, Li Qun has become a popular destination for tourists. Vlad described it as "*the* duck restaurant" in the city, and Mr. Li as the "Mr. Duck" of Beijing. The food and decor are strictly local, but most of the clientele were foreigners that evening.

When we finally sat down, Vlad took charge and immediately ordered three ducks, a spicy pork dish, plates of broccoli and eggplant, and two orders of fried duck bones. (Maybe that's what the mostly eaten ducks were used for?) Along with all of the fixings for Beijing duck—cucumber and onion sticks, pancakes and sauce—our waitress brought out five large bottles of Yanjing beer and placed them on the lazy Susan in front of us. We all took our paper napkins, wiped off our drinking glasses, and poured the cold beer. Before the night was over, we'd ordered another round of beers. It was good company, a truly unique experience, and another excellent meal.

The bill: 647 yuan, or about $8 per person.

$3–$8–$100 per person. That about sums up the restaurant market in China in terms of price. Each restaurant, though serving different markets, provided a quality product, but at substantially different prices. Although I didn't ask, I believe the McCanns would have been hard-pressed to say which restaurant they'd go back to if they had only one more meal in Beijing.

Of the millions of restaurants in China, 99 percent are purely local, with an average price per person of $3 or below. This is the local market, and our dumpling restaurant is representative of that segment. It's important to note, though, that because it's located on the bottom floors of a modern apartment complex, and the place is clean and the food quality high, our dumpling restaurant is at the upper end of this segment. Just around the corner, you could easily find even cheaper local restaurants, and, of course, out of the urban areas things change entirely.

At the other end of the spectrum, each major city will have its share of high-end Western restaurants like the Courtyard, and expensive Chinese restaurants like Lan, but this is a niche market. (These high-end restaurants are now frequented by local Chinese as well as Westerners— a big change from the late 1990s, when the market was more or less limited to foreign businessmen on expense accounts.) Every city will also have local restaurants like Li Qun, which, either because of decor or clientele, are somewhat higher priced than the purely local restaurants—but are still much, much cheaper than the higher-end places.

That's why when people ask me if living in China is cheap or expensive, all I can say is "It depends."

Back to Autos

While China's restaurant industry is more heavily skewed toward the local market, it's still a model that can help us understand other industries. Let's return to autos in China. The headline number, the one that gets all the publicity, is that China produced and sold more than 8 million vehicles in 2007. Even at that number, China is already the third-largest producer of vehicles in the world, trailing only the United States and Japan.

But that's only part of the story. Every year, China produces as many as 40 million gasoline and diesel engines for use in transportation. (Mr. Ni Hongjie, executive director of the China Internal Combustion Association, estimated that China produced 11.4 million diesel engines and 28.5 million gasoline engines in 2005.) These include engines used in conventional vehicles, of course, but also included are the small gasoline engines used in the 21 million motorcycles produced and sold in China each year; the two- and three-cylinder diesel engines used in three- and four-wheeled agricultural vehicles; and the countless one-cylinder diesel engines that are bolted onto a chassis and a frame to form the infamous "inkfish" that I mentioned previously.

The foreign/local segment of the transportation market is the headline number, the 8 million conventional vehicles that look like the trucks, buses, and passenger cars that you might find on the streets of New York, Tokyo, or Paris. While the joint ventures with global auto companies like General Motors and Volkswagen completely dominated this segment of the market ten years ago, local companies like Chery and Geely have been gaining market share rapidly and now account for nearly one-third of passenger car sales in China.

The local market in transportation consists of the roughly 32 million nonconventional vehicles produced each year and used primarily by the 750 million people living in China's countryside. This segment of the market is served entirely by local Chinese companies.

As is true for most industries in China, both segments are extremely fragmented, and becoming more so. Before China's accession to WTO, there were only thirteen different kinds of passenger cars produced in China. At last count, only five years later, there are 165 different brands with 278 different models being produced here. Of the 64 separate legal entities making passenger cars in China today, 22 are foreign-invested enterprises—representing nearly every assembler involved in the global automotive industry—and 42 are purely local Chinese companies. Global players like General Motors, Toyota, and Volkswagen share a meaningful percentage of the market with little-known local companies like Chery, Geely, and Great Wall. New local Chinese companies emerge every day.

Looking at the entire market for mechanized transportation in China today, the "vehicle menu," if you will, includes a BMW 5 Series that can be purchased for RMB 457,000 ($60,130); a Toyota Camry for RMB 193,000 ($25,400); a Buick Regal for RMB 153,800 ($20,240); a Hyundai Elantra for RMB 84,800 ($11,160); or a Geely Meiri or Chery QQ for about RMB 35,000 ($4,600) at the low end of the foreign/local market. And then the price levels break yet again. In the local market, a motorcycle can be purchased for as little as RMB 2,000 ($260), a three-wheeled agricultural vehicle for RMB 10,000 ($1,320), and a four-wheeled for RMB 20,000 ($2,630).

Since I first came to China I've been fascinated with the local market for transportation and the role it might play in the future development of China's automotive industry. From the very beginning, I've traveled extensively throughout China's inner provinces, where agriculture still accounts for a major portion of employment and economic activity. It's always been obvious to me that these nonconventional forms of transportation fill a basic need, and that the dominant players in the agricultural vehicle market might well evolve into manufacturing more conventional vehicles. Coming from their low-cost base, they'd have some natural advantages as they move upmarket.

The former chairman of BAIC, An Qing Heng, and I have always had a special relationship because we share a common vision in this regard. In 1997, I spoke at an automotive conference in Detroit and devoted a significant portion of my presentation to a discussion of the agricultural vehicle market. Chairman An, who was also speaking at the conference, was in the audience listening to my presentation. He approached me afterward and told me how surprised he was to hear a foreigner speak on that topic. Ever since, we've had a kind of special bond. At our company's tenth anniversary celebration, I asked Chairman An to say a few words, and he again referenced our common interest in agricultural vehicles.

Under Chairman An's direction, BAIC took a significant equity ownership position in a leading agricultural vehicle producer that began to move upmarket, targeting the truck and commercial vehicle segment. Beiqi-Foton is now one of the largest producers of light- and heavy-duty vehicles in China; they've successfully made the transition from China's purely local market to the higher-technology segment of the China market, where they now compete with foreign and Chinese manufacturers alike. The next inevitable stop for Beiqi-Foton is the global market, and they've already done a joint venture with Cummins for engines in preparation.

Another source of future global car assemblers is China's vast motorcycle industry. After all, Honda, one of the major Japanese assemblers and a leading global car company, began life as a motorcycle producer in Japan in the 1950s. Why not one or two of the hundreds of Chinese motorcycle companies?

Probably the best example of the potential for this to happen is Geely. Based in entrepreneurial Zhejiang Province on China's east coast, Geely isn't quite a global assembler—yet. But it's well on its way. After years as a motorcycle manufacturer, Geely broke into the auto-mobile business in 1996 and, along with Chery, has become one of the leading Chinese producers of passenger cars.

In 2005, Geely announced its intentions to export to the United States; in October of 2006, the company reached an agreement with Manganese Bronze, owner of London Taxis International, the U.K.-based manu-facturer of the city's trademark black cabs, to produce the cabs in Shanghai. "London's Black Cabs Go East in

Economy Drive" was the headline of an article that ran in the *New Zealand Herald*. Given how quickly things happen in China, it won't be long before the Geely brand is recognized worldwide.

Other motorcycle companies are now following Geely's lead. In January of 2006, the Chongqing-based motorcycle manufacturer Lifan launched its Lifan 520 sedan. In March, Zhongshen, another Chongqing motorcycle maker, started producing minivehicles. Both companies plan to gain a foothold in the market by developing products that meet the affordability requirements of consumers in China's agricultural sector, the same market they serve with their motorcycles. As the income levels of these consumers move up, they'll be able to afford increasingly more expensive models—and Lifan and Zhongshen will be waiting for them with products.

The Components Sector

Turning to the components sector, the story again is increasing fragmentation. We conservatively estimate that there are well over 20,000 companies competing in our space. That includes about 1,500 foreign-invested enterprises, 3,500 state-owned enterprises, and more than 15,000 private companies. Because many of these private companies aren't registered, it's impossible to get an exact number—but we know our estimate is low. In December of 2005, Taizhou City (Geely's hometown) took out a full-page ad in the local newspaper claiming that there were more than 8,000 components companies in Taizhou. The *China Economic Times*, in its December 20, 2006, edition, put the number of components suppliers in Taizhou at 3,240. Whether it's 3,000 or 8,000, if there are even close to that many components companies in Taizhou alone, how many might there be throughout the country?

In piston rings, for example, we estimate that there are about 400 piston ring companies in China. ASIMCO and its three largest competitors together share about 60 percent of the market, and the top six have almost 80 percent; the remaining 394 companies share just 20 percent of the business. In air compressors, we have 65 percent of the market, but there are still a dozen other compressor manufacturers out there. We estimate that there are more than 100 companies making starters and alternators in China, and many of them had booths at the National Agricultural Exhibition Center.

Now, for the perspective: outside of China, there are only five—five!—serious players in piston rings globally, three in compressors, and four or five in starters and alternators. In China, the story is pretty much the same everywhere you look. An overcrowded market exists in just about any product you can think of.

The obvious conclusion is that the market should and will consolidate, as it has in other countries. But when? Since I first came to China in 1993 every analysis of the auto market has concluded that the industry is too fragmented and will soon consolidate. And yet, year after year, the industry has become even more fragmented. Taking piston rings again as an example, we estimate that five years ago there were only 145 piston ring companies in China, less than one-half the number today. Because a growing local market will accept even the lowest levels of technology and quality for the right price, there is no reason to believe that this trend toward fragmentation won't continue for a long time to come.

WHOM DO ALL of these companies sell to? Well, they have several markets to keep them busy.

First, 8 million trucks, buses, and passenger cars need components. Only the top tier of component suppliers are able to serve this segment due to its requirements for higher technology and quality.

Second, there are all those makers of unconventional vehicles such as agricultural vehicles and "inkfish" and the one-cylinder diesel engines, all of which need parts. These vehicles employ very rudimentary technologies and are a market for many of the lower-quality suppliers.

Third, China is the largest producer of motorcycles in the world. The more than 21 million motorcycles made in China every year need engines and other components.

Fourth, parts break and components wear out, so the aftermarket (spare parts) business is very big and growing. Much of the competition in the aftermarket is based on price alone and provides a natural outlet for China's smaller private companies. Over time, distribution will consolidate, but it'll be many years before quality standards are high enough across the board to weed out some of these companies.

Finally, global demand for the competitively priced, lower-technology products that these companies are capable of producing shows no sign of slowing. Components exports, including engines, took another big jump in 2006, increasing from $15.8 billion to $21.8 billion. While some of the components exported out of China are sold to the leading car and truck assemblers, much of the product finds its way into aftermarket channels outside China, where again price is a prime consideration.

Going Global

To develop into truly global suppliers, China's components companies need to improve their managements and put in place systems that lead to consistent quality. Most won't make it, but some will. As they improve their managements, quality, and technology levels, they will be able to compete not only in the purely local market, but also in the foreign/local market. From there, the step to the global markets is a lot shorter. Like Beiqi-Foton in trucks, and Geely in cars, I expect to see some from this sea of components companies make it all the way to the international markets.

In 2004, Chairman Wang asked me to speak to Yuchai's suppliers at its annual supplier meeting, held that year in Chongqing. (He has since left Yuchai, and his new company, Yangdong Diesel, is another example of the development cycle I see for purely local companies. Traditionally Yangdong has been a supplier of engines to the agricultural market, but Chairman Wang is orienting the company toward the passenger car market in China and ultimately the global markets.)

Our plane from Beijing the evening before Yuchai's supplier meeting was diverted to Chengdu due to fog, and seven of my managers and I had to make a harrowing all-night drive just to make it to Chongqing in time for my 8:30 A.M. presentation. But even with all that, I was still more than happy to have made the trip. Yuchai is our largest customer and China's largest diesel engine maker, producing over three hundred thousand engines per year. Because a typical Yuchai engine sells for less than a comparable engine in more developed countries, the majority of Yuchai's suppliers are local Chinese companies. I was one of only a few foreigners among the five hundred people there.

After the meeting, Mr. Gao, the general manager of one of the suppliers, a medium-sized, state-owned company based in Chongqing, approached Henry and said that he'd like to come see me in Beijing to discuss a potential cooperation between our two companies. Henry later asked me what he should tell him, and I said that I would of course be happy to meet him.

When we met several weeks later in the conference room in our offices in Beijing, Gao explained that he wanted to work with ASIMCO because he was looking for ways to improve his management. Yuchai, one of Gao's most important customers, was upgrading the quality of its products to meet the increasing expectations of its China customers, and to make the "leap outside of China," as Chairman Wang had so aptly put it at the supplier meeting a few weeks before. All of Yuchai's suppliers, including Gao's company, were under pressure to upgrade their quality and technology levels.

He didn't speak English, so Henry translated for both of us.

"Capital isn't my problem," Gao told me from his seat across the table. "We listed our company on the Chinese stock market several years ago and raised some money. Also, we made some money by selling the land at our downtown location and moving our factory farther outside the city."

"Our problem," he said, looking at me and the display of our products in the showcase behind me, "is how to improve our management."

Of course, I said that we would be happy to work with him, but as often happens in these meetings I didn't see a logical path to a cooperation. Gao was sincere in what he wanted—I believe that—but he didn't offer any specific suggestions on how exactly we might join forces. Not knowing what was really on his mind, I couldn't be very specific either.

Though nothing came of it, what interested me about this meeting was the concern that Gao expressed with the quality of his management. Ten years before, my meeting with him would have been all about capital. As he plainly put it, capital is the least of his problems today.

As this story indicates, even China's state-owned sector is changing, particularly with regard to small to medium-sized companies. The central government has urged local governments to get out of the asset management business and to focus on running their governments. As a result, the local governments have been restructuring the companies under their control. Some, like my friend from Chongqing, have been able to list their shares on one of China's stock exchanges, but this is not an option available to all.

In most cases, though, this means distributing shares in the underlying companies to key management and employees. Management buyouts, or MBOs, are as widespread a phenomenon in China today as they were in the United States during the 1980s. (Sometimes, these buyouts are referred to as MEBOs, or management employee buyouts.) A large number of the small and medium-sized state-owned companies in China have now been privatized. Anxious to shed the employment and pension obligations of loss-making businesses, the local governments have, in effect, spun off the companies they control to management and employees. In many cases, these are cashless transactions, where the management and employees do not have to put up capital to pay for the company; instead, they give up pension or other claims in exchange for equity in the company. In many cases, the general manager might end up with 20 percent or more ownership. Significant ownership in turn introduces a strong profit incentive, and many of these companies are developing into formidable competitors.

An example of this is the Hunan Oil Pump Co., Ltd., located in the city of Hengdong in Hunan Province. For years an unprofitable factory under the jurisdiction of the local government, the company, now restructured and owned by its management and employees, has improved its quality and is supplying all of the major diesel engine companies in China, including Dongfeng Cummins, a Cummins joint venture in China. In 2006, we surveyed our diesel engine customers and found that they were generally happy with Hunan; obviously, the company has done a good job of serving the marketplace and getting a good lock on the foreign/local market for its products in China. And guess what? Hunan is now beginning to export its products overseas.

In summary, China's motor vehicle industry—at both the assembly and the components level—is already big and is developing quickly. Many of the local companies can't compete with today's global leaders on quality or technology, but the vast local market in China provides a battleground tilted in their favor and gives them more time to develop their managements, quality, and technology. Geely has progressed from local motorcycle assembly to competing in the foreign/local segment of the passenger car market, and it is now taking the first steps toward penetrating overseas markets. Others, like Beiqi-Foton and Yangdong Diesel, will follow.

Hotels and Hair Salons

Not all foreigners are standing idly by. Some astute businesspeople are eyeing the vast local market in China and making plans to get a piece of it.

One of my close friends in Beijing is Mitch Presnick, the president and CEO of Super 8 Hotels (China) Co. Ltd. Mitch is the epitome of an Old China hand, and I've known him since I first arrived in Beijing. Born in Brooklyn, Mitch first came to China in 1988. He learned Mandarin in Beijing and worked in public relations, ultimately becoming the China manager for Edelman, where he advised companies like Anheuser-Busch on their China public relations strategies. He's well known in China circles and has served as the vice chairman of the American Chamber of Commerce in Beijing.

In 2004, Mitch became interested in China's economy hotel market, the roughly 80 percent of China's approximately ten thousand starred hotels that are designated two- and three-star. China's hotel industry generates about $12 billion in revenue yearly; foreign-run hotels, which are typically four- or five-star and have superior management and brands, account for approximately one-third of industry revenues—even though there are only about a thousand of them. Mitch's idea was to bring a brand, better management, and an international reservation system to the local market for economy hotels.

With some former associates, Mitch formed a company that obtained the rights to franchise Super 8 motels in China, and he's now in the process of putting together a chain of economy hotels that will number upwards of three hundred in 2008. His strategy is to go straight for the local market, targeting room rates in the 200-yuan range.

Another good friend of mine, Eric Costantino, is the French founder and owner of ERIC Paris hair salons. Eric owned the largest private chain of salons in the south of France before coming to China in 1996. His salons in Beijing and Shanghai are at the upper end of the market in China, and they've become the salons of choice for China's celebrities, actresses, models, and up-and-comers. (When President George H. W. Bush came to Beijing, Eric was called on to provide a trim.) Eric has been featured in numerous magazines and is the hairstylist of choice for fashion designers in Beijing and Shanghai.

While his traditional salons cater to China's rich and famous, Eric saw enormous potential in the local market for hair and beauty, and he entered into a deal with Carrefour to place Salon 88 shops in all of their stores. Salon 88s provide a woman's cut starting at 28 yuan ($3.50)—more than Wilson might want to pay, but well within the means of China's fashion-conscious young women.

THE POINT IS that whatever the product—restaurants, autos, hotels, or hair care—there's a large local market that coexists with a smaller, higher-priced, higher-technology segment that began to develop when China opened up in

1978. These two markets will not stay separated. As shown by Geely, Beiqi-Foton, and countless other examples, the lines between them are already starting to blur, and ultimately the two will fuse into one.

The introduction of an entirely new universe of entrepreneurial, fast-moving, and low-cost local competitors to a market that already includes all of the global players has made China the most competitive market in the world. How the global and local players fare, and how these two markets begin to come together, will not only determine how the Chinese market develops, but also will likely change the competitive landscape of just about every industry outside of China.

Chapter 15

China's Technology Gap

Two thousand six was designated the year of innovation at ASIMCO Technologies. To encourage our managers and engineers to innovate and to become more confident in their own ability to develop new technologies and products, we began a system of quarterly innovation awards. Starting in the first quarter of 2006, and continuing every quarter since then, top management sifts through a dozen or so nominations submitted by the general managers and picks the product or process innovation that promises to have the biggest impact on the company. The winner receives an RMB 10,000 check and an invitation to present his or her innovation to all of the general managers at the next quarterly meeting. A plaque on a wall at headquarters memorializes both the person and the innovation. It's worked. The innovations submitted in each quarter have improved in quality, and the selection of the winner has become increasingly more difficult with each passing quarter.

To get the technology message out to all of our employees, we also instituted the Kevin Li Memorial Scholarship, in memory of our first chief technology officer, who succumbed at a relatively young age to cancer in 2005. Every year, five scholarships are awarded to deserving sons or daughters of employees of ASIMCO who are pursuing university degrees in engineering, science, or technology. In addition to the scholarship, ASIMCO invites all the recipients and their families to fly to Beijing, all expenses paid, to attend an awards ceremony at the general managers meeting held just before Spring Festival.

There was no more touching moment for me than when I presented the certificates to the first group of scholarship winners, their proud parents standing beside them, in February 2007. The first group included three women and two men. Four of the students were accompanied by one parent, and the fifth, a young lady from rural Anhui Province, came with both parents and her younger sister. Two of the parents were in management; the others included a cook, a security guard, and a machine operator. Four of the five students (and their families) had never been to Beijing before. It was a moving event and one of the nicest things we have ever done as a company.

Why did we feel the need to emphasize innovation, science, and technology by instituting these two programs? In any country, innovation is key to industry leadership. Despite its current lack of development capability, this will also be true in China. But in China at the present moment, it is particularly difficult to create a culture of innovation. A technology gap with the rest of the world in most industries must first be closed, and an insecurity complex among Chinese regarding their own ability to innovate must be overcome.

When China rejoined the rest of the world in 1978, after thirty years of isolation under Chairman Mao, it entered a world that had changed dramatically from the one it had left—in every way, but particularly with regard to technology. Led by the rapid postwar economic and industrial development of the United States and the emergence of a reconstructed Japan, gains in technology had changed the landscape of every industry. With no pressures from a competitive market economy to spur development, China was stuck in the 1950s, a thirty-year time warp behind the rest of the world. Even now, after thirty years of openness, China as a country still struggles with this "technology gap." How it resolves this struggle will have an enormous impact on the global economy.

Unlike Japan, which had the opportunity to completely rebuild its economy and industrial infrastructure with overt support from the United States and other countries, China has had no natural or obvious mechanism by which to rehabilitate itself technologically. India, the world's other large emerging economy, benefited from its ties to the British Empire, receiving technology transfer from British companies as early as the 1960s. The Indian economy has long since weaned itself from dependence on foreign technology and is gaining a reputation for innovation. China didn't even begin to receive technology transfer from abroad until the 1980s, when the promise of the large China market began luring foreign companies into bringing their technology here.

That the technology gap still exists to the extent that it does in China is due to two factors. First, foreign companies have historically been reluctant to transfer their latest technologies to China, for fear that the intellectual property inherent in this technology would be copied. Second, China hasn't yet developed its own product development capability. Vibrant capital markets that have encouraged and rewarded innovation in more-developed economies are not part of the China scene today. The low level of investment that Chinese companies currently make in R&D activities relative to their Western counterparts is common knowledge. China has pulled itself up by its bootstraps by being a "make-to-print" country, not one that is known for product development. The country's emergence as a sustainable economic powerhouse will hinge on its ability to change both perception and reality in that area.

The Intellectual Property Debate

In 2003, I made a presentation at the Global Leadership Conference (GLC) held every year at the lush Greenbrier Resort in West Virginia. Perhaps the leading automotive conference in the United States, the GLC is attended by several hundred CEOs and senior management representatives of companies involved in both vehicle assembly and components supply. One of the topics I was asked to address was the subject of intellectual property rights (IPR), everything from the propensity of Chinese companies to produce counterfeit, or "fake," products, to their readiness to copy designs.

This was a tough task. What could I possibly say about intellectual property violations in China that would be new and helpful? That they're bad? That they undermine the country's reputation in the global markets? That they inhibit product development initiatives within China? That they discourage the flow of technology to China? All of these things are true, but what else is new?

I could make some standard comments about ways to counteract IPR violations, and cite the aggressive legal strategies some employ to close down offending factories, but I knew full well that those strategies take a great deal of time and resources and aren't terribly effective. I could call for more aggressive action by the U.S. government to pressure China's central government to get tougher on these violations, but I knew that wasn't likely to bring about results. Or, I could try, as some have, to attribute the violations to different moral and ethical standards on the part of the Chinese, but I knew that violations like this occur all over the world—including in the United States. Pejorative statements about the character of any people don't seem to me to be the answer to these larger macroeconomic questions.

The more I thought about it, the more I realized that pure economic analysis can go a long way to explain why IPR violations occur, and why they're so prevalent in China. IPR issues occur most frequently with products that meet three criteria: (1) they have a high selling price relative to manufacturing cost, which occurs most often with branded products; (2) they're easy to manufacture; and (3) they are sold to the retail market. This last point is particularly important, because it begins to point to at least a partial solution.

Consider the types of products that have these three characteristics. Callaway golf clubs? Yes. Mont Blanc pens? Yes. Louis Vuitton bags? Yes. DVDs? Yes again. All of these are products that have a high price, are relatively easy to manufacture, and are sold retail—and all are regularly knocked off by Chinese manufacturers. You've seen those Louis Vuitton bags on the shoulders of women walking down your city streets, whether you (or they) know it or not.

In any market, products are sold either to other businesses, "B to B," or to consumers, "B to C." In general, B to B products are harder to knock off, because the customer (a business) is buying more than the individual product. It's buying the supplier's quality and management systems, its service network, its development capability, and its ability to constantly improve the product. All of this has to come in a price package that's competitive, of course, but the supplier's price doesn't have to be the lowest in town if the supplier is good at delivering on other aspects of the value proposition. A pure B to C transaction is most likely a onetime event and is heavily driven by price—especially in a market like China's, with its different affordability standards.

Tougher legal enforcement is only one part of the solution, and it doesn't completely explain why these kinds of IPR violations occur in China but not in the United States. Part of the answer also lies in the differences between China's distribution system and that of more developed economies. In China, distribution is highly fragmented, while in the United States those processes have been concentrated and consolidated. As a result, B to C transactions in China are pure, onetime B to C transactions, while in the United States most traditional B to C transactions also contain a strong element of B to B.

It's somewhat technical, but it's important to understand how it works.

When China's economy was centrally planned, all goods were distributed by state-run distribution organizations, which meant that distribution was highly concentrated. When Deng took the economic handcuffs off in 1978, distribution became a natural outlet for the entrepreneurial instincts of the newly liberated Chinese. Anybody who could scrape together a bit of capital could get into the distribution or trading business, and these businesses began to pop up all over China.

In the process, the proliferation of trading, wholesaling, and retailing enterprises brought down the state-owned distribution companies, which were used to having a monopoly position and captive markets free from competition. They were ill-equipped to compete with the more nimble, private, trading-oriented enterprises that were thriving. As the smaller companies as a group gained market share, and the state-owned enterprises faded from the scene, China's distribution system as a whole became exceedingly fragmented.

These new distribution businesses stayed small, though, because they had no access to the capital they needed to grow their businesses. In most cases, the only source of capital was whatever could be borrowed from relatives. The banks, the only real source of institutional capital in China, made "policy loans," but generally didn't know how to lend to private enterprise. Used to making loans based on relationships, bankers were unable to analyze a balance sheet, an income statement, or a business plan and to make a credit judgment based on the figures alone. And on top of all that, China's regulations, until it entered WTO, prohibited foreigners from engaging in distribution at all. All companies have faced enormous difficulties distributing their goods across the country, but until WTO accession changed the rules, foreign capital was not available to provide a fix.

For all of these reasons, distribution in China remains highly fragmented. The small private companies that form the core of the industry tend to be short-term-oriented, because there is such heavy competition on price. When you combine that with a lack of effective legal enforcement, the integrity of the supply chain—in a structural sense, not an ethical one—is lacking. Interested only in price, retailers and distributors don't always insist on "quality" products that are "real" and not fake. There's no legal downside to selling a counterfeit product, and low price, more than anything else, is the key basis for negotiation. In the fragmented, chaotic, price-sensitive distribution world of China, the counterfeiter thrives.

This deeply flawed system is often cited by multinationals as one of the biggest obstacles to doing business in China. In their home markets, multinationals are used to dealing with larger distribution organizations that take a long-term view in their business models. These companies have the capital resources necessary to use the latest logistics tools to achieve national distribution. The capital markets in places like the United States have looked favorably on companies that can capitalize on the economies of scale inherent in distribution and have rewarded them with more capital.

In the auto parts business, organizations like NAPA and AutoZone have consolidated distribution. Examples abound in other industries, too: Wal-Mart in general merchandise, Barnes & Noble in books, Staples in office products, and Home Depot for the do-it-yourselfers in the home improvement market. Each of these organizations has consolidated the distribution of products in their respective industries, and they often take heat for it. At one time or another, many have been criticized for bringing about the downfall of mom-and-pop retailers like local hardware stores, corner delis, and independent booksellers.

In the United States, these larger distributors are large buying organizations that form an interface between the supplier and the ultimate consumer. Like any business, these organizations purchase products on the basis of price, but also on the basis of management, integrity, quality, service, innovation, and all of the other factors that differentiate suppliers. To protect its own reputation, the wholesaler or retailer understands that when it sells a product to a customer, it's telling the customer that the product being purchased is exactly what it's purported to be. If the product comes in a Bosch box, it'd better be a Bosch product. If it isn't, the U.S. legal system is there to intervene. In this way, selling B to C in the United States subjects a supplier to the same disciplines as selling B to B. Little such discipline exists in China's retail market today.

Whenever the issue of IPR violations or counterfeiting comes up, there's often an undertone to the conversation, the implication being that part of the problem is that the Chinese operate by a different set of ethical standards. That may or may not be true, but I would contend that the same set of circumstances will produce the same result in any country.

Picture a teenager in the United States, sitting at the computer and illegally downloading music off the Internet. Same set of factors. Music, in CDs or any other medium, has the three characteristics I listed above: its price is high relative to its cost to manufacture, it's easy to make (not in terms of the talent involved in the artistic side of it—purely in a production sense), and it sells to the retail market. An individual sitting at a computer terminal is the ultimate in retail distribution.

The Internet has opened new channels of distribution that didn't exist before. In most cases, it has put decisions about consumer purchases back into the hands of the consumer, taking these decisions away from the large distributing organizations. Prior to the Internet, teenagers often only heard about artists whom the larger companies owned, and if they wanted to buy a record, a tape, or a CD, they had to pay a relatively high price for it. Now, they have a greater choice of music and can often get it for free. It shouldn't be any surprise that copyright infringement is one of the hottest topics in the entertainment industry.

When you look at it in this context, you can begin to answer some of the most common questions about IPR issues in China.

Why do they exist? Because high prices for the products and relatively low manufacturing costs provide a great incentive to copy, and because the distribution system doesn't have the scale or coherence to perform the policing function that it does in other countries. The lack of a legal system that enforces IPR compliance is a contributing factor, but fixing the legal system by itself isn't the solution.

What's needed to improve the protection of IPR in China? Probably the single most important change is the development of a more concentrated, less fragmented, more disciplined distribution system. It would go a long way toward eliminating many of the most flagrant violations. As part of China's accession to the WTO, its distribution system is now open to foreign investment—and, thankfully, the consolidation is starting to occur. Carrefour, the giant French retailer, now has over ninety-five hypermarkets in China and plans to open twenty more each year, penetrating not only first-tier cities like Beijing but also smaller second- and third-tier cities. Wal-Mart is not far behind, and many large China wholesalers and retailers are beginning to emerge.

Why doesn't the central government more rigorously prosecute IPR violations? Because, as I covered in Chapter 12, China is a much more decentralized country than most people realize. Local courts, like the local banks, are heavily influenced by local government officials. These officials, in many cases, have agendas that are at odds with the longer-term goals of the central government. Why should a local government close down a factory making counterfeit DVDs when that factory pays VAT and provides employment in the area?

And now, the real question: are my products safe from IPR violations? If they possess those three characteristics, my guess is that they're going to get knocked off in China until the distribution system changes sufficiently. If they're sold to another company, difficult to make, and reasonably priced given the manufacturing costs, they're probably better protected.

That answer is, in a sense, counterintuitive. Most companies are worried about bringing their most proprietary and highest-technology products to China for fear of losing their intellectual property. I'd argue that these products may be easier to protect. As I'll explain later, a number of measures can be taken to help protect a product's underlying technology.

Thorny issues like intellectual property violations will take a long time to solve. It's going to require real legal reform, the development of a more robust distribution system, and China making the transition from being a make-to-print country to developing new technologies and products. When Chinese companies and inventors have as much to lose in terms of intellectual property as their foreign counterparts, my guess is that reform will come about much faster.

In the meantime, creating a viable, legal option—in the same way that the music industry in the United States has done with downloading music—may offer at least a partial solution. With pirated video games selling alongside DVDs on the streets of China, U.S. video game developers have not been willing to create games for the Chinese market. Recently, though, many U.S. companies have started to make successful online games in China. They've created a legal distribution system of "use cards" that operate like phone cards and allow a player to log in to the game for a certain period of time. The amount that a person in China pays to play is a fraction of what's paid in the United States, but the model works because of the economy of scale.

Protecting Intellectual Property Rights

As the China market grows larger, companies have no choice but to bring their latest technologies to China. This naturally raises the question of how to protect intellectual property while the changes in China's distribution and legal systems unfold. There are a few simple things that a company can do.

First, it's absolutely vital that all of your technology and all of your products that are patented elsewhere also be patented in China. Enforcing patent rights remains a problem, and purely legal approaches seldom work in China, but it's not even possible to defend your company's intellectual property if you haven't applied for patent protection in China.

Second, you have a better shot at protecting valuable technology if you transfer it to a wholly owned company in China. This doesn't protect you from individual employees walking off with your technology, but it does make it more difficult for other companies to do so.

Third, you can do your best to keep key processes and aspects of the technology separate from one another by placing them in different facilities in China, which makes it harder for one person to see and understand the entire process. You should also carefully consider whether it's wise to outsource key components. In many products, the key to the technology is in the components. It might be perfectly safe to teach a supplier how to make such components in more developed countries, but in China it's probably a better decision to keep them in-house.

IPR will continue to be a big issue—and problem—in China for some time to come. I've laid out a couple of the steps you can take to protect yourself, but the reality is that the problem won't be solved until China's technology gap finally closes.

Closing the Technology Gap

"The Chinese can copy, but they can't create" is a comment I hear all the time. Given how isolated China has been, and how quickly it has wanted to catch up to the rest of the world, it's understandable that the country's focus has been solely on getting access to technology in any and every way possible. Ethical considerations aside, IPR violations are simply one of the means available to the Chinese as they seek to close the gap.

But China's ultimate objective—and the objective of every local Chinese company—is to reduce its reliance on imported technology, to move up to more advanced, higher-value-added products, and to become a global leader in technology. Every day, I see signs that the central government is encouraging innovation, and that local companies are relying more heavily on self-development. I have to believe that many companies have similar innovation programs to ours.

China has no choice but to become an innovative country, for the simple reason that many of the problems it faces will require different solutions than those found in more developed economies. The disparity in income levels across the country will force this to happen. China's companies will have to find a way to satisfy the functional requirements of the marketplace, all the while keeping the price of products within the affordability standards of the majority of the country's population.

Most people who drive cars take for granted what a car actually does. They don't appreciate the level of technology required for a car to accelerate quickly and stop on a dime. Modern cars and trucks incorporate vast amounts of materials, product and process technology; as emissions and environmental requirements change, the level of technology that goes into vehicle design and production increases dramatically. For this reason, following China's technology road map in autos can serve as an example of how China might evolve technologically in other industries.

When China established First Auto Works in 1953, companies in the States and in Europe had been manufacturing vehicles for at least thirty years, so China was on the low end of a thirty-year technology gap with the developed countries in autos and trucks. Until 1984, when Beijing Jeep was formed, China's auto industry was a completely local affair. Even though the Chinese hoped to encourage foreigners to bring in technology by opening up the auto industry to outside investment, very little real technology transfer occurred. After an initial growth spurt, where the annual production of vehicles increased from about 700,000 units in 1991 to almost 1.5 million units in 1995, there had been little growth. In 2001,

China produced about 2.3 million trucks, buses, and passenger cars—barely 800,000 more than six years before.

When China entered the WTO in 2001, all of this began to change. The market grew significantly, increasing in increments of roughly 1 million units per year, to the point where China now produces more than 8 million vehicles a year and is the third-largest vehicle producer in the world. At the same time, customers raised their expectation levels. They were no longer content to have older-technology products and models. They wanted the best quality and highest-technology models from around the world, the same models that American, European, and Japanese consumers were buying.

Because of these two factors, a bigger market and higher expectations, technology has streamed into China and the technology gap has begun to close. How do I know it's not completely closed? Because China is still importing components. From 2002 to 2004, the amount of components imported into China increased from $3.4 billion to $11.3 billion—a staggering jump—and exceeded the amount of components exported from China in every single one of those years. Quite simply, the materials, process, and product technologies required to produce the components used in top-of-the-line modern vehicles simply didn't exist yet in China, and so they had to be imported.

When I explained this to audiences prior to 2005, I would tell them to watch the pattern of components imports. "When those numbers begin to level off and decline," I'd say, "you'll know that the technology gap is closing."

In 2005, that's precisely what happened. For the first time, imports of components declined to $10.4 billion, despite the fact that unit production of vehicles increased by 15 percent. Also for the first time, exports of components exceeded imports, with exports shooting up by almost 50 percent, to more than $15.8 billion. The year 2005 was the inflection point.

The question now is "What happens from here?" Most industry experts predict that China will move from having the world's third-largest auto industry to having its second largest by 2010. I believe that between now and then, any company in the auto industry that has any useful know-how or technology is going to have to get it into China. If a company's technology or product is not in the world's second-largest market, how much will it really be worth?

Make no mistake about it, the technology gap is closing, and it is closing fast. Global assemblers are transferring technology and know-how to local Chinese suppliers in order to develop a reliable supply base in China. Global components companies are expanding their operations in the country, bringing their latest technologies and designing advanced systems for Chinese assemblers. The CEO of a major transmission company told me that his company was designing a new transmission for a Chinese assembler.

"When we're done," he told me, "our customer will have the most advanced transmission in the world."

Chery, the fast-growing Chinese car company, is also taking lessons from Chrysler as it prepares to produce compact models for the American market to be sold under the Chrysler label. Ask FEV, AVL, and Ricardo, the leading engine design houses, who their biggest customers are, and Chery, Geely, and other Chinese assemblers will be at the top of the list.

By 2010, when China is the second-largest vehicle producer in the world, it will be on a level playing field technologically with the rest of the world. That's when things will really become interesting, as China moves to become the world's largest automotive producer, and by far its largest market, by 2020.

In developing such a large automotive industry, China will run head-on into three very strong constraints to its growth.

The first will be affordability. It's one thing to provide vehicles for everybody in Beijing and Shanghai. It's another to get them to the 750 million people who live in the countryside. The market wants more affordable conventional vehicles, and Chinese makers are scrambling to figure out how to deliver them.

The second constraint will be fuel availability. Even with the industry at its current level, China's leaders are traveling the world negotiating long-term supply contracts with oil-producing countries. China does not have enough of its own energy reserves, and obtaining enough energy to fuel its economy is a very real concern.

The third constraint is environmental impact. If China puts another 100 million vehicles on its highways, that's going to stress the planet. Even if China doesn't care—which it does—every other country around the world is going to be very concerned about how the growth of the China market and its transportation sector will impact the environment. Over the last ten years, satellite photographs have shown that nitrogen dioxide levels have increased by 50 percent across northeast China, where the bulk of China's population lives. Pollution has become China's "unwanted export" as clouds of polluted air have now appeared over the northwestern part of the United States. Unfortunately, China is an environmental accident that has already happened.

China's auto industry, like the country at large, is beginning to come under enormous, unprecedented pressure to solve these problems. As a result, I believe China's auto industry is likely to become an early adopter and developer of new technology. Any technology that can be useful in solving any one of these three constraints— affordability, fuel economy, and environmental impact—will get a ready hearing in China, even more so than in more established markets. In more developed and wealthier countries, the pressure on affordability and fuel efficiency simply isn't as strong. It's inconvenient for Americans to pay over $3.00 a gallon for gas, as they have in 2006 and 2007, but this is intolerable for the vast majority of China's population. In China, fuel efficiency isn't a matter of political correctness or presidential approval ratings: it's a matter of economic life and death. If China is restricted in its ability to move people and goods around the country, it can't continue to grow. It's that simple.

Some of these problems may actually be easier to solve in China than in more established countries. Introducing new technology in an established market like the United States often threatens to obsolete existing infrastructure and can encounter stiff resistance from entrenched vested interests. In China, there is most likely no existing infrastructure to obsolete. In most areas, China has a blank page to work with.

Consider the telecommunications business. In 1994, Ai Jian told me that he wanted to have a telephone installed at his home, but he had been advised that there was a six-month waiting list for landlines. The tele-communications infrastructure in China obviously had not kept pace with the growth of the economy. What did China do? Did China hurriedly erect a bunch of tele-phone poles and string them with wires to catch up with demand? No. China went right to the latest cellular technology, skipping over landlines entirely. China went from no phones to cell phones in one step.

In transportation, the conditions are ripe for China to do just the same thing. As China adopts, and indeed develops, new technologies, and as these technologies gain scale in the large, rapidly growing Chinese market, they'll then more than likely set the standard for the global automotive industry. And when this happens, China will have made the switch from an importer of technology to an exporter. In the process, the entire $2 trillion global automotive industry will have been turned on its head.

The acute environmental dilemma that China faces is how to deal with the vast portion of its population that can't afford to use conventional transportation—cars, trucks, and the like—and relies on cheaper, polluting, unconventional vehicles. The double-income professional couples in the larger cities, or the wealthy entrepreneurs who've started businesses all over China, can easily afford to purchase cars with the latest emissions technology. But most of these vehicles are well beyond the reach of the 750 million people living in the countryside who make roughly $500 a year. A growing vehicle population in Beijing and the other major cities in China clearly adds to the environmental problem, but the tens of millions of motorcycles, agricultural vehicles, and inkfish in use today in China's purely local market are a much bigger problem. Most of them have very rudimentary engines and fuel systems that are creating an environmental nightmare.

Innovation occurs when an unsatisfied market demand is combined with a lot of smart people. Somewhere out there lies a technological solution. Somebody will figure out how to create more fuel-efficient and environmentally friendly vehicles, which at the same time meet the affordability needs of the China market. Perhaps the ultimate solution will come from engineers in Detroit, Stuttgart, or Toyota City. But it's equally likely that the solution will be developed by Chinese engineers in Beijing, Shanghai, Changchun, or Wuhan, engineers who instinctively understand China's lower cost perspective and design with that difference in mind. Out of that vast pool of China companies that sell entirely to the purely local transportation market in China may emerge the truly elegant solution that satisfies all requirements. In our fuel business, we are working on possible solutions and are being encouraged by our customers to do so. I know that other Chinese companies are also hard at work. Whoever finds this solution will unlock one of the biggest opportunities of the twenty-first century.

Chapter 16

Establishing a Business
in China

As Beijing prepares to host the 2008 Olympics, there's hardly a news program, magazine, newspaper, or even board meeting where some aspect of China isn't one of the key topics. General knowledge about China is high, and most people realize that this country is already having a significant impact on the global economy—and that its future impact will be even more pervasive. What everybody wants to know is "How do I get in on it? How do I set up my business there? What are the three or four things that can help get me started?"

The first advice I give on this front is simple: don't be intimidated. China has always had an air of mystery about it, and plenty of people will encourage your perception that you'll never be able to understand it. To be sure, the country is big and complicated, the people tend to hide their true feelings, and the language is completely different from (and more complicated than) what most in the West are used to. But the country does have a logic. If you rely on your experience, use your good judgment, and spend the time, you'll be able to find it. And as you do, step-by-step, China won't seem quite so mysterious.

I also suggest relying more on firsthand observation than taking at face value what others have to say about the country. China is big, complicated, and changes rapidly. When I first came to China, I spoke to as many people as I could to get the broadest possible range of information. But I also tested what I was being told against what I was seeing on the ground. It was amazing to me how many times the two were different. It wasn't that the advice I'd gotten was wrong; it was just out of date. Trust your instincts. In the end, your own experiences and observations will be more useful to you than anybody else's.

The Language Barrier

One of the first questions people ask me when they learn that I've been in China since 1993 is "How's your Mandarin?"

When I say "Nonexistent," they look at me in disbelief.

To lighten it up, I often add, "I learn one word every year, and I'm now up to fifteen words. When I've been here for five thousand years, I'll finally be able to have a conversation with one of my Chinese colleagues."

Language is one of the reasons why doing anything in China takes twice as long as it does anywhere else. First-time visitors don't need to do much else other than try to order a cup of coffee in order to figure this out. I'm always amused by the stories people tell me. If you order an ordinary cup of coffee, you've got a chance. But God forbid if you try to order decaf, or Sweet & Low instead of sugar. Much of what is common to Westerners is completely foreign to the Chinese, and even those who speak English will have a difficult time understanding idioms and quick speech patterns.

And, like everybody else, the Chinese don't like to admit that they don't understand. They'll nod knowingly, and then go off and bring you something completely different from what you ordered. I wish I had a nickel for every time I ordered a cold glass of water and got a glass of hot instead. Didn't the waiter's nod mean that he understood me? (To the Chinese, the Western preference for ice water is odd, much the way the Brits find it hard to understand why Americans like their beer cold.) When in doubt, a Chinese waiter will always bring you hot water, because that's how they drink it themselves. And forget about trying to order an iced tea in all but the most Westernized restaurants. "Ice" and "tea" in China just don't mix.

Wouldn't speaking the language make it that much easier for me to work in China and function as the head of ASIMCO? Sure it would. If I were proficient in Chinese, my life would be much easier—but that's a big "if."

What amount of effort would it take for me to get my Chinese up to a level where I could rely on it in business?

The answer is, a great deal. Chinese is an extremely complicated language. You can learn it to a level that helps in daily life—directing a taxi driver, ordering in a Chinese restaurant, asking for directions—but mastering it to where you can use it in business is another story. The people I know who've done it have spent at least two years studying intensively.

I was forty-two when I left Wall Street to set up a business in Asia, and the second career I started was making automotive components in China. That decision came with two inherent difficulties. First, I was an American Studies major at Yale and had never studied China or Chinese. Second, my first career was in finance, and I had no experience in manufacturing or in the auto industry. Because I had to learn both a new country and a new industry, I simply had no time to spend two years or more learning a new language. My value add is my knowledge of the way capital markets work; my experience gathering capital, management, and technology resources for growing companies; and the vision and broader perspective I gained from twenty years on Wall Street. It's not my ability to speak Chinese.

Studying the language part-time isn't a realistic option, at least not for me. It would help a bit in getting around China, but I'd never gain the level of proficiency necessary for a business context. And the idea of coming home from a busy day at work and hitting the language lesson plan isn't terribly appealing, either.

Even if I did somehow manage to achieve proficiency,

I'd still be concerned about what I might miss if I didn't have an interpreter. Wilson speaks English as well as anybody in China. But he admitted to me that if he's sitting in a roomful of Westerners, he only gets about 70 to 80 percent of what's being said. How much would I miss in a comparable situation? And how much can anybody ever afford to miss? For this reason, we always do translations at our general managers meetings, even though most of our top managers speak both languages. With important information, it pays to take a bit more time and make sure that everyone understands.

One image I've never been able to get out of my mind is a dinner I had with a relatively senior government official when I first came to China. This person, who was in his fifties, was quite proud of the fact that he was learning English. No problem there. But at the dinner, he insisted on stumbling through sentence after sentence. I give him credit for trying, but quite frankly he sounded like a seven-year-old, and that's the image of him that I carry around to this day. I can't even imagine how I'd sound in Chinese. I'd rather pick battles that I at least have a chance of winning.

Maybe this is all one big rationalization for not having taken the time to learn the language. That's part of it: languages have never been my thing. But I do believe that too much emphasis is put on the language, and not enough emphasis is put on gaining a more substantive understanding of China and how it works. There's this sense that if you don't speak the language you can't possibly understand China; there's also the equally wrong notion that anybody who speaks the language *does* understand China. I've seen plenty of instances where this isn't the case.

Having said all of that, I would advise any young person with a serious interest in doing business here to learn the language. Early in your career, you can devote time to doing it the right way. All three of my kids started taking Chinese in high school, continued through college, and took language courses in China. Carleen has managed to learn enough so that she can get around pretty well. If you can do it the right way, like my kids, by all means do it. If you can't, but you still want to learn it for your own personal gratification, like Carleen, then by all means go ahead if that's important to you. But don't let the language present your first insurmountable hurdle to getting started here. Strictly in terms of business, my advice is to spend the time learning how China works and leave the language to linguists.

Dealing with Chinese Culture

It goes without saying that China's culture is different from what most Westerners are used to. But again, as with the language, I've found a tendency on the part of Westerners to be overly concerned about it. Before some-one's first trip to China, I'm often asked, "Are there any customs or cultural issues that I should be sensitive to so as not to offend the Chinese?" I always tell first-time visitors to relax and not be overly concerned about these issues. The Chinese don't expect you to understand their culture, and they're perfectly happy to explain their traditions and practices. Besides, there is no way that you will learn enough in the one or two weeks before a trip, or on the plane ride over, to significantly increase your effectiveness. If a Westerner makes a mistake or does something wrong, it's readily excused. No one's going to be offended. On matters of etiquette, I've always been able to get by simply by watching what others do and following suit. In a pinch I can always whisper a question to one of my Chinese colleagues.

More to the point, though, is trying to understand a bit about the Chinese personality. Everybody is different, and generalizations are always dangerous, but there are a few things to keep in mind.

First, no matter how straightforward or outwardly aggressive Chinese may appear to be, they are very sensitive—much more so than Westerners. They don't like to be embarrassed. Where you might be able to tease a Westerner in public, this is generally not a good idea here. "Face" is extremely important, and "loss of face" a serious matter. Being told "no" publicly is, for example, a loss of face. Better not to be so direct. Deliver the bad news privately.

Second, in virtually all of my early meetings in China, the concept of "mutual trust" was mentioned. It happened so frequently that I began to think of it as a platitude, like apple pie and motherhood. The more I am in China, though, the more I realize the importance of establishing real trust with your Chinese partners, the local government, your customers, or your employees. It's very simple. Chinese will be offended and standoffish if they sense that, despite your words, you do not trust them. On the other hand, there is nothing they won't do for you if they believe that you do.

Third, the Chinese are respectful of seniority and authority, but don't expect even your closest subordinate to tell you when something is wrong. They don't want to give you bad news, to complain, or to appear to be critical. Only with a great deal of urging will you be able to find out their true feelings about another colleague, or some new initiative that you're considering. This couldn't be more different from Westerners, who at the drop of a hat will tell the CEO how he or she should be running the company. The Chinese will talk to one another about all of this, but they're not going to talk to you.

My best example of this aspect of Chinese behavior is one of our former general managers, a quiet, unassuming, and very sensitive person. In describing him, colleagues would say he's a "very traditional Chinese."

Sometime after we got started, I began to circulate monthly results to all of the general managers. Without thinking twice about it, I listed the name of each general manager in the order in which the joint venture or operating unit was established. First on the list was the name of whoever happened to be the general manager of our Anhui operation, because that was the first company we formed.

The joint venture managed by this particular general manager was formed somewhat later, so his name was somewhere in the middle.

This went on for years. Little did I know that this person felt slighted each time his name wasn't listed first. After all, the business he ran was usually one of our best-performing units. It was only in passing that someone brought this to my attention. Once I heard that, I could understand how he felt. I hadn't intended to slight anybody—doing it in order of formation was logical—but I could see why he might think that he should be listed first. What surprised me was that this had been a sore point for years, but nobody had dared mention it to me. If this had happened in the States, I'd have known about it immediately. From then on, I always put this manager's name at the top of the list on anything that I circulated, and I became more sensitive to these seemingly little things.

My last bit of advice on the cultural side is that you need to learn how to be patient and how to listen when you're working in China. The surface is typically just part of the story. You've usually got to go layer by layer, peeling the onion, before you get to the true meaning or motivation. My biggest mistakes in China have occurred when I've overreacted, not taken enough time to listen, and not tried hard enough to put myself in my counterpart's place to better understand his or her perspective.

Dos and Don'ts

When companies first start thinking about China, they believe that the first, and biggest, hurdle to overcome is the language barrier. Though it's important, the language issue should fall farther down on the list; in the name of solving it, I've seen companies make some crippling mistakes.

When companies come to China, they tend either to hire the first remotely qualified Chinese speaker they meet, or they delegate the "China" job to a junior member of management. My advice is to take just the opposite approach. Pick somebody senior in your organization who has a thorough understanding of the company's business and is well regarded at headquarters, and don't worry too much about the language. A person who knows the company's operations and is in good standing with colleagues will have much better luck at getting the resources and support necessary for success in China. You can always hire a translator.

What people don't realize is that somebody who speaks Mandarin but grew up in Singapore, Taiwan, Hong Kong, or the United States simply can't be expected to know much about Mainland China. It's a country unto itself. Speaking the language helps, but unless you're a native Mainland Chinese and have spent most or all of your life in China, we all start from the same place when we try to figure out how the place works.

At the request of a friend, I spoke about China with the CEO of a $60 million Midwestern manufacturer of specialty engineering equipment. When I called him on the appointed evening from my home in Beijing, the CEO told me that his company had more than a 50 percent market share in the United States and had begun seeing strong interest in its products from China. The company had hired an agent, a Chinese national, and export sales to China were growing. He wanted to know whether he should think about setting up a manufacturing facility here.

"How much do you think your revenue opportunity might be if you manufactured in China?" I asked him.

Straight off, he said, "I think we could do as much as $40 million."

Hearing that, my advice was clear. "If the market is that big in China, you'd better start producing here," I told him. "Your product is a labor-intensive, assembled product. With transportation, the imported price is already pretty high. And given the high labor content, there's plenty of room for a Chinese company to reverse-engineer your product and sell it for a great deal less."

He saw the point and agreed.

But I wasn't quite done. "Losing sales in China isn't your biggest problem if you don't start manufacturing here," I added. "How long do you think it'll be before your Chinese competitors begin to eye your market, and those higher prices, in the United States? If you don't get over here, your 50 percent market share at home could also be in jeopardy."

This was a sobering thought for him; I could hear it

through the silence at the other end of the telephone. I had just told him that, in many ways, it was "worse" than he might have thought, and that he needed to worry about a lot more than just the prospective size of the market in China. The whole future viability of his company might be at risk.

I'm pretty sure I ruined his day, and that he was sorry I'd called. After a long silence, he asked, "How should I go about setting up a manufacturing facility?"

"The first thing I'd do," I said, "is pick someone at the company whom you trust, and who's willing to spend the next three to five years in China. His job will be to figure out your game plan and put together a good local management team."

He thought about it for a second, and then said glumly, "That's my first problem. I don't have anybody here who would be prepared to do that."

I wish I could have given him different advice, but there just isn't some consultant out there who can do it all for him. It might have made him feel better to think that there was, but it wouldn't have been true. There are plenty of professionals who can help you set up an operation in China, but the involvement of a senior person from the company is the only way to ensure success. If China's that important to the future of your company, then somebody senior had better step up and take responsibility.

I like to use John Mooney, CEO of Sachem, Inc., a medium-sized chemical science company with plants in

Texas, the Netherlands, and Japan, as an example of the right way to do it.

John's son, Sean, works for one of our shareholders, and he e-mailed me one day saying that his father was going to be in town and he wanted to get together to talk about doing business in China. On a Saturday in late October of 2003, John came over to my office in Beijing, and we sat for several hours and discussed some of the major issues involved with doing business here. Afterward, he and his wife, Kay, joined Carleen and me for dinner at the Courtyard.

During our discussion, John told me that his company needed a presence in China. He believed it was so critical to the future success of the company that he decided not to delegate the job to somebody else. Instead, he decided to take it on himself: he and Kay planned to move to Shanghai for several years.

As he explained it, "The business is running well enough that I can leave that to the rest of my management team. China's too important to leave to anybody else." It was the right decision. (Apart from the business side of things, it was obvious that both John and Kay were looking forward to the move to Shanghai.) The company began building its China plant in 2006.

Whoever takes on the China role at your company needs, first and foremost, to assemble and develop a good local management team. We've been through it earlier in the book, but I stress it again here because it really is the first job that needs to get done. It was the first thing we tried to do in early 1993; in retrospect, I could have done a better job, but I learned from my mistakes and we've now got an excellent local management team. While the conventional wisdom is that the way to succeed in China is to find a good partner, I believe that for the long term, outsourcing management to another organization, no matter how good a partner it might be, is a mistake.

In picking a local team, I also caution managers not to confuse language capability with ability. If a Westerner has two Chinese on his staff—one with great experience and ability but no English, and another who speaks perfect English but is much less capable—I guarantee you that the Westerner will spend more time with the latter, and probably go there first for advice.

In a sense, this is just human nature. I find myself still doing it after fifteen years here. It's easier to converse in English, and it's painfully more difficult to work through translation, but sometimes the most valuable members of the company don't have language capability. To tap the full potential of a company's human capital in China, you've got to find a way to hear everybody's views.

From a talent pool point of view, more and more Chinese in their twenties and thirties, particularly those in the larger cities like Beijing and Shanghai, are learning to speak English. Most Chinese over forty do not, and outside the major cities language capability falls off considerably. Given the shortage of management talent in China, I think it's unwise to exclude these individuals from your potential management pool. (Having a good core group of local Chinese managers will help you here, because it'll matter a lot less if some of the other managers don't speak English.) That's why we are now devoting more attention to our ASIMCO Leadership and Management Development programs. Many talented young managers in our organization work at our factories in the inner provinces and have no English capability. We want to reach down into our company and develop as many of them as we can.

Site Location

Too often, I see companies picking manufacturing sites for the wrong reasons. In most cases, companies pick a location because it offers the best living conditions for the company's expatriate managers. I believe that this is a mistake, and another strong argument for developing local management—because then you can feel free to pick the site that makes the most sense in terms of pure economics.

While China is a low-cost country, costs can still vary widely. Just as costs around major cities like New York, Chicago, and Los Angeles will be higher than other areas in the States, so, too, employee and other costs will be considerably higher around Beijing and Shanghai. With greater competition for scarce management talent, management turnover is also more likely to be higher in the major cities.

As I discussed in a previous chapter, China's local

governments are very development-oriented, and they'll go to great pains to make the investment environment in their cities as favorable as possible. As a result, economic development zones, which provide the infrastructure necessary to establish a manufacturing facility, can be found in virtually any sizable city in China. Depending on whether a given economic zone is authorized by the central government, the province, or the local government, tax and other incentives may vary somewhat. Otherwise, they all offer more or less the same advantages.

I'm a big proponent of the "big fish in a little pond" approach to site location. In most of the cities where our factories are located, we're one of the biggest taxpayers and most important companies in the area. It only makes sense that the local officials tend to pay a bit more attention to your well-being if you're an important business in their city.

In one of our locations, the local government worked quietly for more than a year to qualify our business for special tax treatment. Even though some of the tax rebate that we eventually received as a result of their effort came from the local government's share of our previously paid taxes, they still lobbied hard to have us qualified because it was good for our business. We should probably have known about this special tax status and worked toward it ourselves, but we didn't. That didn't stop them, though, from taking the initiative and going out of their way to help.

One cautionary note regarding site location: be

careful in cities where there hasn't been at least some level of foreign investment. In some cases, the local governments can be somewhat parochial and narrow-minded. Referrals from other companies that have operations in any city are vital in gauging whether this is the case.

Getting Started

The Chinese have an oft-repeated saying, "A journey of a thousand miles begins with a single step." After being in China for over fifteen years, I've learned to take everything step-by-step, one step at a time.

The first obvious step is to buy a ticket to Beijing or Shanghai and see for yourself. Talking about China is one thing, but being here is another. You need to be here, even if it's just for a short period of time, if you want to learn about the country. Like Chairman Mao, who said, "Conclusions invariably come after investigation, and not before," I recommend that you come over as soon as possible and start piecing things together yourself.

And don't make it too complicated. If you're coming for a week, don't worry about filling up a five-day schedule. Lawyers, accountants, consultants, and others doing business here will be more than happy to talk to you, and you can learn a great deal from them. Most people look forward to meeting with visitors from their home country, and you'll find them eager to share their experiences. Set a couple of key appointments, but keep your schedule fluid and leave plenty of time for referrals.

You'll be amazed by how much you can absorb in one week.

Living and Working in China Today

If somebody asks me in casual conversation where I live, and I say, "Beijing," the first question is almost always "Beijing, China?" as if to confirm that they've heard me correctly. "What's it like?" is always the immediate next question.

Obviously, Beijing and China are a great deal different than they were in 1993, when Carleen and I first arrived. At the time, Western housing was difficult to find and was limited mostly to a number of "villa"-type communities that had been developed close to the airport. That's where we lived, in one development or another, until 2004. The villas were user-friendly, and the truth is that there wasn't much incentive to move into the heart of the city. There simply wasn't much going on.

That has all changed. Today, you can find every type of restaurant in Beijing, and there's plenty of nightlife. A good friend of ours, Henry Li, is credited with starting "Bar Street" in Sanlitun by opening his Public Space bar, and he's since gone on to open one nightclub after another. A host of others have followed Henry's lead, and now more than one hundred separate bars are listed in the Nightlife section of the *Insider's Guide to Beijing*.

The restaurant industry in particular has exploded over the past ten years in Beijing. Depending on your mood, you can find just about any type of food: Western, French, Indian, Thai, Mexican, Spanish, Greek, Brazilian, Italian, German, Japanese, Russian, Korean, and Vietnamese. Although nobody knows the actual number, I was told by the head of BAIC, which has a joint venture with Hyundai, that there are at least one million foreigners living in Beijing, with more than two hundred thousand Koreans and Chinese/Koreans alone. Given the number of Korean restaurants that have sprung up recently here, I shouldn't have been surprised. Even North Korea has gotten into the act with a number of restaurants, complete with Mandarin-speaking North Korean waitresses.

In addition to the many local Chinese restaurants where you can find good basic food, there are also places now that feature food from every part of China. Whether you prefer Sichuan, Hunan, or Shanghai cuisine, you can find great restaurants in Beijing that specialize in each. Another big change has been the development of upscale, high-end Chinese restaurants. Lan, part of the South Beauty chain of restaurants, opened in Beijing in 2006. Designed by Philippe Starck, the restaurant was built for a reputed 300 million yuan, and it seats a thousand. Restaurants like this simply didn't exist ten years ago.

Apart from bars and restaurants, Starbuckses have also sprung up all over China. If someone had told me ten years ago that coffee selling for more than $2 would be popular in China, I would have looked at them like they were crazy. But Starbucks has now become the in place for the up-and-coming young professional set. You can see them there at all hours, sipping on lattes, working on their computers, talking to a friend, or reading a book.

As Beijing developed, we found ourselves going into town more and more frequently. In 2004, tired of the drive back and forth, Carleen and I decided to take an apartment in the Sanlitun Diplomatic compound, near the embassy district and convenient to Beijing's restaurants and social life. The compound was built in the 1950s to provide office space and apartments for the embassies of some of the smaller countries that had diplomatic relationships with Beijing. The Soviet-style architecture won't win any prizes, but we love the high ceilings and big rooms, and the fact that the building is solid and meant to last. As more and more Western-style housing has become available, the state-owned company that owns the property was amenable to renting an apartment to people outside the diplomatic community, and we jumped at the chance.

Since then Beijing has continued to boom. In one weekend in 2005, we were invited to attend the first China Open here, which Serena Williams won, and the first Formula One racing event in China, which was held in Shanghai. (Having two world-class sporting events on one weekend in China was inconceivable in 1995.) Concerts, fashion shows, wine tastings, and specially catered dinners are becoming more frequent, too, as singers, musicians, wine merchants, chefs, and fashion designers from around the world flock to this country, anxious to build a following with the new China consumers.

Travel has also gotten much easier since the days of our Long March. In the past, I would never have been caught traveling in China without a book to read. Long car trips and endless waiting in airport sitting rooms packed with people (and filled with smoke from about five feet above floor level to the ceiling) meant that you had to have some way of taking yourself to another place. A good book was one way to do that.

Though still crowded, nearly all of the airports in China are clean and modern. Virtually every city of any size has built a new airport within the past five years. And one other major change: no smoking! Airports in China today are, thankfully, smoke free.

The aircraft used by China's airlines were often another surprise in the early days. It took me a while to figure out that I needed to instruct my assistant to check the equipment on every flight, and to book me only on the flights that involved aircraft with names that I recognized—Boeing, Airbus, or McDonnell Douglas at that time. Before I realized this, I had some pretty harrowing trips.

On a trip in 1997 to Ürümqi in the far northwest corner of China, Carleen and I were horrified when the bus from the Beijing airport terminal stopped in front of a massive plane that looked like it was meant to carry cargo. As we entered the ground-floor door leading to the steps that took us up through the cargo hold and into the passenger section above, I noticed some writing on the plane that said, "Leased from Air Volga." This was not encouraging. My first thought was about whether anybody had any incentive to maintain the aircraft, and my second was about whether they even had enough spare parts for a plane like that. The four-hour trip seemed like it took forever. On another flight, we boarded a small Tupolev, which only carried ten people. I swore that I could see the ground below through a hole in the floor.

There's no need for my assistant to check anymore. China has been one of the world's largest purchasers of aircraft over the last ten years, so the fleet here is one of the most modern on the globe. Bob Johnson, a friend of ours who's been training pilots in China for Boeing for a number of years, told me that the safety record for Chinese airlines is among the best in the world. That was reassuring.

If you don't mind paying the extra $100 or so to fly business or first class on most flights, it's well worth it. While first-class travel isn't such a luxury in other parts of the world, first class and VIP really mean something in China. If you fly first or business, there are virtually no lines at the special check-in counter where you get your boarding pass and check your bags. They give you a special security line, too, and I can't remember ever waiting more than about five minutes to pass through it. In some airports, an attendant will literally escort you from the counter, walking on a long red-carpet runner through security to the lounge, where she (it's always a woman) will find you a seat. If your plane is leaving from a remote part of the airport, special buses whisk you to the departure gate.

In the post-9/11 environment, air travel in China is far less stressful today than it is in the States. I can comfortably arrive at the airport an hour from departure and not worry at all about missing my flight. Within fifteen minutes of arrival, I'm typically sitting in one of the airline lounges having a cup of coffee.

And then there's that special "airport massage" to send you off to your next destination. Anywhere else, if the alarm goes off as you go through security, a male security guard is called over for the men and a female guard for the women. Not so in China. Here, a young female security guard beckons from the other side of the security check, wand in hand. I swear they look disappointed if the alarm doesn't go off, and that a subtle smile comes across their faces when it does. Man, woman, boy, girl—it doesn't make a difference. The same guard will pat you down and run her wand all over your body. Some consider this to be the highlight of every flight.

Living Outside the United States

Another question I get asked a lot is "What do you miss most living in China?"

That's a tough one to try to explain. Until you've lived here, you don't really appreciate how well developed a country like the United States is. Service levels are higher, everything is easier and more readily available; the place just works. China's a lot more variable.

Being a foreigner living in China, you're often

reminded that it isn't your country. Most people would be annoyed to discover that they're being charged a higher price by a shopkeeper than other customers, but it happens all the time here. Because a country like the United States is more developed than China is, many Chinese believe that foreigners can (and should) pay more and routinely charge them a higher price than they would a local. No matter how good a foreigner's Chinese might be, they'll never get the same price.

Carleen and her friend Katy were shopping for furniture one Saturday afternoon in Beijing. When they found something that they liked, they began negotiating with the store owner—who politely told them that, as a matter of policy, she didn't negotiate prices. The listed price was final. Fair enough, they thought. That's the way it works in the rest of the world.

But when the shopkeeper left to wait on another couple, Katy, whose Chinese is pretty good, heard the Chinese couple try to dissuade the owner.

"Why don't you charge the two foreigners more and give us a discount?" they asked. In their minds, this was perfectly acceptable. To her credit, the shopkeeper kept to her policy.

Those kinds of hassles aside, most of the basics are now available here, and living in Beijing, Shanghai, or any of China's major cities is no longer a hardship tour. What we miss most are the little things. Forget about catching a movie on Saturday night, for example, or turning on the TV on a Sunday afternoon and watching your favorite

NFL team. The only football you're likely to see on TV in China is a soccer match between two cities you've barely heard of. (In fairness to my European friends, they seem to be quite happy with the sports coverage in China.) If an NFL game happens to be televised live, as they sometimes are during the playoffs, you might have the choice of waking up at 2:00 A.M. to watch if it's an afternoon game in the States, or canceling all of your Monday morning meetings if it's on a Sunday night. Naturally, the meetings never get canceled.

Being in China and missing holidays in the States is tough, especially if there are parents, children, and grand-children back home. (At the end of August of 2006, we had our first grandchild, little Bobby, born to Sara and her husband, Bob.) On the Fourth of July, Memorial Day, and Labor Day, when everybody in the States is taking a long weekend and firing up the barbecue, we're in the office.

One holiday that we miss in particular is Thanksgiving. Since we've been in China Carleen and I have never made it back to the States to celebrate. The time between Thanksgiving and Christmas is so short that it doesn't make sense for us to make the round-trip twice in six weeks. We've always opted to be home for Christmas and New Year's instead.

During our first year in China, it didn't even dawn on either of us that we were going to be spending Thanksgiving in Wuhan, of all places, until we boarded the plane in Beijing on Wednesday afternoon. The thought was a bit of a downer, but our mood brightened considerably when we pulled up to our hotel in Wuhan and saw a large sign draped above the front door: "Join us for Thanksgiving Dinner." Underneath, in smaller letters, it said, "Turkeys Imported from the U.S."

Encouraged, I turned to Carleen and said, "See, this won't be so bad."

Unfortunately, the flight bringing the turkeys was canceled, and they never made it to China. Like millions of Chinese that evening, we ate duck instead.

From that day forward, Carleen was determined never to miss a Thanksgiving Day celebration again. Every year, we host Thanksgiving dinner for our friends at our apartment in Beijing. At first Carleen had to order the turkey months in advance, but now many stores carry them and they're in abundant supply. The guest list has grown in size over the years so that we now cook two turkeys, and it's become somewhat of an international affair. A number of our friends in Beijing are from Europe, Australia, China, or parts of the world where people have heard of Thanksgiving but don't really know what it means. We enjoy telling them, they enjoy hearing about it, and we all enjoy the celebration. While Thanksgiving has turned out to be a happy occasion for us in Beijing, it's still not quite the same as being with family in the States. That's the part we miss most.

THOUGH CHINA'S CHANGED a great deal over the past ten years, so have we. People who know us would say that

Carleen and I are relatively easygoing and patient, and that we both have a pretty good sense of humor. To whatever degree we possessed those traits before we came to China, though, we've had to take them up a couple of notches since we've been here. Daily occurrences in China can be so frustrating, so aggravating, and so perplexing that it's impossible to be here for any length of time unless you step back and see the humor of it all. You simply have to accept China for what it is, and you can't get too worked up about a lot of what happens.

If you sweat the small things, you'll condemn yourself to a life of frustration. You might not get your coffee the way you want it. It might take three tries to get ice for your drink. And you might never get that order of white toast. You just can't let it bother you. I'm not trying to apologize for China, but the simple fact is that the country is going through its adolescent stage. Like any adolescent, sometimes the ears are too big, or the skin isn't just perfect, but eventually it all sorts itself out. What China will become is anybody's guess. In one way or another, though, all of us have a chance to shape its future in some small way.

Chapter 17

Challenges of Running a Business in China Today

Whatever you've read about China before you make your first visit, it's almost impossible to be fully prepared for the scope of what's being created here: looming cranes everywhere, Shanghai's blossoming skyline, Beijing's sprawling cityscape, immense traffic on six-lane expressways, modern restaurants, and visible signs of increasing affluence everywhere all speak of a large country on the move. Parts of China are now so modern that it's entirely possible to spend a week or two here with the Chinese characters on the signs serving as the only reminders that you're in China. In Beijing or Shanghai, you can stay at one of many five-star hotels, eat at upscale restaurants on a par with anything else in the world, and drive off in the latest-model car to visit modern factories located in any one of China's many economic development zones.

We call this "China Light." It's not the China I first experienced in 1993, and in many ways it's a bit misleading. All of the new development around the urban areas encourages the notion that doing business here is just like doing business in New York, London, or Paris. That's a dangerous misimpression to have.

After experiencing China Light, it's difficult for many visitors to imagine that "China Heavy," or the less-developed side of the country, even exists. But it does, and if you look for it you'll see it even in major cities like Beijing, where New China sits side by side with remnants of Old China. Modern skyscrapers tower over two-hundred-year-old buildings below; luxury cars pass people on bicycles; and vegetable stands sit next to retail stores selling the latest, most upscale fashions. In the more rural areas, where the bulk of China's 1.2 billion people live, life goes on much as it has for the past several hundred years. New China is emerging there, too, but less quickly and less visibly.

After listening to me describe the many issues and problems we faced in the mid-1990s, people often ask me, almost wishfully, "But Jack, China has changed a lot, right? It's no longer the 'Wild West' [or East, depending on your point of view]. Surely it must be getting easier to do business here, right?"

Well, yes and no. Many things *are* easier. Because China now has more than $1 trillion in foreign currency reserves, converting yuan to a hard currency is much easier. For most projects, government approvals come more quickly, and foreign practices and requirements aren't quite so foreign as they once were. Support services—legal, accounting, financial—are now readily available. Having a joint venture partner is no longer required in most industries, and establishing a wholly foreign-owned enterprise is routine.

But, for all of this, China remains one of the most difficult places in the world to do business. In the previous chapters, I've discussed some of the larger challenges: building a local management team, dealing with local governments, heeding the lower cost perspective, and understanding the two different markets that exist here and what it all means for technological leadership. In this chapter, I'll review the list of additional challenges you face here. Some of these are unique to China, while others are faced by companies in other countries as well. My purpose in mentioning the latter is to make sure you understand that China-based companies aren't exempt from some of the broader global issues that affect all companies worldwide.

Intense Competition

Competition is fierce in China. It comes not only from foreign players, but also from the seemingly endless supply of local companies. Consolidation will not come as quickly as many think. China's two markets tolerate a wide range of quality and technology. Creditors' rights aren't enforced in the courts to nearly the same degree as they are in other countries, so out-and-out bankruptcies and plant closures don't happen as much. Ignoring obligations, able to run on low overhead, and sometimes supported by a banking structure more motivated to keep the plant going than to collect principal and interest, companies can limp on indefinitely, churning out products well past their point of economic viability. Because these companies aren't attractive acquisition candidates, you can't count on merger and acquisition activity to rationalize the competitive structure in the same way it has in other countries. The net effect of all of this competition, of course, is to create downward pressure on pricing.

How can you compete in this marketplace? One of the answers is to install management systems that ensure consistent quality, and focus on innovation, product development, and new products. In the early years of a product's life cycle, when the number of competitors is limited, profit margins are at their highest. As the market develops, and more companies in China learn how to make a product—which is inevitable—margins will come down.

The good news is that customers in China are raising the bar on reliability and quality. They want to deal with companies that can help them improve their products and make them more competitive. Because the quality standards have been lower in China, and because China's not yet known for innovation and new product development, the opportunity is there for companies that can deliver a value proposition that includes world-class quality and product development, along with cost competitiveness.

Dealing with Chinese Customers

Chinese customers are exceedingly price conscious (though what customer isn't?), and they don't always pay as promptly as Western customers do, but by and large I enjoy dealing with them. They appreciate that few companies in China can deliver consistent quality and also help them upgrade their own technology levels, so when they identify a company that can do this for them, they treat the relationship like a partnership.

An example: we don't have contracts with our key customers in China, something that surprises most people. At the beginning of the year, our Chinese customers tell us how many engines and vehicles they plan to build, and, if we're not the sole supplier, what our share will be. We negotiate a price, and, unless something changes significantly, that's the price for the year. It's quite simple. Chinese customers are less bureaucratic and act quickly. If you're one of many suppliers providing a certain product, it'll be difficult to get a good price or a share of the business. But if you're providing a value-added product and service, they treat you like a partner, and they're loyal.

The Global Cost/Price Squeeze: Made in China?

In 2003, the global prices of virtually every raw material began to rise. The price of copper began climbing, never stopped, and is now more than four times its 2003 level. Steel prices, as I mentioned before, had nearly doubled by the beginning of 2004. Rubber prices are more than double their level in 2003—and the list goes on.

With some exceptions, raw material prices in China are the same as they are everywhere else. If anything, prices of some may be higher because they have to be imported, adding transportation and other costs to the purchase price. In the face of a highly competitive market and unforgiving competition, manufacturers in China have had to deal with the margin squeeze caused by high raw materials prices just like everybody else has.

As everyone knows, strong demand in China was one of the principal reasons for the rapid rise in raw material prices. Looked at from a macroeconomic point of view, China literally shot itself in the foot. While it was creating overcapacity and lowering the price of virtually every manufactured product sold in the global marketplace, it was also raising the price of every manufacturing input. This price squeeze, which was basically "made in China," benefits consumers everywhere, who can still buy products at ever-lower prices, even though those products now cost much more to produce.

China began to deal with this issue in 2006, when it began to discourage lower-value-added industries, which use a great deal of natural resources, and to encourage the production of higher-value-added, higher-technology products. As mentioned previously, China passed regulations that disallow the VAT rebate when certain products, like steel, are exported. In addition to raising the price of China's steel in the global markets and discouraging the creation of additional steel capacity, this may have the effect of lowering the price of steel in the China market. With approximately 100 million tons of excess steel capacity, and with the global markets increasingly less attractive as an outlet, China's steel producers will have to compete even harder in the domestic steel business.

Markets Do Go Down in China

With all that you hear about China and its pace of economic growth, it's easy to believe that markets only go one way in China: up. In truth, though, they do go down, too, just like they do everywhere else.

We found this out firsthand in 2005, when our core market, the heavy-duty truck market, declined by 38 percent. Despite favorable long-term prospects, a number of different factors (most notably, the cyclicality brought about by China's five-year planning cycle and uneven enforcement of certain regulations that set load limits on trucks) coincided to cause a severe drop in sales. The China market is great on the way up, but it's treacherous on the way down. Compounding the difficulty of dealing with market cycles is the lack of reliable information about what is going on in the marketplace. Unlike developed markets where dependable industry inform-ation and market analysis are more available, the flow of information in China is less complete. Not surprisingly, we find that our best source of information is our own sales force.

Management Turnover

Management will be the key issue facing business leaders in China for some time to come. With global companies expanding or establishing their operations in China, and with local companies trying to improve their existing managements, retaining key employees is already a serious problem. Competition for professional managers is especially heated in the major cities, and salary levels and other forms of compensation are on the rise.

Even though you have to provide competitive salaries and benefits, money isn't enough to keep good managers. Young, professional Chinese managers understand that the growth of China's economy is creating opportunities for everybody. Every day, they see their classmates getting exciting new jobs with multinationals or Chinese companies, or getting rich after starting a new business. Talented employees need to believe that their employer is providing them with the same opportunity for success. If you're not, they're going to leave, no matter what the pay.

My advice, if you want to keep your best people, is to empower your Chinese managers, expand their responsibilities, give them new opportunities within the company, and provide training so that they can develop their skills. This is what Chinese managers will respond to. If they see new opportunities going to outsiders, feel that their jobs don't carry real responsibility, don't believe they're trusted, or believe that the company has a "glass ceiling" where the top jobs go only to Westerners, no amount of money will keep them.

Localizing and empowering Chinese managements can help you address management turnover, too. With local Chinese managers in charge of your factories, you can cast a wider net for management talent because not all have to have English language capability. Using local managers also allows you to consider establishing factories in more remote locations where turnover, by definition, will be lower. IBM put its factories in small cities in upstate New York, because it found that there was less turnover. The same is true in China. The Chinese are family oriented, and the grandparents often assume the responsibility for watching the grandchild while both parents work. If at all possible, Chinese managers will prefer to work in their hometown; if a company there provides a good job and opportunity, there's little incentive to leave.

Another key element is that wages for factory workers have remained stable in the smaller cities where we've established our businesses. While wages might be rising in southern China, the fact remains that 50 percent of China's workforce is still in agriculture. Although this is 20 percentage points lower than it was in 1978 when reforms began, and each year there's another 1–2 percent shift from agriculture to industry, China's got a long way to go before it reaches the 10 percent level that experience in Japan, Korea, and Taiwan suggests marks the transition from an agrarian economy to an industrial one. China needs to spread economic development more evenly across the country, and the government provides a number of incentives for companies to locate in less-developed areas. I recommend that companies look seriously at locating factories where the supply of labor promises to remain strong, and where, incidentally, management turnover will be less of an issue.

Transportation of Goods

When I'm asked if distribution is a problem in China, I have to first clarify whether the question refers to the logistics of getting goods around the country or the wholesaling and retailing functions. Most people assume that moving goods from one place to another in China is a big problem. I can honestly say that it's not been a big one for us.

While it took longer in the past for us to physically deliver our products, customers have accepted this as part of the territory. In my fifteen years in China, I've never heard anybody say that we lost a sale, or a sales opportunity, because we couldn't physically get the product to the consumer. With all of the investment in transportation infrastructure, delivery times are shorter today than when we first started.

Products in China are transported by rail, truck, or boat. The railway system is extensive, and if shipments can be planned and scheduled (and time isn't of the essence) this will often be the cheapest alternative. Another low-cost alternative is to move things by boat. Companies along the Yangtze River, for example, have the option of loading their goods onto barges and shipping to other cities along the Yangtze, or to the port city of Shanghai to be exported. The Three Gorges Dam project will further improve water transportation by making it possible for oceangoing vessels to travel into the interior, all the way to Chongqing.

Most important, in the 1990s, the Chinese government did what President Eisenhower did in the 1950s: it began to build an interprovincial highway system. Between 1996 and 2003, China invested an average of almost $30 billion per year on its highway system, and more investment is planned. In the Eleventh Five-Year Plan, which began in 2006, China has a "7918" plan for new expressways: seven routes radiating from Beijing; nine north/south routes; and eighteen east/west routes. China's 30,000 kilometers of expressways at the end of 2003 will be increased to 55,000 by 2010, and to 85,000 by 2020.

The highway system is already significant, and you can now drive by car or truck to any of China's major cities—something that was virtually impossible as recently as ten years ago. The growing use of trucks to move goods around the country is one of the reasons why the heavy-duty truck business has grown so quickly and is in fact already about the same size as it is in the United States.

When I first came to China, it might have taken upwards of a week to ship a fuel pump from our factory in Hengyang in the southern part of China to Dalian Diesel in the far north, but that distance has never been an obstacle to doing business with them. Today, with the highway system in place, that trip takes just three days by truck.

Ten years ago, most of our factories were a one-and-a-half-hour plane trip and a four- to eight-hour drive away. Today, the plane takes the same amount of time, but the car trip is down to two hours or less in most places. There's no question that the time it takes to move around the country has shortened considerably. But even ten years ago, it wasn't the problem that most people assume it to have been.

Distribution

Having the ability to distribute, as opposed to transport, your product to all segments of the market is another story. This is a problem that Chinese managers have to deal with that their colleagues in other countries might not. As discussed earlier, distribution channels in China have been extremely fragmented, making it almost impossible to achieve national distribution without Herculean effort.

An example: five of our operating units sell to the aftermarket in China, and numerous independent studies have listed ASIMCO as one of the major players in the aftermarket across China. Since our products are used in trucks and vehicles that travel all over the country, we have to be able to get our parts to all corners of China.

To accomplish this task, we are in touch with two thousand separate dealers and have dealings with five hundred. The largest dealer we sell through has sales of approximately RMB 500 million, or $65.7 million U.S. There's no single organization that we can go to in order to achieve national distribution. And our experience is not unique: the same set of circumstances would apply to virtually any product in China.

Fortunately, this situation is starting to change. Due to the WTO and the opening of distribution to foreign investment, the industry is starting to consolidate. I expect most of these problems to clear up in the coming years. In fact, I believe that distribution will be one of the biggest growth opportunities in China, for the same reason that it's been an attractive industry in the United States. Better distribution allows companies to more efficiently and inexpensively get their products into the hands of the consumer, and both consumer and company benefit.

The Lack of Functional Capital Markets

The average savings rate in China is estimated to be 50 percent, and anywhere from $150 billion to $200 billion in hard currency reserves flows into the country each year as a result of new foreign direct investment and trade surpluses. In other words, there's plenty of capital here. The problem, as I've mentioned before, is that there's no way to distribute that capital efficiently to the businesses that need it.

At our various operating companies, we have local currency loans with the major state-owned banks to finance working capital, but they're short-term and generally have to be repaid by the end of one year. The banks are good about rolling over loans, extending them another year, but that assumes that operations are going well. If not, the banks will insist that the loans be repaid. Needless to say, it's very difficult to run a business with that type of financing.

On new projects, where we're building new buildings and plants, there are too few financing options. In the United States, we'd have an entire menu to choose from: longer-term bank loans, private placements of long-term debt with insurance companies or pension funds, sale leaseback financings, or equipment financings. At the corporate level, we could raise equity in the stock market, negotiate a revolving credit with a bank or group of banks that would provide financing for up to seven years, sell mezzanine securities in the high-yield market, or raise private equity from a wide range of sources. We'd also be able to choose from among a dozen of the big investment banking firms for advice and help in the financing if the amounts being raised were large enough. And even if the financing needs were more modest, there are still a slew of midsized firms and boutiques that would be only too happy to help.

In China, few of these options are available.

The Legal System: Difficulties of Enforcement

Contrary to what most people think, China does in fact have a body of law and a legal system, including courts and arbitration panels where grievances can be brought. On December 29, 1993, the National People's Congress adopted a Company Law, which has been refined over the years and was last modified in 2006. The point is that China already has laws on its books. The difficulty lies in enforcement.

There's an International Arbitration Tribunal in Beijing, made up of both Chinese and Western judges, where a contractual dispute with a Chinese partner (or something of that nature) can be taken. When I was researching the idea of setting up a business in China, I was told that a foreign investor or company could get a fair hearing in arbitration, and that foreign companies had actually prevailed in a majority of the cases. I have found this to be true.

During the course of our history in China, we've had three cases that have gone to arbitration, two that we brought and one that was brought by one of our Chinese partners. What we didn't realize at first, but soon learned, is that prevailing in arbitration and getting an arbitral award is actually only the first—and the easier—step in the process. Having the arbitral award enforced is the second and harder part. Because the job of enforcement reverts to the Chinese court system, the party with better relationships in the area in which the grievance occurred has a substantial advantage.

In the first case, we were new at the game and thought winning in arbitration was everything. With the tribunal's ruling in our hand, we marched off to court in Harbin, the site of the complaint—only to find that our Chinese partner already had the system wired. Despite several years' worth of efforts, we got nowhere.

The second case was the one you read about in Chapter 8, where the general manager and our Chinese partner in Anhui had set up a competing factory in violation of a noncompete agreement that he'd signed only months earlier. Right was clearly on our side, and we won in arbitration. But this time, we lined up support from the local government ahead of time. Armed with a favorable ruling, we asked them to help and got what we wanted in one meeting, presided over by the party secretary. We never even had to go to court.

In the final case, a Chinese partner that we had bought out—with the blessing and encouragement of the local government—made claims against us and took us to arbitration. (The local government was as frustrated as we were with the actions of the Chinese partner over the years and believed we could better develop the business if it were wholly owned.) The case wasn't credible and we won rather easily. At all times, the local government was on our side, so enforcement wasn't an issue.

My best advice on legal actions is to avoid them at all costs and use them only as a last resort. The outcome is uncertain, and it's going to take time—no matter what. In all three arbitration cases, even though they were open and shut according to any objective legal adviser, it took a year to go through the arbitration process. If you then have to go to court to enforce the award, you can easily add on a couple of years. And that whole time, the business that's the subject of the dispute will be in turmoil, with a cloud of uncertainty hanging over it. Under these circumstances, given the competitiveness of the Chinese market, final victory will probably be Pyrrhic, if it ever comes at all.

Maybe the best reason to avoid legal action in China is that once you go down that path, all other avenues for resolving a dispute are foreclosed. We had this experience in each case. Once we had filed for arbitration, the local and provincial governments took the position that the matter was being resolved through the legal system, and they didn't want to interfere. Once the legal gauntlet is thrown down, you have no choice but to see it through to the end. In my experience, negotiation is a better way to go.

All that said, the legal system is evolving and improving every day. With government support and help from international legal experts, the body of law governing commercial transactions and contracts in China is becoming increasingly sophisticated. It's no longer so different from the legal frameworks that exist in the most developed countries. But the key link remains enforcement through the judiciary system, and in this area personal relationships will continue to play an important role for some time to come.

Chapter 18

"Where Is It All Headed?"

On Tuesday, February 27, 2007, the Shanghai stock market plunged by 8.8 percent. The meltdown on China's Black Tuesday was the largest since February 18, 1997, when the market had declined by 8.9 percent. Almost ten years to the day before Black Tuesday, the collapse in 1997 had been triggered by a rumor that Deng Xiaoping, China's beloved leader, had died. In 2007, the damage was due to a rumor that China might institute a capital gains tax and raise interest rates in order to slow the blistering growth of its economy.

The causes of the two crashes were different—one was political, and the other economic—but there was an even bigger difference. In 1997, China's market decline barely caused a ripple in world stock markets. In 2007, it shook markets around the globe.

In the United States, China's largest trading partner, the DJIA declined by 3.3 percent, wiping out $737 billion in stock market value in the single biggest decline since September 11, 2001. In Brazil, which sells steel, soybeans, and iron ore to China, the market fell by almost 7 percent. In London, the FTSE 100 suffered heavy losses, declining by 2.31 percent under pressure from sliding mining stocks. In Paris, shares of Arcelor Mittal, the world's largest steelmaker, declined by 5.61 percent. And down under, shares of BHP Billiton, the giant Australian mining company that has prospered while supplying China, lost 6.16 percent. Investors everywhere were concerned about a softer steel market and less demand for iron ore and other commodities.

The global reaction to the stock market decline in Shanghai was all the more remarkable given that foreigners are limited in what they can invest in China's stock market. Very little foreign capital was directly involved. Though it had grown considerably over the previous two years, stocks on the Shanghai stock exchange in February of 2007 were worth a little more than $1 trillion, less than 6 percent of what U.S. shares were worth. On that Black Tuesday, the loss in value of U.S. stocks nearly exceeded the value of all of the companies listed in Shanghai.

Given this, the impact on global markets seems like it's somehow out of proportion—unless, of course, you realize that stock markets are a reflection of the larger economic reality. And the reality is this: a potential economic slowdown in China isn't good for anybody. If there were ever any doubts that China had become integral to the global economy, or that Caterpillar (or other companies like it) were staking too much on the

China market, they were erased that day. On February 27, 2007, China sneezed, and the world caught a cold.

THE QUESTION LOOMING on everybody's mind now is "Where's China headed?" If the country's influence has become so pervasive in less than thirty years of economic development, with less than 500 million of its 1.2 billion people truly participating, what will China's position be in a hundred years, fifty years, or even ten years' time? Some have said that the twenty-first century belongs to China, just as the twentieth belonged to the United States. How will the United States, the world's largest economy, deal with China's rise? How will other countries?

Of course, nobody really knows the answers to these questions. At Tom Brokaw's retirement party in New York City in December of 2004, he said that his one regret was that he wouldn't live long enough to see how China played out. That's a pretty important comment, coming from somebody of his stature. The truth is that China is here to stay, and future Tom Brokaws will be busy reporting the China story for many, many years to come. As you have probably sensed from the previous three hundred pages, I'm generally optimistic about China's chances for success. As they say here, I believe the country has "a very bright future."

That's not to say, though, that I think China's perfect, or that I like everything about it. China has its problems, and it's not going to be simple smooth sailing from here on out. From the early 1900s, when the United States began its transition from an agrarian economy to the largest industrial and military power in the world today, it had to withstand a major depression, numerous recessions, several stock market crashes, a savings and loan crisis, oil shocks, double-digit inflation, assassinations, race riots, Watergate, two world wars, a "police action" in Korea, the cold war, the threat of nuclear annihilation, Vietnam, 9/11, and, as of this writing, a war in Iraq. The road ahead for China will have at least as many bumps, and perhaps more.

One glaring difficulty the country faces is the great disparity of income between the haves and the have-nots. China's history is punctuated with uprisings of the peasants against the ruling class. For China to remain stable, the hope for a better day has to become a reality for a greater portion of the population.

Inefficient use of capital, as I've discussed on a couple of occasions, is another big problem. The amount of capital required to generate an additional 1 percent growth in the country's GDP increases each year. Unless China develops a better way to channel capital to the individuals and companies that can use it best, the country won't be able to reach its full economic potential.

High birthrates in the 1960s under Mao, in combination with the one-child policy of recent times, has given China a large, young population. Nothing could provide a better foundation for China to become the "workshop of the world," as it has done over the past thirty years. But in the coming decades, today's disproportionately young population will become disproportionately old. The United States got rich before it became old. China may become old before it becomes rich, particularly if capital isn't put to more efficient use. Today, six adults support every child. In the future, one working adult may have to support as many as six aging parents and grandparents. Unless the country can afford a good system of health care, this will be an enormous strain.

The environment is a huge issue already. You only have to spend a day or so here to see how bad it already is. Hell-bent on economic growth, China has been polluting its air and water for many years now, and the damage to the environment is only going to increase in the years ahead. Like the bar tab at your favorite watering hole, the cost of the environmental damage isn't closely watched because it doesn't have to be paid every day. Ultimately, though, you have to settle up.

Despite the understandable reasons for why violations occur, intellectual property rights have to be protected in China if the country is ever going to fully transition from "make to print" to innovation. This is important not only to ensure China's standing in the world, but also for a more fundamental reason: to address issues like the environment, solutions that meet the unique needs of the China market will be necessary. Solutions developed in other economies may not be applicable, particularly if they don't meet China's affordability standards. The ability to innovate and to develop new products and technologies to solve its own problems will be critical to China's future development.

In this book, I've counseled you to recognize that the legal system operates differently in China than it might in your home country, and to approach legal issues in the Chinese way if at all possible. Nonetheless, until China creates a more transparent legal system and a truly independent judiciary, it's difficult for me to see how the country can continue to develop indefinitely. At some point, an absence of the rule of law will act as a giant brake on China's development. How can truly efficient capital markets develop, for example, if property rights can't be protected (or contracts enforced) objectively, predictably, and reliably?

Information doesn't flow freely in China, and this will continue to grow as a problem until it gets addressed. Even Google, committed as it is to making all information in the world available to everyone, has found it necessary to bend to China's wishes in this regard. Political and human rights issues aside—and I by no means wish to minimize these concerns—the free flow of information is essential to efficient capital markets and technological development, two of China's greatest needs.

If this sounds like a long list of problems and a very bumpy road, that's because it is. No matter how great China's past and prospective progress and accomplishments may seem, never underestimate the problems the country faces, and will continue to face for quite some time.

* * *

So, IN LIGHT of all this, how can I be optimistic?

It all goes back to those early days of traveling in China, when I witnessed firsthand the spirit of the Chinese people. It wasn't just the personable, development-oriented government officials; the obviously well-educated professionals; or the clever entrepreneurs (who could make a buck anywhere) whom I came across. In truth it was the ordinary Chinese, the laborers doing incredibly hard work, stoically and peacefully. It was the lack of despair in the face of almost impossibly difficult living conditions and poverty. It was the optimism shared by just about everyone for the better day that tomorrow might bring for them and for China.

When I was eighteen years old, I made my first trip to New York City, to visit Columbia University. The first thing I noticed was that everyone in New York walked faster and talked faster than the people in Pittsburgh. That's the way I feel about China. Everyone here is walking faster and talking faster—and the pace has been picking up, not slowing down. The combination of a large pool of human capital, a strong work ethic, a traditional emphasis on education, and a burning desire to succeed—and to do it quickly, to make up for lost time—will ultimately enable China to overcome the difficulties it will surely face in the coming years.

When I want inspiration, I take a trip to the Great Wall. It's my favorite place in China. Most people go first thing in the morning, but I like to be there late in the afternoon. By then, all of the tourists are gone, and you have the wall to yourself. There's nothing quite like standing on top, looking out over the mountain ranges and the setting sun on the horizon.

Everywhere you look, you see different parts of the wall. The Chinese didn't simply build the wall on one ridge, and they didn't pick the lowest ones, either. They picked the highest, and they built on every conceivable ridge that an enemy might try to cross. You might question the wisdom of building a four-thousand-mile wall, but I have a different take. To me, any nation that can conceive of such an immense project, and then have the patience and perseverance to see it through over a two-thousand-year period, is not one you should ever underestimate.

THE TWO FINAL questions I'm always asked are "Knowing what you know now, would you do it all over again?" and "How long do you plan to stay there?"

The answer to the first question is easy. It's a definite yes. Though my journey here has been much more difficult than I first imagined, this has been an incredible experience, and I wouldn't trade it for all the world. What I've learned over the past decade and a half will serve me well in the years ahead, and I intend to continue to put that experience to good use.

Apart from the business side of things, I take great

personal satisfaction from the fact that what we are doing as a company is making such a positive and visible impact on the lives of so many. Handing out scholarships to those five deserving students in February 2007 was worth all of the effort it took to get our company to that point. Walking into a two-room schoolhouse in Shanxi Province, packed with eighty or so first- to eighth-graders, and seeing how diligently they were all working, despite the fact that the lone teacher had to divide his time between the two rooms, was truly inspirational. If they are willing to work so hard to try to get ahead in the face of such odds, don't they deserve a little help? Knowing that the investment that ASIMCO and Caterpillar made in our foundry there undoubtedly opened up new opportunities for them (as well as for their parents) is extremely gratifying, to say the least. Don't get me wrong: I didn't come to China with altruistic motives. But if you can have a once-in-a-lifetime business and personal experience—and, at the same time, help so many others—that's a pretty compelling proposition for me.

Last but not least, Beijing and China are a real kick.

An example: In early March of 2007, Carleen and I were spending a quiet Sunday evening at home. Quiet, that is, until the fireworks erupted. It turns out that that particular day was Lantern Festival, the last day of the Chinese New Year, when fireworks are set off to drive out the evil spirits. I've seen fireworks in the United States, of course, but they're nothing compared with what you see in the country that invented gunpowder. From our sixth-floor apartment in Sanlitun, we have a 360-degree view of Beijing. Beginning at about 7:00 P.M. (as if on a timer) and extending well into the night, the whole of Beijing was illuminated in bright flashes of light. Everywhere we looked, fireworks were going off. It was breathtaking.

As we stood on our balcony and surveyed the scene, Carleen gasped, "Oh my God, they're setting them off on the Third Ring Road!" It was as if we were standing on the sixth floor of an apartment in New York, looking at fireworks being set off simultaneously up and down Park, Madison, and Lexington Avenues; Central Park; the West Side Highway; and in Greenwich Village.

The answer to the second question, about how long I'll stay, is also simple. I'll stay as long as it's fun. Despite the difficulties, it's been a fun ride. I've met so many interesting people from all over the world, and the unexpected experiences, like those fireworks, only add to the allure. Beyond that, there is the constant sense here that, every day, history is being made right before your eyes. There's never been a country of China's size going through what China is going through in such a short period of time, and it will never happen again. The way I look at it, I have a front-row seat at the greatest show on earth.

I can't wait for the next act.

Jack Perkowski was a working-class kid from western Pennsylvania who got a football scholarship to Yale and went on to a successful career as an investment banker for Paine Webber. After twenty years on Wall Street, he asked himself whether he had the guts to do something completely different. He chucked his New York City lifestyle and bet the farm on China at a time when it was seen as an emerging economy, not the powerhouse it is today. He is now chairman and CEO of ASIMCO Technologies, among China's largest makers of automobile components, with twelve thousand employees in seventeen plants in eight provinces.

Acknowledgments

Undertaking a project of this magnitude would not have been possible without the strong and unflagging support of a loving spouse. First and foremost, I would like to thank Carleen, my wife, friend, and partner in China. Carleen has been with me from day one on this journey, giving up a comfortable life in New York to travel with me all over China and to help set up the business. Her adventurous spirit has enabled me to indulge mine, and her total support and confidence in me has helped me through all of the rough spots that are part and parcel of doing business here.

I am also very fortunate to have three wonderful children: Sara, Doug, and Libby; and a great son-in-law, Bob Cusimano. Along with Carleen, they have all patiently read through countless versions of each chapter, giving me their thoughts, insights, and recommendations. Since they have been intimately involved with China and my adventure in that country, their advice provided the first reality check of what I had written. Through her experience in the media, Sara has had a unique exposure to a world vastly different from my own as an investment banker and manufacturing executive in China, and she provided valuable advice as I navigated a world unknown to me.

Truth be told, this whole project might never have gotten under way were it not for Tom Friedman, whom I got to know when he was interviewing me for *The World Is Flat*. He set the wheels for this book in motion with his comment "You know, Jack, you have a book in you."

William Morris Agency, LLC, my agent, has done a first-class job representing me. I had the pleasure of meeting Jim Wiatt, head of the firm, in 2004, and he introduced me to Grace Chen, who was on her way to Shanghai to set up the firm's office there. I was extremely flattered when both Grace and Joni Evans, who then worked in the New York office, endorsed the idea of William Morris representing me in this endeavor. Their enthusiasm for the project from the very beginning encouraged me to begin the long, hard process of writing a book, and I want to thank them both for their confidence in me.

In terms of turning *Managing the Dragon* into a reality, Wayne Kabak, co-chief operating officer of William Morris in New York, has been the consummate professional. Wayne has guided me through the process of getting a book published, patiently explaining each step of the way. Wayne's astute comments on the book proposal and the initial drafts of the manuscript enabled us to present a professional package to publishers, and his advice on selecting a publishing firm could not have been more on point.

I could not have asked for a better and more supportive publisher than the Crown Publishing Group. John Mahaney, my editor, immediately appreciated the potential for a book of this type and understood what I was trying to accomplish with its publication. His insights and editorial suggestions greatly improved the manuscript. In addition, John assembled a first-rate team at Crown to work on the project, including Lindsay Orman, assistant editor; Laurie McGee, copy editor; Patricia Bozza, senior production editor; Jie Yang, production manager; and Lauren Dong, designer.

One happy coincidence of choosing Crown is that it is part of the Random House organization, where Marcia Baumann is a senior marketing executive. Marcia is a close friend, a former roommate and classmate of Carleen's, and someone I have gotten to know over the past twenty years. Long before the first word appeared on paper, Marcia provided insights into the publishing business as I toyed with the idea of perhaps writing a book some-day about my experiences in China.

Jeff Himmelman, a Phi Beta Kappa English major at Yale, and I formed an effective team in writing *Managing the Dragon*. Jeff brought strong technical skills, a balanced perspective, a deep intellectual curiosity about China, and experience working with authors on similar projects, which gave me confidence in the product we were creating. He taught me how to make the story and lessons come alive, and enabled me to take the book to a level that would not have been possible without his involvement. Communicating by e-mail over a six-thousand-mile distance and twelve-hour time difference, Jeff and I edited and reedited drafts of the manuscript, passing them off to each other in cyberspace and demonstrating yet again just how fluid the world has become.

Lu Zaihou, a true veteran of the China automotive industry who worked for ASIMCO from 1994 to 2000, helped me to fact-check the manuscript. Given his extensive knowledge and experi-ence in China and China's auto industry, as well as his firsthand knowledge of ASIMCO, I was delighted to have him looking over my shoulder ensuring that I presented the facts correctly. As always, Pauline Au and Sophy Wang, my assistants in Beijing, were tireless in their support, helping me to fact-check names, places, and numbers.

Like all industries, the world of publishing is being reshaped by the Internet. Scott Silverman, a good friend and veteran marketing executive in Beijing, immediately recommended that I create a blog or website when he first heard of the book. Working with a group of professionals that he organized in Beijing, Scott drove the launch of www.managingthedragon.com in June 2007 as a vehicle for communicating my ongoing thoughts, and those of others doing business in the country, on important developments in China.

There are also a host of people who didn't have a direct impact on the creation of the book but who deserve serious thanks. I begin here with Joe Wirth, the head football coach at North Catholic High School in Pittsburgh, who counseled me to look to the Ivy League and steered prospecting coaches from those schools my way. Though he would not have referred to it as such, Coach Wirth had noticed the *guanxi* provided by the alumni networks of the Ivies, and he advised that it was an opportunity I should not pass up if I had the grades to be admitted. The wisdom of his advice was immediately confirmed by the tremendous support that Jim Mourkas and Bob Egan, two Pittsburgh-area Yale alumni, gave to my Yale application and then also to me during my years in New Haven.

At Yale, I was very fortunate to play football under Carm Cozza, the school's legendary head coach. Over his long career as the head football coach, and then as both head coach and athletic director, Carm coached hundreds of Yale players. I know that all of them, like me, are extremely grateful to him for the lessons that he taught and the values that he instilled in us as individuals. No discussion of my career at Yale would be complete without a mention of Tony Gaslevich, my best friend there who has remained a close friend all these years. No matter how much time has passed since our last visit, we always pick up where we left off as if it were only yesterday.

Malcolm MacGregor, whom I got to know while growing up in Pittsburgh, first introduced me to the value of a Harvard Business School education, and then helped me to find managers willing to come to China while he was with Boyden Associates' Pittsburgh office. Michael Johnston was my boss at PaineWebber and gave me my first opportunities to manage, first as head of the real estate group and then as head of investment banking. I will always be grateful to Mike for the confidence he placed in me. He has remained a dear friend and supporter and has followed closely my activities in China.

I want to make special mention of Wilson Ni and Henry Huang, two individuals who have worked closely with me in China for more than ten years. In addition to their many contributions to ASIMCO, they have taught me a great deal about China and how the country works. I greatly appreciate their patience in answering my many questions about China's history, culture, and business environment. I would also like to thank the countless employees, managers, and general managers of ASIMCO; government officials; and representatives of our Chinese partners—too numerous to mention—who have provided me with valuable insights into China over these years. It has been possible to mention only a few of them in the body of the book, but I have benefited from my association with a very broad cross-section of Chinese government and business leaders since first coming to the country. Gaining their perspective has enabled me to put what I see happening in China into a broader and more realistic context.

ACKNOWLEDGMENTS

In Beijing, Carleen and I are blessed with many close friends who, like us, have made China an important part of their lives and are establishing interesting businesses in the process. As mentioned in the chapter on China's two markets, Eric Costantino and Katy Sinnott are building the largest chain of hair salons in China, and Mitch Presnick has brought Super 8 motels to the country. Both concepts address the large local market in China, and my exposure to them has provided me with yet another insight into how the China market works.

Managing the Dragon draws upon my life experiences, my experiences in China, and the efforts that went into writing the book itself. It has been a fun book to write, because it has given me a reason to reflect and to remember those who have played an important role in my life. Some have been directly involved in what I have done in China, while others have had nothing to do with the country but have helped me prepare for the journey that ultimately brought me here. Wherever our paths have crossed, my association with a wide range of family, friends, classmates, and business colleagues has provided the background and texture that have made the book possible. To everyone who has helped, I want to take this opportunity to say thanks and to tell you that your past and continued support is greatly appreciated.

Index

Index

The Millionaire Mind
Thomas J Stanley, PhD

The groundbreaking *New York Times* bestseller that examines what makes a millionaire

Exploring the ideas, beliefs, and behaviour that have enabled millionaires to build and maintain their fortunes, Thomas J Stanley provides a fascinating look at America's financial elite. For example:

- What were their school days like?
- How did they respond to negative criticism?
- What are the characteristics of the millionaire's spouse?
- Is religion an important part of their lives?

The author uncovers surprising answers, showing readers just what it is that makes the wealthy prosper while others feel dejected or beaten by life. *The Millionaire Mind* delves deep into the minds of America's wealthy and answers universal questions with solid statistical evidence in an approachable, anecdotal style.

'Readers with an entrepreneurial turn of mind will devour
The Millionaire Mind because it provides road maps on how
millionaires found their niches'
USA TODAY

A Bantam Paperback

9780553813647

Hug Your People

The proven way to hire, inspire and recognize your team and achieve remarkable results

Jack Mitchell

Today, when social networking is the hottest buzz word and 'relationships' are things that can happen virtually, top CEO and inspirational speaker Jack Mitchell is totally committed to bringing back the human connection in our businesses and our lives.

Now, in *Hug Your People*, Jack shares his 5-step plan for creating a winning team . . .

- Be NICE – because how you treat one another is as important as how you treat your customers . . .
- Learn to TRUST – it's a crucial part of building strong working relationships
- Instil PRIDE in your team and the work they do; give them all the 'tools' they need to do their jobs well . . .
- Try to INCLUDE your team in decision-making processes; you can't do it alone, so reach out for their input . . .
- Generously RECOGNIZE the contributions made and celebrate victories, big and small, because they all count . . .

Simple, unpretentious and fun, *Hug Your People* is a morale-boosting blueprint for success. With its blend of anecdotes and practical advice it will inspire you to build an energized, focus team, the type of team that lies at the heart of every great organization.

'Totally inspiring. Jack Mitchell takes you on a journey that is as much about life as it is about business. This book will help you become a better leader and make you a better person'
Howard Behar, author and director of Starbucks

'Jack Mitchell is the grand master at motivating and inspiring employees to perform brilliantly'
Richard J. Harrington, President and CEO, The Thomson Corporation

9780553820089